Latin Prose Composition Workbook
For the Middle Forms of School
M. A. NORTH
A. E. HILLARD

ISBN **1450513573**
EAN-13 **9781450513579**

Book text and illustrations from public domain, unless otherwise credited. Formatting and cover design all rights reserved by Clark Highsmith.

Alacrity Press, 2010

This primary source for this book is:
LATIN PROSE COMPOSITION
FOR THE MIDDLE FORMS OF SCHOOLS
M. A. NORTH, M.A. ASSISTANT MASTER AT CLIFTON COLLEGE AMD
THE REV. A. E. HILLARD, M.A HEAD MASTER OP DURHAM SCHOOL
SIXTH IMPRESSION (fifth Edition)
RIVINGTONS
34, KING STREET, COVENT GARDEN
LONDON, 1904

This book is a product of its time. Some of the terms and views expressed by the author may reflect common values and usage of his day and may be contrary to modern values and should be viewed in that context.

ALACRITY PRESS

LATIN PROSE COMPOSITION WORKBOOK

FOR THE MIDDLE FORMS OF SCHOOLS

BY

M. A. NORTH

A. E. HILLARD

Revised by Clark Highsmith

Contents

PREFACE (*from 1904 edition*)	5
PRELIMINARY EXERCISES	6
SEQUENCE OF TENSES	21
FINAL SENTENCES	22
CONSECUTIVE SENTENCES	26
INFINITIVES	38
PARTICIPLES	43
TIME, PLACE, SPACE	53
INDIRECT STATEMENT	61
SE, IPSE	64
TENSES OF THE INFINITIVE IN INDIRECT STATEMENT	65
PRICE AND VALUE	72
PARTITIVE GENITIVE	74
DATIVE VERBS	76
PASSIVE OF INTRANSITIVE VERBS	83
DIRECT COMMAND OR PETITION	85
INDIRECT COMMAND AND PETITION	87
WORDS THAT MAY INTRODUCE STATEMENTS AND COMMANDS	90
DATIVE OF PURPOSE, OR PREDICATIVE DATIVE	96
ABLATIVES OF ORIGIN, SEPARATION, ASSOCIATION	98
ABLATIVES OF RESPECT AND MANNER	100
GERUNDS AND GERUNDIVES	107
SUPINES	112
DIRECT QUESTIONS	118
INDIRECT QUESTIONS	121
SUBORDINATE CLAUSES IN INDIRECT STATEMENT, ETC.	131
IMPERSONAL VERBS	134
RELATIVE WITH THE SUBJUNCTIVE	144
GERUND AND GERUNDIVE EXPRESSING OBLIGATION	152
VERBS OF FEARING	158
CAUSAL CLAUSES	164
QUIN	170
QUOMINUS	173
TEMPORAL CLAUSES	182
QUUM	188
DUM	191
QUUM AND DUM	194
CONDITIONAL SENTENCES	202
PRONOUNS AND ADVERBS	212
CONCESSIVE CLAUSES	220
COMPARATIVE CLAUSES	227
ORATIO OBLIQUA	233
THE ORDER OF WORDS IN THE SIMPLE SENTENCE	250
THE COMPOUND SENTENCE	252
PREPOSITIONAL PHRASES	255
SYNONYMS	257
MILITARY VOCABULARY	260
GENERAL VOCABULARY	263
ANSWER KEY	276
INDEX	298

PREFACE (*from 1904 edition*)

The authors wish to explain one or two points with reference to the use of this book.

The arrangement of subjects is meant to adapt it for school use. If a definite section of the book be assigned to each Form, and the division suggested in the Table of Contents be adopted for this purpose, each Form will deal with some new kind of clause in the Compound Sentence, the first with Final and Consecutive Clauses, the second with simple Indirect Statement, and so on. **Pari passu** those subjects are dealt with that concern the structure of the simple sentence (Participles, Case Constructions, &c.). In dealing with the Cases the book does not treat each case as a whole, but gives the most necessary constructions (*e.g.* those of Time and Place) to the lowest Forms, and other constructions later on.

The Vocabularies given for the separate exercises are meant to be an important part of the work. They are meant to be learned and kept up by revision. The authors have tried to bring in all words commonly required in Latin Prose Composition below the sixth Form, and any uncommon words required in an exercise have been given in notes, and not included in the vocabulary to be learnt. These Vocabularies are placed together at the end of the book, so that they may not be before the eye of a boy when he does an exercise in school.

The authors have tried to write the exercises so that no word or construction may be required which has not previously been given. This applies to the "connected pieces" (which begin from the lowest Form) as well as to the sentence-exercises. Each piece has been written expressly for the place in which it stands.

Each exercise is marked either [A] or [B]. This is to divide the section assigned to a Form into two term's work. Either the [A] exercises or the [B] exercises will make a complete course, and contain sufficient practice in constructions. But it is recommended that the Vocabularies of both [A] and [B] exercises should be learnt in any case, and of course the Eules and help given at the head of exercises are not repeated.

After some hesitation the authors have added a "General Vocabulary," collecting all the words given in the separate Vocabularies. This is meant to assist short memories, but not to supply again constructions, genders, etc., which should have been learnt in the separate vocabularies.

At the end of the book will also be found some further help in the way of Vocabulary: (1) A list of Military phrases grouped together; (2) A list of the most useful Prepositional phrases; (3) A list of the commonest Latin Synonyms. These are to be learnt or referred to as occasion requires.

The rules on the Order of Words in Latin are grouped at the end of the exercises. This seemed better than scattering them throughout the book, or trying to bring each in where first required. But the more elementary of them are required in the earliest exercises. Before beginning this book a boy should be able to translate simple sentences (including easy questions and commands) into Latin, and should understand the rules of agreement, the use of the Passive Voice, the simplest uses of Pronouns and Prepositions, and the easiest Case constructions. (Ablative of Instrument, Agent, Cause; Dative of Indirect Object and Possessor; Accusative after Factitive Verbs, etc.) But for the occasional revision of this elementary work the "Preliminary Exercises" (**A** to **K**) are prefixed.

The thanks of the authors are due to many colleagues at Clifton for suggestions, and especially to the late Mr. E. N. P. Moor, to Mr. W. W. Asquith, and Mr. E. H. C. Smith, for kindness in reading through proofs. They wish to acknowledge also the great assistance given them in making the vocabularies by Mr. K. D. Budworth, of Magdalen College, and Mr. E. G. North, of Keble College, Oxford. It should be mentioned that the book has been used in a privately printed edition at Clifton College during the last two terms, and that the present edition has therefore benefited by the experience thus gained.

Clifton College, April, 1895.

Editor's Note: The original book was a traditional textbook, There was no answer key provided to students and the special vocabularies were seperated from the exercises. The intent was that the exercises would have been worked out by the student on notebook paper. This workbook version was created with the self-learner in mind. It was inspired by a commuter who tired of juggling a grammar, textbook, answer key and notebook paper while on a train.

PRELIMINARY EXERCISES

These Exercises from *A* to *K* are meant to supply occasional practice in the more elementary rules not covered by this book. As they are not intended to be included in the course of the book, a separate vocabulary of the harder words is given at the foot of each.

Editor's Note: *No answers were provided in Answer Key for preliminary exercises.*

Exercise A.
ACTIVE AND PASSIVE;
ABLATIVE OF INSTRUMENT AND AGENT.

1. The land was ruled by a good king.

2. The soldier was killed by an arrow.

3. The boy killed the bird with a stone.

4. The Roman general was defeated by Hannibal.

5. The soldier killed the peasant with a sword.

6. We have been conquered by the enemy.

7. The walls were defended by the citizens.

8. Our city was built by Romulus.

9. The Romans fortified their city with a wall.

10. Gaul is separated from Britain by the sea.

11. A high wall defends the camp.

Preliminaries

12. We are loved by our friends, and we love them.

13. We shall not be conquered by the enemy.

14. The camp is defended by a long wall.

15. The citizens defended the city.

16. Cities are defended by the citizens.

17. We have taken the camp.

18. The camp has been taken by us.

19. They are teaching the boys.

20. The boys are taught by books.

Exercise A	
arrow, sagitta.	**build**, aedificare.
stone, lapis ; *gen*. lapidis.	**fortify**, munire.
peasant, agricola, *m*. 1st decl.	**separate**, dividere.
defend, defendere.	**friend**, amicus.
	teach, docere.

Exercise B.
COMMAND; REMOTER OBJECT.

1. Give me this book.

2. Do not give him a sword, but give him arrows.

3. Let us go, and let them remain here.

4. Do not go home, but return to us.

5. Let him go away now, but come again.

6. Keep these books. Do not lose them.

7. Let us fortify the city with walls.

8. Do not let us return to the city.

9. Boys, obey your masters.

10. Let us spend the winter in the city.

11. Do not remain at home.

12. Let them build ships. Let them not be afraid of the sea.

13. Do not give me the book.

14. This is Caius's book — give it to him.

15. Do not let us remain here.

16. Let him be killed.

17. Do not be afraid of the sea.

18. Citizens, defend the city with your arms.

Preliminaries

19. Give me the letter.

20. Let all return to the city.

Exercise B	
book, liber ; *gen.* libri.	**lose**, perdere.
sword, gladius.	**fortify**, munire.
remain, manere.	**obey**, parere, dat.
(to) home, domum.	**spend** (*time*), agere.
at home, domi.	**winter**, hiems ; gen. hiemis.
return, redire.	**build**, aedificare.
again, rursus.	**be afraid of, fear**, timere.
keep, servare.	**defend**, defendere.
	letter, epistola.

Exercise C.
APPOSITION; COMPOSITE SUBJECT.

1. Romulus, son of Mars, was the first king of the Romans.

2. Obey the king, the father of his country.

3. You and your brother will be killed by the enemy.

4. Caius and I are well.

5. The youths were killed by their father, Brutus.

6. You and I and our friends will set out.

7. The king and queen are dear to all of the citizens.

8. By good laws Numa, the second king of Rome, benefited his country.

9. Both men and women were killed by the soldiers.

10. All of us love life, the greatest gift of the gods.

11. The king lost his kingdom and his riches, the things most pleasant to him.

12. Citizens, obey me, your king.

13. Neither the king nor his sons will be killed.

14. The king and his son Caius have been killed.

15. He and I will go away.

16. Give the letter to me, your king.

17. She and her brother have been sent home.

18. His father, the king of Italy, has sent him.

19. I have come to you, my own brother.

20. Both the men and the women are good citizens.

Exercise C	
obey, parere, *dat.*	**benefit**, prodesse, *dat.*
country (fatherland), patria.	**both men and women**, et viri et feminae.
to be well, valere.	**gift**, donum.
youth, juvenis.	**lose**, perdere.
friend, amicus.	**kingdom**, regnum.
set out, proficisci	**riches**, divitiae.
dear, carus.	**pleasant**, jucundus.
	letter, epistola.

Exercise D.
QUESTIONS; USE OF RELATIVE.

1. Who saw the man, who killed the king?

2. Did you, who were present, see him?

3. Did not Marius, the Roman general, conquer the Teutones?

4. He was not killed by the enemy, was he?

5. Has he lost the presents which you gave him?

6. What general conquered the Teutones?

7. What did you buy for your brother?

8. I have lost the book which I bought for my brother.

9. Whose son are you?

10. Were you not present?

11. Surely he did not say that.

12. What name is dearest to you?

13. This is the book that I lost.

14. What cities has he taken?

15. By whom was he killed?

16. Am I not your father?

17. He did not say that, did he?

18. She is not the woman, whose son was present.

19. What city do I see?

20. What man's house have you bought?

Exercise D	
to be present, adesse.	**buy**, emere **dear**, carus.
lose, perdere.	**woman**, mulier.
present, donum.	**house**, domus.

Exercise E.
FACTITIVE VERBS; VERBS GOVERNING TWO ACCUSATIVES.

1. The people elected Pompey consul.

2. Marius, who was often elected consul, was a great general.

3. You have often asked me for advice, which I cannot give you.

4. He was thought a good general by all.

5. You wished to conceal the sword from me, but it was given me by the slave.

6. You have been taught many things by your master.

7. Did I not teach you Greek?

8. The general asked the consul for the soldiers.

9. Marius, who became the enemy of Sulla, killed many Roman citizens.

Preliminaries

10. You and I will hide this from our friends.

11. He, having been made king, did not ask his people for advice.

12. We were asked for the sword, which we had concealed from our father.

13. I was asked by Caius for a sword.

14. They were thought to be very wise.

15. I hid from Caius the sword for which you asked me.

16. Were you not taught Greek by your master?

17. They became consuls, because they were thought to be wise.

18. Why did you hide this from Caius?

19. You, who did this, were not elected consul by the citizens.

20. The man, whom you asked for advice, has taught me many things.

Exercise E	
ask. rogare.	**Greek** (*language*), Graeca lingua.
teach, docere.	**friend**, amicus.
hide, conceal, celare.	**people**, populus.
elect, creare.	**sword**, gladius.
consul, consul, -sulis.	**wise**, sapiens.
advice, consilium.	**because**, quod.

Exercise F.
DATIVE OF POSSESSOR; SIMPLE USES OF *SE, SUUS, IPSE, IS.*

1. He killed himself with his own sword.

2. He has a garden which was given him by his friend.

3. He bought the house for himself and his wife.

4. I have never seen him himself, but I have seen his children.

5. His children ask him for bread, which he cannot give them.

6. He has given his children the bread which they asked him for.

7. They have ships and sailors, but they have not many harbours.

8. He wished to conceal his opinion from me, but I asked his friends.

9. You Gauls fear Caesar and his army.

10. He led his army against the Gauls, and took their camp.

11. The citizens themselves wished to make him consul.

12. We have many friends, whom we do not often see.

13. I myself will give you his sword.

14. We ourselves have many ships.

15. He himself gave me his own sword.

Preliminaries

16. I killed him, because he wished to make himself king.

17. I had many friends once, but now I have few.

18. I asked you for their bread.

19. They gave us their sailors and ships.

20. We ourselves have been taught many things by him.

Exercise F	
garden, hortus, -i.	**sailor**, nauta *m*.
buy, emere.	**harbour**, portus, -us
wife, uxor, oris.	**opinion**, sententia
children, liberi.	**fear**, timere.
bread, panis, is *m*.	**once**, olim, quondam.
	few, pauci.

Exercise G.
ABLATIVE OF CAUSE; WORDS GOVERNING ABLATIVE.

1. A state which has a good king enjoys peace.

2. Relying on the courage of his soldiers, he led them against the enemy.

3. They died of fear.

4. Oxen feed on grass, and lions on flesh.

5. We use riches, and wish to get possession of them.

6. Relying on his wings, Mercury had no need of a ship.

7. A man who performs his duty is worthy of praise.

8. The enemy wish to get possession of our camp.

9. Through his help I can now use my sword.

10. We have need of the soldiers we have asked him for.

11. A man who is contented with little is worthy of a happy life.

12. We shall often use the books which you have given us.

13. You seem to me to be worthy of praise.

14. We have no need of these ships.

15. They attacked the city, relying on the courage of their soldiers.

16. I did this through the advice of Caius.

17. By his courage he took the city.

18. Did you use the riches which were given you?

19. Many men have died of hunger.

20. You, who perform your duties well, have many friends.

(*For words -which govern the ablative see Vocabulary 42.*)

Exercise G	
state, civitas.	**help**, auxilium.
die, mori.	**little** (*noun*), parvum (neuter of parvus).
flesh, caro, carnis.	**happy**, beatus.
riches, divitiae.	**book**, liber, -bri.
wing, ala.	**often**, saepe.
duty, officium.	**hunger**, fames.

Exercise H.
EASY PREPOSITIONAL PHRASES.

1. Among the captives.

2. At the house of Caius.

3. Over and above the dowry.

4. Before his feet.

5. Without a ransom.

6. From him.

7. With his friends.

8. With you.

9. Because of his age.

10. Owing to his joy.

11. Through fear.

12. Kind towards the poor.

13. To advance towards the city.

14. Through the river.

15. In the presence of,the king.

16. Through scouts.

17. By the king.

18. From the fame of his deeds.

19. From that time.

20. Out of the bravest soldiers.

21. He was sent to him with gifts.

22. As hostages.

23. For so great a service.

24. Instead of horses.

25. On the nearest hill.

26. Into his alliance.

27. Under the general himself.

28. At my house.

29. To go under the earth.

30. About terms of peace.

31. Before a year.

32. Round about the city.

33. On this side of the mountains.

34. Besides the messenger.

35. Except the poet.

36. Against Antiochus.

37. About a thousand men.

38. Around the mountain.

39. Within the camp.

40. Outside the gates.

41. Below the city walls.

42. In the power of the enemy.

43. Behind the horseman.

44. According to the laws.

45. Contrary to the laws.

46. Adjoining the camp.

47. As far as his head.

48. Near the garden.

49. The army was sent under the yoke.

50. It lies under your eyes.

Exercise H	poor, pauper.	terms, conditiones.
captive, captivus.	scout, explorator.	messenger, nuntius.
dowry, dos; *gen.* dotis.	gift, donum.	poet, poeta, *m.*
ransom, pretium.	hostage, obses; *gen.* obsidis.	horseman, eques.
age, aetas.	service, meritum.	garden, hortus.
joy, gaudium.	nearest, proximus.	yoke, jugum.
fear, metus, -us.	alliance, societas.	lie, jacere.

Editor's Note: For some unknown reason, no *Exercise I* or *J* was included in the original book.

Exercise K.
PREPOSITIONS.

1. He came into the city with ten soldiers.

2. After one night he set out against the enemy.

3. In front of the house there is a field.

4. I cannot go across the sea without ships.

5. He was killed by his brother at a feast, amid all his friends.

6. He spoke to me about your house in your presence.

7. He went round about the city, and saw the walls.

8. He came towards me, and called out, "Who is in the city?"

9. The camp is on this side of the river, the army is beyond the city.

10. On account of the war no one goes outside the gates.

11. Besides these men we have no army in the city.

12. We saw him on the road.

13. He was brought by the soldiers into the presence of the king.

14. They escaped from prison without my knowledge.

15. They sailed past the island in a boat.

16. We sailed as far as Spain (Hispania).

17. They live near the island of Corsica.

18. He did this in sight of all.

19. I did this because of my friendship towards you.

20. Were you not going towards the city?

21. Men who live underground.

22. He led an army over the mountains against the tnemy.

23. After the battle they were killed outside the city walls in the presence of their friends.

24. Before daybreak they came close to (under) the walls of the town.

25. I killed him after these things, not on account of them.

Exercise K	
field, ager ; *gen.* agri.	**sail**, navigate.
feast, cena.	**boat**, linter; *gen.* lintris. *f.*
prison, carcer, -is.	**friendship**, amicitia.
	daybreak, prima lux.

SEQUENCE OF TENSES

<u>Rule 1</u>. The tenses in Latin are divided into two groups :
A. Primary tenses —

Ind.	**Subj.**
Present.	Present.
Future.	Perfect.
Perfect *with* 'have.'	

B. Historic tenses —

Imperfect.	Imperfect.
Perfect *without* 'have.' (Aorist.)	Pluperfect.
Pluperfect.	

Where we have a dependent sentence with its verb in the Subjunctive, the tense of the Subjunctive is determined by the tense of the principal verb. Primary tenses follow Primary, Historic tenses follow Historic.[1]

The English will generally make it quite clear which of the two Primary tenses, or which of the two Historic tenses, is required in each case.

Exercise 1.

In the following sentences Latin requires the dependent verb to be in the Subjunctive. Say (without translating) what *tense* you would put it in.

1. They have come in order that they *may conquer* us.

2. They sent money that we *might buy* our freedom.

3. We had already succeeded so well that we *hoped* to win.

4. We are so tired that we *cannot* work.

6. He ran so quickly that no one *could* catch him.

6. We do not know what he *is doing*.

7. Have you heard what he *has done*?

8. They did not know what the island *was* like.

9. We shall ask what he is *doing*.

10. We asked whether the war *had been finished*.

11. I do not know how many ships there *were*.

12. We were wondering why you *feared* us.

13. Tell me why you *are* afraid.

14. We shall work in order that we *may become* rich.

---

1. The Historic Present may be regarded either as a Primary or as a Historic tense. The Imperative is always followed by a Primary tense.

FINAL SENTENCES

Rule 2. Final Sentences (*i.e.* sentences expressing a *purpose*) have their verbs in the Subjunctive, introduced by *ut* when positive, by *ne* when negative.

EXAMPLES.
Laborant pauperes ut divites fiant.
Poor men work to become rich.

Se receperunt ne consilia ab hostibus cognoscerentur.
They retreated in order that their plans might not be discovered by the enemy.

Exercise 2 [A].

1. I am going to the city to buy bread.

2. He went to the city lest he should see his father.

3. We have gone home[1] to see our friends.

4. We shall go to Caesar to ask for peace.

5. Do not send me to ask for peace.

6. We were running fast that we might not be caught.

7. I have bought a horse that I may not be tired.

8. Give him a sword that he may not be killed.

9. You had gone to Italy to see the king's son.

10. We were sent to ask for peace.

---

go, eo, ire, ivi, itum	**friend**, amicus, -i.	**fast, quick**, celer; adv. celereiter	**kill, put to death**, interficio, -ere, feci, -fectum; occido, -ere, occidi, occisum.
city, urbs, urbis *f.*	**ask for**, rogo, 1.	**catch, take, capture**, capio, -ere, cepi, captum.	
buy, emo, emere, emi, emptum.	**peace**, pax, pacis, *f.*		
bread, panis, is, *m.*	**send**, mitto, mittere, misi, missum.	**horse**, equus, -i, *m.*	**give**, do, dare, dedi, datum.
see, video, -ere, vidi, visum		**tired, weary**, fessus, defessus.	**king**, rex, regis.
home, domus, -us, *f.*	**run**, curro, ere, cucurri, cursum.	**sword**, gladius, -i, *m.*	**son**, filius, -i

1. **domum**.

Exercise 3 [A].

1. The enemy retreated in order to avoid a battle.

2. We shall send 200 men in order that we may hinder the enemy's march.

3. They marched quickly so that the enemy might not learn their plans.

4. We advanced to the top of the hill[1] to see the enemy's camp.

5. He is marching with Caesar so that he may not be accused by us.

6. We work in order to become rich.

7. They have come to ask for arms from us.

8. In order that we may not think you a coward, fight bravely.

9. He did this in order that a poor man might not be consul.

10. We ought not to do this to be praised.

---

retreat, serecipere, -cepi, -ceptum; pedem referre, rettuli or retuli, relatum.
avoid, vito, I.
battle, pugna, proelium.
hinder, impedio, 4.
march, *n.* iter, itineris, *n.*
march, *v.* iter facio; contendo, -ere, -di, -tum.
learn (=discover), cognosco, -ere, -novi, -nitum.

plan, consilium, n.
advance, pro-gredior, -i, -gressus, procedo, -ere, -cessi, -cessum (so conjugate *cedo* and all its compounds).
camp, castra, -orum, *n. pl.*
accuse, accuso, I.
work, *v.* laboro, I.
work, n. labor, -oris, m.; opus, -eris, *n.*
become, fio, fieri, factus sum.
rich, dives, -itis.

arms, arma, *n. pl.*
think, puto, I.
coward, ignavus.
brave, strong, fortis, validus.
poor (a poor man), pauper, -eris.
consul, consul, -ulis.
ought, debeo.
praise, laudo, I.

---

1. **summua collis.** So with some other words :
    the middle of the *stream* = **medium flumen.**
    all of *us* = **omnes nos.**
    the rest of the *army* = **reliquus exercitus.**
    the whole of the *dfy* = **tota urbs.**
    the end of the *year* = **extremus annus.**
   In all these Latin use *adjectives* where English uses the words 'rest,' 'all,' 'middle,' etc., as nouns.

Exercise 4 [B].

1. I was sent to ask for peace.

2. I shall do this in order to help my friends.

3. They have gone away lest they should be seen.

4. They had gone away that they might not be seen.

5. We will leave the sick that we may not be hindered.

6. To help our friends we are willing to suffer pain.

7. To help us they had marched very quickly.

8. He did this in order to become consul.

9. They retreated that they might not be killed.

10. Let us go to the top of the hill to see the plain.

> **help**, juvo, -are, juvi, jutum, *acc.*
> **subvenio**, -ire, -veni, -ventum, *dat.*
> **sick**, aeger, -ra, -rum.
> **suffer**, patior, -i, passus.
> **pain**, dolor, -oris, *m.*
> **plain**, campus, -i, *m.*

Exercise 5 [B].

1. In order not to be accused myself,[1] I accused my friend.

2. We ought to praise good men to make others good.

3. To avoid the enemy march very quickly.

4. We left the sick so that we might not be hindered.

5. I have not come to avoid my enemies.

6. To be safe stay in the city.

7. All of us will come with you,[2] so that you may be safe.

8. Do not come in order to save me.

9. In order that the enemy might not take the city the whole of the army set out.

10. That they may not be caught by the enemy do not send many men.

---

1. 'ipse,' in agreement with subject expressed or understood.
2. 'tecum.' 'Cum' follows its case in the same way in **mecum, lecum, nobiacum, vobiscmu. quibuscum**.

---

safe, tutus.
stay, remain, maneo, -ere, mansi, mansum.
save, servo, I.
whole, totus, omnis.

CONSECUTIVE SENTENCES

Rule 3. Consecutive Sentences (*i.e.* sentences expressing a *consequence*) (have their verbs in the Subjunctive introduced by **ut**. When the consequence is negative we have **ut non, ut nemo, ut nullus, ut nunquam**, *etc.*, according to the sense.[1]

EXAMPLES

Tantum est periculum ut omnes terreantur.
So great is the danger that all are frightened.

Tam celeriter se receperunt ut hostes eos capere non possent.
They retreated so speedily that the enemy could not catch them.

Exercise 6 [*A*].

1. The soldiers are so brave that they always conquer the enemy.

2. He has done this in such a way that we do not praise him.

3. The enemy were so many that all our men were afraid.

4. He escaped so quickly that no one[2] could catch him.

5. The battle was fought[3] so fiercely that all the soldiers were killed.

6. The danger is so great that no ships can be saved.

7. So deep is the river that no one can cross it.

8. They have conquered the enemy so often that now they despise them.

9. Their fear was so great that they did not dare to cross the river.

10. So great a storm had arisen that all the sailors were terrified.

---

1. The sequence of tenses is the same as for Final clauses, with one exception; viz. the Perfect Subj. is often used after a historic tense. But only use it thus when (a) the result is "*momentary*," not continuous, and (b) the result actually did follow. *e.g.* **Tantus erat ardor militum ut nemo tuotum terrae senserit.** *The soldiers were so engrossed that no one felt the earthquake.*
2. **Nemo** is a noun, '*nobody*' '*no one*' **Nullus** is an adj., '*no*', '*none*.'
3. **Pugnatum est** — *the battle was fought.*

Exercise 7 [A].

1. We were so tired that we remained in the plain.

2. Are you strong enough to defeat the enemy.

3. The snow was so deep that we did not set out, but remained in the camp.

4. He has said this so often that now I am weary.

5. So numerous[1] were the enemy that they easily took the city.

6. The tree was so high that it fell, and lay on the ground.[2]

7. We were not brave enough to return to the battle.

8. Such was his courage that all men praised him, and wished to follow him.

9. He has done this so easily that he is not tired.

10. These trees were of such a kind that we could not climb them,

---

1. *so numerous* = **tot**.
2. *on the ground* = **humi**.

Exercise 6
- **so great**, tantus.
- **such**, talis.
- **so many**, tot (*an indecl. adj.*)
- **so often**, toties
- **so** (with *adv.* and *adj.*), tam.
- **so** (=in such a way), ita.
- **so** (=to such an extent), adeo.
- **conquer, defeat**, vinco, -ere, vici, victum.
- **be afraid, fear**, timeo.
- **our men**, nostri [omit men]
- **escape**, effugio, -ere, -fugi.
- **fierce**, ferox; *adv.* ferociter.
- **danger**, periculum.
- **ship**, navis, -is, *f.*
- **deep, high**, altus.
- **river**, flumen, -inis, n. fluvius, -i, *m.*
- **cross**, transeo, -ire, -ii, -itum.
- **despise**, despicio, -ere, -spexi, -spectum.
- **fear**, metus, -us, m.; timor, -oris, *m.*
- **dare**, audeo, -ere, ausus.
- **storm**, tempestas, -tatis, *f.*
- **arise**, co-orior, -iri, -ortus.

Exercise 7
- **enough**, satis.
- **snow**, nix, nivis.
- **set out**, proficiscor, -i, profectus.
- **easily**, facile.
- **tree**, arbor, -oris, *f.*
- **fall**, cado, -ere, cecidi, casum.
- **lie**, jaceo, -ere, jacui.
- **return**, redeo, -ire, -ii, -itum.
- **courage**, virtus, -tutis, *f.*
- **climb**, ascendo, -ere, -di, -sum.
- **follow**, sequor, -i, secutus.

Exercise 8 [*B*].

1. Let us work in such a way that all men may praise us.

2. So many soldiers had arrived that the camp was full.

3. We have crossed the sea so often that we do not fear storms.

4. He asked me so often that I gave him the book.

5. The forces of the enemy are so great that we cannot despise them.

6. We were so greatly terrified that we all fled.

7. So many men were killed that we did not fight again.

8. They are such cowards (so cowardly) as not to dare to return into battle.

9. We are strong enough to save you.

10. We were not strong enough to fight against them.

11. They are so strong that they are always willing to work, and do not[1] become weary.

---

1. *and . . . not* = **neque**. Never put '**et**' before a negative; *e.g.* do not say '**et nunquam**,' but '**neque unquam**'; do not say '**et nulla navis**,' but '**neque nils navis**.'

Exercise 8
arrive, advenio, -ire, -veni, -ventum.
full, plnus.
sea, mare, -is, *n.*
book, liber, -ri, *m.*
fly, fugio, -ere, fugi, fugitum.
again, rursus.
idle, cowardly, ignavus.

Exercise 9 [*B*].

1. The tree was so high that it fell

2. The sea is so great that we cannot cross it.

3. Will the snow be so deep that we cannot set out?

4. The sailors were so terrified that they left the ship.

5. He was so brave that he crossed the sea, and returned home.

6. The hill is so high that we cannot climb it.

7. The boys were so idle that I did not praise them.

8. He is so brave that he ought to be praised.

9. Such was his courage that all men praised him.

10. The island is of such a kind that I do not wish to see it.

11. They worked so well that they became rich, and were praised by all.

Exercise 9
leave, relinquo, -ere, -liqui, -lictum.
home, homewards, *acc.* of domus, -us, *f.*

Exercise 10 [A].

In the following exercises Final and Consecutive sentences are mixed. When the sentence is negative remember that a negative final sentence **always** begins with *ne*, a consecutive sentence **never** does. Therefore for

"*that no one*" use **ne quis** in a final, **ut nemo** in a consecutive sentence.
"*that no . . .*" use **ne ullus** ,, **ut nnllu** ,, ,,
"*that never*" use **ne unquam** ,, **ut nunquani** ,, ,,

1. We have come to defend the walls.

2. There is no one here so brave as to climb the walls alone.

3. The wall was made so high that no one might ever climb it.

4. The wall was made so high that no one could ever climb it.

5. I am so tired that I cannot work.

6. The messengers, who were sent to ask for peace, have returned.

7. The laws which the Romans made were so good that no one wished to break[1] them.

8. Speak about[2] me so that he may never accuse me again.

9. The rich helped the poor so that they might not die of[3] hunger.

10. He was so hurt that he died.

1. **Violare.**
2. When *about* or *of* means *concerning* use **de..**
3. *Of* here means *by*, denoting cause or instrument. Therefore use simple abl.

> **Exercise 10**
> **defend**, defendo, -ere, -fendi, -fensum.
> **walls**, muri, m.; moenia, n. pl.
> **alone**, solus.
> **law**, lex, legis, f.
> **speak**, loquor, -i, locutus.
> **die**, morior, -i, mortuus.
> **hunger**, fames, -is, f.
> **hurt**, laedo, -ere, laesi, laesum.

Exercises

Exercise 11

1. He was sent to ask for peace, that the citizens might not die of hunger.

2. The messengers arrived so quickly that no one died.

3. Go away quickly that no one may see you.

4. We defended the walls so well that the enemy retreated, and did not take the city.

5. The snow was so deep that many men died of cold.

6. Set out quickly that no one may see you.

7. Are you brave enough to set out alone?

8. Do not do this, lest you should seem to be a coward.

9. We have made the ditch deep that no one may cross it.

10. The ditch was made so deep that no soldiers could cross it.

Exercise 11
citizen, civis, -is.
messenger, nuntius, -i.
go away, abeo (like eo).
cold, frigus, -oris, *n.*
seem, videor, -eri, visus.
ditch, **trench**, fossa.
soldier, miles, -itis.

Exercise 12 [*B*].

1. So many weapons were thrown that no place was safe.

2. His shield was large enough to defend him.

3. That no one may be idle, this work has been given to all.

4. They were so cowardly that they retreated, and did not defend the city.

5. Our forces are great enough to repel the enemy.

6. We put him to death that he might not hurt us.

7. He is so brave that he does not fear the enemy, but loves battles.

8. He did the work in such a way that all men praised it.

9. Be brave that we may praise you and call you a friend.

10. He went away so quickly that we never saw him again.

Exercise 12
weapon, telum.
throw, jacio, -ere, jeci, jactum.
place, locus, -i, *m.*
shield, scutum.
repel, repello, -ere, reppuli, repulsum.
call, appello, I.

Exercises

Exercise 13 [B].

1. He sent so few men that we could not defend the walls.

2. We shall return so quickly that you ought not to fear danger.

3. The man who[1] dares to despise his enemies is brave enough to conquer them.

4. No man is so brave that he is never afraid.

5. We have come to help you so that nothing may hinder the work.

6. He bore a shield so that no weapon might hurt him.

7. He bore so big a shield that no weapon could hurt him.

8. They all were put to death so that no messenger might ever return home.

9. I am accused by so many men that I dare not defend myself.[2]

10. In order never to be conquered never be afraid.

1. **Is qui.** Wherever '*the man*' or '*men*' is equal to '*he*' or '*those*' translate by '*is.*'
2. **me ipsum.**

Exercise 13
few, pauci.
bear, fero, ferre, tuli, latum.

Exercise 14 [*A*].

A poor soldier was one day leading a mule laden with gold which had been sent to Alexander[1] the Great. The mule was so tired that it could no longer bear the burden, and the soldier was compelled to carry the gold himself. But by chance Alexander himself was following the man, and he admired his kindness so much that he said, "My friend, try to carry the gold home, for I give it all to you."

1. **Alexander**, -dri.

Exercise 14	
mule, mulus, -i, *m*.	**carry**, porto, I.
lead, duco, -ere, duxi, ductum.	**by chance**, casu, forte.
laden, oneratus.	**follow**, sequor, -i, secutus.
gold, aurum.	**admire**, miror, I.
long (*of time*), diu; **longer**, diatius.	**kindness**, beneficentia, humanitas, -tatis, *f.*
burden, onus, -eris, *n*.	**try**, conor, I. *followed by Inf.*
compel, cogo, -ere, coegi, coactum.	

Exercise 15 [*A*].

The enemy advanced quickly to capture the city. There were so few soldiers in the city that they were hardly able to defend the walls. But reinforcements were advancing, and they resolved to resist bravely, that these might arrive and defeat the enemy. The attack was so fierce that the walls were almost taken, but at length the fresh forces arrived, and the enemy retreated. So great was the joy of the citizens that they went to the temples, and gave many gifts to the gods.

Exercise 15
hardly, vix.
reinforcements, supplementum, novae copiae.
resolve, constituo, -ere, -ui, -utum.
resist, resisto, -ere, -stiti, dat.
attack, (onset, charge), impetus, -us, *m*.
almost, paene, prope.
at length, tandem.
joy, gaudium, laetitia.
temple, templum, aedes, *f.* [*sing. only*].
gift, donum.
go, se conferre.
god, deus, dei.

Exercise 16 [A].

The soldiers, who had been marching all day,[1] were so tired that they could scarcely climb the hill. Some, in order to march quickly, threw away their arms; others were so exhausted that their friends carried them. But their courage was so great that at last they came to the top of the hill, and saw the enemy's camp. Here they hid themselves that they might not be seen by the enemy.

1. *Acc.*

Exercise 17 [B].

They had been so often defeated by Caesar that they sent messengers to him and asked for peace. In order that they might not wish to fight again, Caesar asked them for hostages, which they gave him. But the army of the Gauls was so great that Caesar was not willing to remain near them, and he went away. Lest the enemy should follow he led his soldiers very quickly, and before night they came into their camp.

Exercise 16
hill, collis, -is, *m.*
throw away, abjicio, -ere, -jeci, -jectum.
some...others, alii...alii.
exhausted, confectus labore.
hide, celo, I.

Exercise 17
hostage, obses, -idis, c.
near, prope, *acc.*
army, exercitus, -us, *m.*
night, nox, noctis, *f.*

Exercises

Exercise 18 [*B*].

A Persian,[1] who had been banished from Persia, came to the city of Athens[2] to see Cimon. He brought much gold and silver, in order by presents to make Cimon his friend. "Do you bring this money to buy my friendship?" asked Cimon. " I wish to make you my friend," replied the Persian. "Take away the money," Cimon said, "lest I should think you an enemy. Friendship is not bought and sold."

1 *Persian* = **Persa** 1 decl. *m*. **Cimon**, *gen*. **Cimonis**.
2 *Athens* = **Athenae, -arum**, f. pl. '*The city of Athens*' = '*the city Athens*' in Latin, the two nouns being in apposition.

Exercise 19 [*B*].

Pyrrhus, the Greek, gave money to Fabricius, the Roman general, that he might betray the Roman army. But no present was great enough to tempt Fabricius. A Greek came to the Roman camp that he might receive a reward, and then kill the king. But so upright was Fabricius that he sent the man back to the king to be punished by him.

Exercise 18
banish, expello, -ere, -puli, -pulsum.
bring, affero, afferre, attuli, allatum (**of persons**), adduco.
take away, aufero, auferre, abstuli, ablatum.
money, pecunia.
friendship, amicitia.
sell, vendo, vendere, vendidi, venditum.
buy, emo.
silver, argentum.

Exercise 19
Greek, Graecus.
general, dux, ducis; imperator, -oris.
betray, prodo, -ere, -didi, -ditum.
present, donum.
tempt, tempto, I.
receive, accipio, -ere, -cepi, -ceptum.
reward, praemium.
upright, probus.
send back, reddo (*like* prodo).
punish, punio.

INFINITIVES

Rule 4. The simple use of the Infinitive is as the subject or complement of a finite verb. It thus corresponds to the English verbal noun in *-ing*.

e.g. **laborare est orare** = *working is praying.*

Here '*laborare*' is the subject of '**est**,' and '**orare**' is the complement, just as, in the sentence "**laborare est difficile**," '**difficile**' is the complement. This last sentence we usually translate "*It is difficult to work*," but the Latin is "*To work is difficult*," and '**laborare**' is a true subject.

All verbs whose meaning is incomplete in itself require a complement, and this is usually in the Infinitive. We call it the **Prolate Infinitive**.

e.g. **volo abire** = *I wish to go away.*
conor laborare = *I try to work.*
possum vincere = *I can conquer.*
te sino proficisci = *I permit you to depart.*

Exercises

Exercise 20 [A].

1. Hoping is easier than believing.

2. Those who wish to command ought to learn to obey.

3. He was thought to be a good general.

4. It is the duty of[1] all soldiers to be willing to die for their country.

5. Cease to be idle, and learn to work.

6. We have determined to go to the help of our friends.

7. These men are not accustomed to fight.

8. Did they seem to you to be true friends?

9. The general decided to pitch his camp on a hill.

10. They did not dare to lie.

11. Were you not compelled to leave your home?

12. They do not allow us to remain in the city.

---

1. Lat. '*it is of all soldiers*' (Genetive). So with such phrases as '*it is (the part) of ...*' and '*it is (the nature) of ...*'

Exercise 20
Words which take Prolate Infinitive.
be able, possum, posse, potui.
ought, debeo.
be accustomed, soleo, solere, solitus.
dare, audeo, audere, ausus.
wish, am willing, volo, velle, volui.
not to wish, be unwilling, nolo, nolle, nolui.
prefer, malo, malie, malui.
desire, cupio, cupere, -ivi, -itum.
determine, statuo, constituo.
begin, incipio ; coepi, -isse.
cease, desino, desinere [*for perfect use* destiti].
try, conor, I.
teach, doceo, -ere, docui, doctum.
learn, disco, discere, didici.
compel, force, cogo.
allow, sino, -ere, sivi, sltum.
seem, videor.
 Also passives of all verbs of saying, thinking, take Prolate Infinitives.
hope, spero, I.
believe, credo, -ere, -dldi, -ditum.
command, impero, I., *dat*.
obey, pareo, *dat*.
country (= native land), patria.
for, on behalf of, pro, abl.
true, verus.
pitch a camp, castra pono, -ere, posui, positum; *or* castra munio.
lie, mentior, -iri, mentitus.
go to the help of, subvenio, *dat*.

Exercise 21 [B].

1. It is (the part) of good citizens to try to help the poor.

2. Learning is easier than teaching.

3. If soldiers are unwilling to march they are punished.

4. He desires to benefit himself alone.

5. The barbarians are said to be very brave.

6. They determined to follow the enemy into the city.

7. It is pleasant to help those who can help themselves.

8. All men ought to think it disgraceful to lie.

9. Some men are accustomed to rule, others to obey.

10. Those who are accustomed to command others ought to learn to obey.

11. They think it foolish to die for their country.

12. All men ought to praise those who seem to be wise.

Exercise 21
punish, punio; poena afficio, -ere, -feci, -fectum.
benefit, prosum, prodesse, profui, *dat.*
barbarians, barbari.
pleasant, jucundus.
disgraceful, turpis.
foolish, stultus.
wise, sapiens, -entis.

Exercises

Exercise 22 [B].

1. I used to learn more quickly than I can learn now.

2. To complain is useless.

3. He never ceases to complain of his friends.

4. We have decided to remain in the plain.

5. He seemed to me to be very brave.

6. Ruling is more difficult than being ruled.

7. If we try to help others, they are willing to help us.

8. I prefer to remain, you to depart.

9. They determined to work that they might not be punished.

10. They were accustomed to go home with their friends.

11. They were compelled to retreat.

Exercise 22
complain, queror, -i, questus.
useless, inutilis.
of (= *concerning*), de, *abl.*
rule, rego, regno, I.
difficult, hard, difficilis.
man (*as opposed to boy or woman*), vir.

Exercise 23 [B].

1. You ought not to desire to be a man.

2. The general determined to set out against the enemy.

3. Speaking is easier than persuading.

4. You ought never to cease to learn.

5. If we desire to learn we can always have masters.

6. Not helping our friends is the same as[1] hurting them.

7. Punish him if he is unwilling to learn.

8. We decided to defend the city.

9. We have been compelled to buy many things which do not seem to be useful.

10. You force me to speak against my will.

1. *the same as* = **idem ao**.

Exercise 23
persuade, persuadeo, -ere, -suasi, -suasum, *dat.*
master (of pupils), magister, -tri;
(**of slaves**), domlnus, -i.
often, saepe.
useful, utilis.
against one's will, unwilling, invitus, *adj.*

Exercise 24
army, exercitus, -us, *m.*
give up, **surrender**, trado, -ere, -didi, -ditum.
summon, call, arcesso, -ere, arcessivi, arcessitum; convoco, I.
collect, colligo, -ere, -legi, -lectum.

PARTICIPLES

Rule 5. English sentences which require to be translated by participles in Latin are not usually in the Latin form at first. The English has to be *turned*; e.g. "The Greeks, *having captured Troy*, burnt it," cannot go straight into Latin, because Latin has no Perfect Participle Active.

(a) **Wherever possible, make the participle agree with the subject or object.**

  e.g. The Greeks having captured Troy, burnt it. = **Trojam captam Graeci incenderunt.**[1]
  The chiefs were taken and massacred = **Capti duces trucidantur.**

(b) Wherever this is not possible, use the construction called **Ablative Absolute**; *i.e.* a Participle agreeing with a Noun in the Ablative, the whole phrase being an Abl. of Manner or "Attendant Circumstances"; *e.g.* in the sentence "*Having taken the city, he marched on,*" the participle cannot agree with the subject because there is no Perfect Participle Active in Latin, nor can 'the city' be made the object of the verb. We therefore turn it: "*The city having been captured, he marched on*" = **Capta urbe progressus est.**

Exercise 24 [A].

1. The army having been defeated the general fled.

2. Regulus having been given up to the enemy was put to death.

3. Having conquered the enemy the general returned home.

4. Having summoned the citizens he spoke as follows.[2]

5. The soldiers having been captured gave up their arms.

6. Having collected his forces he led them against the enemy.

7. The Gauls[3] having thrown away their arms were taken by the Romans.

8. Having taken the messenger they put him to death.

9. Having killed his brother he fled into the woods.

10. The enemy having captured the messengers put them to death.

---

1. Never write such a sentence as "**Capta urbe, Graeci eam incenderunt.**" The Ablative Absolute is only to be used where the participle cannot agree with subject or object.
2. **haec dixit.**
3. **Galli.**

Exercise 25 [B].

1. Having been made king he tried to benefit the state.

2. Kings having been driven out consuls were elected.

3. The soldiers, throwing away their arms, fled from the battle.

4. Caesar having conquered the Gauls demanded hostages.

6. Our men having taken the chiefs brought them to Caesar.

6. Seizing his sword he tried to kill his enemy.

7. Having taken the camp we set it on fire.

8. Having conquered the enemy the soldiers wished to return home.

9. Having set the prisoners free he sent them home.

10. The Gauls having been defeated asked for peace.

Exercise 25
state, civitas, -tatis, *f.*
drive out, expel, expello.
elect, creo, I.
demand, posco, -ere, poposci; impero, I.
bring (of persons), duco; (of things), fero.
chief, princeps, -ipis.
seize, rapio, -ere, rapui, raptum.
set on fire, uro, -ere, ussi, ustum; incendo, -ere, -di, -sum.
set free, libero, I.

Exercise 26 [A].

1. **Do not invent a Passive Participle of Intransitive Verbs.** Saying "**Caesare pervento**" is as absurd as saying "**perventus est**" for *he arrived*. Latin having no Perfect Part. Active, the only way to render "Caesar having arrived" is "**Caesar quum pervenisset.**"[1]

2. On the other hand remember that **Deponents have Perfect Participles with an Active sense**, though their form is Passive; *e.g.* **locutus** = *having said*, **aggressus** = *having attacked*, **ratus** = *thinking*, etc,

1. My horse having stumbled I was caught.

2. Having said those things the messenger departed.

3. Having come to the gate of the city they halted.

4. Having advanced ten miles our men reached the river.

5. Having seen the enemy's forces our men retreated.

6. Our men being afraid, the general retreated.

7. Having halted we pitched a camp.

8. Being about to die he called his sons.

9. The enemy having set out we retreated.

10. The Gauls having attacked the walls the city was taken by storm.

1. See the first part of Rule 26 after Exercise 189.

Exercise 26
stumble, labor, -i, lapsus.
fall down, collabor.
attack, aggredior, -i, -gressus; adorior, -iri, -ortus; (*of a city, camp, etc.*), oppugno, 1.
advance, progredior.
enter, march in, ingredior.
return, regredior, redeo (like to).
go out, egredior ; exeo (like eo).
be afraid, vereor.
die, morior, -i, mortuus, *Fut. Part.* moriturus.
delay, moror, 1.
exhort, hortor, 1.
gate, porta.
halt, consisto, -ere, -stiti.
mile, mille passus; **two miles**, duo milia passuum.
reach, pervenio ad.
take by storm, expugno, 1.

Exercise 27 [B].

1. Having reached the gates our men tried to open them.

2. Having opened the gates our men marched in.

3. Saving attacked the walls the Gauls took the city by storm.

4. My house having fallen down I went to Caius' house.

5. Having entered the house I called to Caius.

6. Night approaching we pitched a camp.

7. Winter beginning we retreated across the river.

8. His father being about to die he returned home.

9. Having slept in the house he went away early.

10. The messenger having returned brought this answer.

Exercise 27
open, aperio, -ire, aperui, apertum.
call to, appello, I.
approach, appropinquo, I.
winter, hiems, hiemis. *f.*
winter beginning, ineunte hieme.
at my house, apud me.
sleep, dormio.
early, mane [lit. **in the morning**].
bring an answer, responsum refero.
call for, appello, I.

Exercise 28
wood, silva.
small, parvus.
youth, juvenis.
rampart, vallum.
fortify, munio.
resist, resisto, -ere, -stiti, *dat.*; sustineo, -ere, -tinui, tentum, *acc.*

Exercise 28 [A].

1. *"Saying this, he fled"* is a loose way of expressing *"Having said this, he fled"*; and in Latin must be "**Haec locutus fugit.**" *The Present Participle always denotes an action going on at the same time as the action of the principal verb, whatever the tense of that verb may be*; e.g. **Hoc jam moriens dixit** = *he said this while dying.*

2. We must often use participles in Latin where they are not used in English.

(1) **Where English uses two simple verbs joined by "and" or "but"**; e.g. *Numa died and Tullus became king;* = **Mortuo Numa Tullus rex factus est**; *He took him and slew him* = **Captum eum interfecit**.

(2) **Where English uses phrases with prepositions or conjunctions**; e.g. *He was killed while hunting* = **interfectus est venans**; *on the death of Numa* = mortuo Numa; *after advancing a mile* = **mille passus progressus**.

(3) **Where English uses clauses denoting time, cause, etc.**; e.g. *When Tullus was king* = **regnante Tullo**; *As the soldiers would not follow, he remained* = **nolentibus sequi militibus, mansit**.

1. On leaving the wood we saw the camp of the enemy.

2. We departed after saying these words.

3. Saying these words he left the camp.

4. The Greeks returned home after the capture of Troy.

5. When Romulus was ruling Rome was a small city.

6. The youth was killed while fighting for his country.

7. The enemy took the messenger and put him to death.

8. They pitched their camp, and fortified it with a rampart.

9. They collected an army and marched against the enemy.

10. Not being able to resist us the Gauls threw away their arms and fled.

Exercise 29 [A].

1. Having made silence he spoke as follows.

2. He died while sleeping.

3. On the death of Remus Romulus became king alone.

4. Seeing the great walls of the city we did not attack it.

5. Having received reinforcements we were able to resist the enemy.

6. During the consulship of Crassus there was peace.

7. He exhorted his soldiers and led them out.

8. After burning the town we departed.

9. After killing his brother he fled into the woods.

10. Being followed by the enemy we did not halt.

Exercise 29
silence, silentium.
lead out, educo.
town, oppidum.

Exercise 30 [*B*].

1. On their return home they were received gladly by their friends.

2. Having gone out of the city the soldiers returned to the camp.

3. He was killed while trying to save his friend.

4. On the approach of night we left the camp and advanced against the enemy.

6. On hearing this the general resolved to retreat.

6. Saying this he threw himself at the king's feet.

7. This is the tenth year from the foundation of Rome.

8. Having killed the Gaul he buried him in a wood.

9. Having set out at the approach of spring they marched against the enemy.

10. He took these presents and gave them to his son.

Exercise 30
gladly, libenter.
save, conservo, I.
foot, pes, pedis, *m.*
at the king's feet, ad pedes regis.
found (a city), condo, -ere, -dldi, ditum.
From the foundation of Rome, ab urbe condita.
spring, ver, -is, *n.*
bury, sepelio, -ire, -ii, or ivi, sepultum.

Exercise 31 [B].

1. They were attacked by the enemy while fortifying a camp.

2. Some having already gone out of the camp it was attacked by the enemy.

3. The enemy attacked some of them when they had gone out of the camp.

4. Caesar having arrived in the camp the soldiers resisted the attacks of the enemy more bravely.

5. With these exhortations he left his men.

6. Having betrayed the town they went away.

7. Leading back the army into the city he demanded hostages.

8. After the banishment of the kings the Romans had consuls.

9. They left the sick in the camp and pursued the foe.

10. He was killed while pursuing the foe.

Exercise 31
some, nonnulli.
lead back, reduco.
pursue, tequor.

Exercises 51

Exercise 32 [A].

The enemy being now defeated, the general led his men back to the camp, which had been fortified by a rampart. The lieutenant[1] having been left in the camp, had not heard about the battle. When he saw the army at a distance, he went to the top of the rampart to await them. As they approached, he went out and asked them about the fight. But they were so tired that they would tell him nothing, but threw away their arms and went to their tents.[2]

1. **legatus**.
2. **tabernacula**, *n. pl.*

Exercise 33 [A].

The bread being now all eaten, we were dying of[1] hunger. But the general, calling us together, gave us the bread which he had kept hidden in his house; then, opening the gates, he and the soldiers escaped through the enemy's camp. The wounded only being left [behind] in the city, we gave ourselves up to the enemy. They soon left us, taking away much gold and silver from the city.

1. *Of* here means *by*, denoting cause or instrument. Therefore use simple abl.

Exercise 32
at a distance, procul.
await, exspecto, I.

Exercise 33
eat, edo, -ere, edi, esum.
keep, servo, I.
wounded, saucius, vulneratus.
only, solum, modo, tantum.
give up, dedo, -ere, -didi, -ditum.
soon, mox, brevi (*sc.* tempore).
take away, aufero (See 18).
from (out of), ex; **(away from)**, ab; **(down from)**, de.

Exercise 34 [B].

Seeing the enemy the Gauls crossed the river, and breaking down the bridge waited for Caesar's arrival. Caesar did not wish to fight immediately as his men[1] were wearied. Marching therefore into the hills he pitched a camp, then came down against the enemy when they had gone out of the camp and were seeking corn. Having conquered them he sold those whom he had captured, and after repairing the bridge returned to the city.

1. *His men* — **sui**.

Exercise 35 [B].

Returning to the top of the hill the scout saw the enemy slowly advancing across the plain. Coming to the camp he told these things to the general. Immediately our camp was moved, and we set out to the other side of the river. Having broken down the bridge, so that the enemy might not follow us, we marched the whole day through the woods, and as night approached reached the city of Spoletium. Here we determined to collect provisions and defend ourselves. The walls and gates of the city having been made by the Romans were very strong.

Exercise 34
break down (trans.), rescindo, -ere, -scidi, -scissum.
bridge, pons, -tis, *m.*
arrival, adventus, -us, *m.*
immediately, statim, extemplo.
therefore, itaque (first word), igitur (second word).
come down, descendo, -ere, -di, -sum.
seek, peto, -ere, -ivi, -itum.
corn, frumentum.
repair, reficio.

Exercise 35
scout, explorator, speculator.
slowly, gradatim, lente.
tell (= **announce**), refero, nuntio, I.
to the other side of, across, trans.
provisions, commeatus, -us, *m.*; **food**, cibus, -i, *m.*
strong, firmus, validus.

TIME, PLACE, SPACE

Rule 6.

TIME.
To be expressed without a preposition.

Time during which.	Accusative.	e.g.	**Triginta annos vixit.** *He lived 50 years.*
Time when.	Ablative.	e.g.	**Tricesimo anno mortuus est.** *He died in the 50th year.*
Time within which.	Ablative.	e.g.	**Multis annis Romam non venit.** *For many years he did not go to Rome.*

N.B.— **Undeviginti annos natus.**
Nineteen years old.

Tribus ante (post, abhinc) diebus.
Three days before (after, ago).

PLACE.
To be expressed **with a preposition**, except in the case of towns, small islands, domus, rus.

Place whither.	Accusative.	e.g.	**In urbem,** *into the city.* **Athenas,** *to Athens.*
Place whence.	Ablative.	e.g.	**Ex Italia,** *out of Italy.* **Roma,** *from Rome.* **Domo,** *from home.*
Place where.	Ablative.	e.g.	**In urbe,** *in the city.*

But to express *place where* use the Locative of towns, small islands, **domus, rus, humus**; *e.g.* **Romae, Athenis, Corinthi, Rhodi, ruri, humi.**

EXTENT OF SPACE.
To be expressed by the **Accusative without a preposition.**

e.g. **Tria millia pasauum progressus.**
Having advanced three miles.

Tredecim pedes altus (latus, longus).
Thirteen feet high (broad, long).

Castra ab urbe aberant millia passuum ducenta.
The camp was distant from the city 200 miles.

Exercise 36 [A].

1. In the country. At home. From Asia. From Athens. In summer. In the night. All night.

2. He sent the forces to Labienus in the camp.[1]

3. Augustus died at Nola (when) 70 years old.

4. Cicero was consul a few years before.

6. I will go into the country next summer.

6. Ten years I stayed at your house.

7. In three days you will reach Athens.

8. I went to Syracuse in winter. The snow was two feet deep.

9. I saw my friend at Carthage three months ago.

10. The snow was deeper in the country than in the city.

---

[1]. In Latin, *into the camp*," in close connection with the verb of motion. So in **Exercise 37, sentence 7**, '*to go into Italy to see your friends.*'

Exercise 36
country (*as opposed to town*), rus, ruris, *n.*
Athens, Athenae, *f. pl.*
Syracuse, Syracuse, *f. pl.*
Carthage, Carthago, -inis, *f.*
summer, aestas, -tatis, *f.*
next, proximus.
month, mensis, -is, *m.*

Exercise 37 [A].

1. The new ship is fifty feet long.

2. At Messana. At Carthage. At Saguntum. In Sicily. From Florentia. To Pisae.

3. We shall remain at Athens or Corinth for three years.

4. On that day on which the battle was fought.

5. Nine years afterwards in the night I came home.

6. I shall come back to Carthage in nine days.

7. Do you not wish to go and see your friends in Italy?

8. Setting out from Sicily he went to Brundusium, and afterwards to Greece.

9. Will you be at home?

10. Ten days ago I came back to the city from the country.

Exercise 37
long, longus.
Sicily, Sicilia.
Greece, Graecia.
new, novus.
Corinth, Corinthus, -i, *f*.

Exercise 38 [B].

1. The Romans were severely defeated at Cannae.

2. For five days the army advanced.

3. Within 14 days help will come to the city.

4. While marching to Athens he delayed at Corinth.

5. Sailing from Asia to Brundisium he perished in a storm.

6. I am going to the country to see my farm.

7. Hannibal waged war in Italy for 14 years.

8. Three days afterwards he was killed by his brother.

9. On the fifth day a storm arose and compelled us to go to the harbour of Tarentum.

10. Will you come to see my house at Florence?[1]

11. I am now 19 years old, and have never gone to Athens.

12. The enemy having attacked us at dawn we were fighting the whole day.

---

1. See note 1 to Ex. 36.

Exercise 38
severe, gravis.
within, intra, *acc.*
help, auxilium.
delay, cunctor, 1.; moror, 1.
sail, navigo, 1.
set sail, navem solvo, -ere, soli, solutum.
perish, pereo, -ire, -ii, -itum.
farm, fundus, -i, *m.*
wage war, bellum gero, -ere, gessi, gestum.
harbour, portus, -us, m.
Florence, Florentia.
dawn, prima lux.

Exercise 39 [B].

1. Out of Spain. To Rome. At Florentia. From Alba. Into France. To Zama.

2. The city was so beautiful that I remained in it for many years.

3. I have not seen my friends for many years.

4. They stayed in the country all the summer, and on the approach of winter returned to the city.

5. My friends came from Athens to see me at Corinth.

6. He left the camp at sunset and went to the nearest town with one companion.

7. On the following day he pitched his camp about seven miles from the enemy.

8. In the evening they reached the river Allia, which is about eleven miles distant from Rome.

9. This river is thirty feet broad and ten feet deep.

10. On that day he returned to his country, from which he had set out (when) fifteen years old.

Exercise 39
beautiful, pulcher, -ra, -rum.
sunset, solis occasus, -us, *m.*
companion, comes, -itis.
on the following day, postero die, postridie.
about, *adv.*, circiter.
evening, vesper, -eri, m. (*Locative* vesperi *or* e).
be distant, absum.
broad, latus.
deep, altus.
from which, whence, unde.

Exercise 40 [A].

Three days after we crossed a river 45 feet broad. From this river we marched along a good road[1] for four days, and came to Carthage. For a short time we stayed in the city, but for fear of the citizens soon left it and made a camp upon the seashore. Food was brought to the camp from the country every day. At the beginning of spring we marched to Utica, a town which[2] had been captured by the Romans five years before.

---

1 The *way* by *which* one goes is expressed by the Ablative without preposition.
2 In Latin, '*which town.*'

Exercise 41 [B].

For many days we remained within our camp awaiting the enemy's attack. All night we heard their shouts and songs, but by day we did not see them, nor did we dare to go out to explore. Their camp seemed to be pitched about six hundred yards from us, and there was a river between about twenty feet broad. At last we resolved to escape by this river. Accordingly on a dark night we left the camp, and a large boat having been got ready we began to advance up the river without the knowledge of the enemy.

Exercise 40
road, via.
for a short time, paulisper.
shore, ora, litus, -oris, *n.*
every day, quotidie.
beginning, initium.

Exercise 41
shout, clamor.
by day, interdiu.
song, cantus, -us, *m.*
explore, exploro, 1.
yard, passus, -us, *m.*
come between, intercedo, -ere, -cessi, -cessum.
accordingly, igitur [second word].
dark, obscurus.
boat, linter, -tris, *f.*
get ready, equip, paro, 1.
up the river, adverso flumine.
without the knowledge of— *use* inscius.

Exercise 42
The following words govern the ablative:
get possession of, potior, 4.
enjoy, fruor, -i, fruitus.
perform, fungor, -i, functus.
use, utor, -i, usus.
feed on, vescor, -i.
lean on, nitor, -i, nixus (nisus in the sense of **striving**).
relying on, fretus.
contented with, contentus.
endowed with, praeditus.
worthy of, dignus.
unworthy of, indignus.
there is need of, opus est.
I have need of help, opus est mihi auxilio.
booty, praeda.
disease, morbus, -i, *m.*
body, corpus, -oris, *n.*
weak, infirmus.
lot, sors, -tis, *f.*
duty, offcium.
undertake, suspicio.
difficulty, difficultas, -tatis, *f.*
tall, altus.
wing, ala.

Exercise 42 [A].

ABLATIVES OF COMPARISON, QUALITY, MEASURE OF DIFFERENCE; WORDS GOVERNING THE ABLATIVE.

(1) **Quid mollius undā**[1]   What is softer than water?
(2) **Stătūrā fuit humili**.   He was of low stature.
(3) **Multis partibus** (*or* **Multo**) **major est.**   It is much greater.

1. Having gained possession of the enemies' camp, he gave the booty to the soldiers.

2. More citizens were dying of hunger than of disease.

3. My brother was a man of weak body.

4. The wise man is contented with his lot, and performs his duties well.

5. I never saw a house more beautiful than this.

6. Being a man of great courage he remained.

7. Hercules undertook twelve labours of great difficulty.

8. The army, which he has equipped, is much larger than ours.

9. Relying on his wings Mercurius had no need of a ship.

10. He was killed by the arrow which had been shot by the soldier.

11. War was waged much oftener by sea than by land.

12. My brother is two feet taller than I am.

---

[1]. The Abl. of Comparison is only to be used where two things are directly compared with one another by means of a Comparative Adjective. Otherwise use **quam**. The case of the noun following **quam** will be the same as that of the noun corresponding to it in the first part of the sentence.
  e.g.   **Facilius est mihi quam tibi.**   *It is easier for me than for you.*
           Balbi domus quam Caii altior est.   *Balbus' house is higher than Caius'.*
Compare with these —
           Facilior est somnus labore.   *Sleep is easier than toil.*
           Domus muro altior est.   *The house is higher than the wall.*
In these sentences we have direct comparison between the two things denoted by the nouns, and can therefore use the Ablative of Comparison.

Exercise 43 [B].

1. Let us feed on the same food as[1] the soldiers.

2. He is much more like you than Caesar (is).

3. Solon, a man of great wisdom, gave laws to Athens.

4. The walls, which have been built by Balbus, are of great height.

5. We shall be saved more by courage than by our walls.

6. On the march we saw more friends than enemies.

7. No walls are higher than those of[2] Babylon.

8. I admire this house much more than that.

9. The enemy's forces are a little smaller than ours.

10. We were attacked by the enemy with a shower of darts.

11. He was beaten by the bows which the soldiers used.

12. We crossed a river many feet deeper than the Rhone.

13. Our city is many times larger than yours.

---

1. Use the Relative (**eodem...quo**).
2. Omit *those*. So with the words 'that of' in comparisons, *e.g. my house is higher than that of Caius* = **mea domus quam Caii altior est.**

Exercise 43
like, similis.
build, aedifico, I.
height, altitudo, -inis, *f*.
on the march, ex or in itinere.
beat, caedo, -ere, cecidi, caesum.
Babylon, Babylon, -onis, *f*.
wise, sapiens.
wisdom, sapientia.
bow, arcus, -us, *m*.
Rhone, Rhodanus, -i, *m*.
many times (*with comp.*), multis partibus.

INDIRECT STATEMENT

In the sentence "*He said many things*" the verb governs a noun as direct object. In the sentence "*He said that I was unwise*" a clause has taken the place of a direct object. When in this way a sentence becomes the object of a verb of "saying" or "thinking" we call it an "indirect statement."

When the verb of '*saying*' or '*thinking*' is in the Passive the 'indirect statement' becomes the subject, *e.g.* **nuntiatur hostem adesse** = "*that the enemy are near*" *is announced*. So with 'impersonals' like constat (*it is agreed*).

Rule 6.—**When a statement is made dependent on a verb of "saying" or "thinking" the subject of the dependent clause is put in the Accusative, and the verb in the Infinitive.**

Verbs of "saying" and "thinking" include all such verbs as *learn, perceive, know, hear, pretend, inform, hope, promise, threaten* — of which **hope, promise, threaten** are always followed by the **Future Infinitive**. The subject of the Infinitive must always be expressed.

"*I deny*" and "*I say that . . . not*" are both translated in Latin by **nego**. Never use **dico . . . non**.

EXAMPLES

DIRECT STATEMENT.	INDIRECT STATEMENT.
Ille vir bonus est.	**Putamus ilium virum esse bonum.**
He is a good man.	*We think he is a good man.*
Legiones sequentur.	**Dixerunt legiones secuturas esse.**
The legions will follow.	*They said the legions would follow.*
Copiae advenerunt.	**Senserunt copias advenisse.**
Forces have arrived.	*They perceived that forces had arrived.*
Urbs non capietur.	**Negant urbem captum iri.**[1]
The city will not be taken.	*They say the city will not be taken.*
Regrediar.	**Spero me regressurum esse.**
I shall return.	*I hope to return.*

---

[1]. The Future Infinitive Passive is made up of the Supine with **iri**, so that in the sentence '**Dixerunt nos interfectum iri**,' **interfectum** really governs **nos**, being a supine of purpose after **iri**.

Exercise 44 [A].

1. We know that forces will arrive.

2. They say the king is dead.

3. We have heard that peace has been made.

4. It was reported that the enemy had struck their camp.

5. Messengers say that the city has been taken.

6. We perceived that the king would be killed.

7. It is agreed that the citizens are cowardly.

8. Tell your friend that I am ready.

9. We promised to give Caesar arms.

10. Do you not know that the arms will be taken?

Exercise 44
Verbs followed by Acc. and Inf.
think, puto, I.; existimo, I.; arbitror, I.; reor, reri, ratus.
believe, credo.
be sure, pro certo habeo.
perceive, sentio, -ire, sensi, sensum.
understand, intellego, -ere, -lexi, -lectum.
notice, observe, animadverto, -ere, -verti.
learn, ascertain, cognosco, -ere, -novi, -nitum.
know, scio.
not to know, nescio.
hear, audio.
say, dico.
assert, declare, affirmo, I.
inform, tell, certiorem facio.
announce, report, nuntio, I., refero.
relate, narro, I.
cry out, clamo, I.
deny, say not, nego, I.
reply, respondeo, -ere, -spondi, -sponsum.
pretend, simulo, I.
men say, it is said, ferunt.
it is agreed, well known, constat.
promise, promitto, polliceor.
hope, spero, I.
threaten, minor, I.
strike a camp, castra moveo.
ready, paratus.

Exercise 45 [B].

1. We promised to give hostages.

2. It was announced that the city had been taken.

3. They say that fresh forces are at hand.

4. We hope that our men will not yield.

5. It is well known that the Gauls are good soldiers.

6. It is announced that a great disaster has been sustained by our men.

7. It was announced that Caesar had defeated the Gauls.

8. We hope Caesar will be defeated by Ariovistus.

9. They perceived that the camp had been taken by Ariovistus.

10. Did you not think that your friends would come?

Exercise 45
be at hand, adsum.
yield, cedo, -ere, cessi, cessum.
disaster, clades, -is, *f.*
sustain (— **receive**), accipio.
a Gaul, Gallus.
Gaul, Gallia.

SE, IPSE

Latin has no Reflexive Pronoun of the 1st and 2nd Persons, but **ipse** is used as an adj. in agreement with the Pronoun (expressed or understood from the verb); e.g. **tu ipse** = *you yourself*, **mihi ipsi** = *to me myself*, **vos ipsos** = *you yourselves*.

In the 3rd Person **se** is the Reflexive Pronoun, both Masc. and Fem., Sing. and Plu. It has no Nom., and for "*he himself*," "*they themselves*" we must use **ipse**, **ipsi** in agreement with the subject.

Rule 7. In simple sentences "se" refers to the subject of its own clause. In Indirect Statement (Acc. with Inf.) use *se* with reference to the subject of the principal verb; *i.e.* the verb of 'saying.' 'Eum, 'eos' must not be used for the speaker.

The adj. **suus** follows the same rule, and **ejus** must not be used for it.

EXAMPLES.

Ad eum discedite (vos) ipsi.
Go to him yourselves.

Se sua pecunia liberavit.
He freed himself with his own money.

Ariovistus respondet non sese iis sed eos sibi bellum intulisse.
Ariovistus replied that he had not waged war on them (the Gauls), but they on him.

Exercise 46.

In the following sentences translate only the pronouns in *italics*:

1. Cato slew *himself* with *his own* hand.

2. Lentulus *himself* was put to death.

3. He *himself* knows best.

4. Come with me *yourselves*.

5. I sent for *them themselves*.

6. They gave the greatest share to *themselves*.

7. He said *he* did not know *them*.

8. I *myself* told them that *they* would be punished.

9. The king said *he* should set *them* free.

10. The judges replied that *they* did not fix the penalty, but the laws *themselves*.

11. Cato told *his* men that *they* would escape.

12. Who said *he* would give me the money?

Exercise 46	Exercise 47
None.	**deceive**, decipio, fallo, -ere, fefelli, falsum.
	arrival, adventus, -us, *m*.

Exercises

TENSES OF THE INFINITIVE IN INDIRECT STATEMENT

<u>Rule 8.</u>—If the time referred to by the Infinitive is the same as the time of the verb of saying or thinking, the Present most be used. Otherwise use the Perfect or Future according to the tense of English.

The tense of the Infinitive is always the tense that was used by the speaker in Direct Statement; *e.g.* "*He said he was ill*" The actual words were, "I *am* ill" Therefore use the *Present* Infinitive.

EXAMPLES

(a) **Caesar per exploratores cognovit et montem a suis teneri et Helvetios castra movisse.**
Caesar ascertained through scouts that the mountain was being held by his own men, and that the Helvetii had moved their camp.

Exercise 47 [*A*].

1. Few men knew that the walls had been taken.

2. Have you heard that the king's army is advancing?

3. He does not believe we shall ever finish the journey.

4. He says we shall not finish the journey.

5. Promise that you will not follow me.

6. I hope to give it you within a few days.

7. The soldiers cried out that they had never been conquered, and would not now yield.

8. I pretend to be his friend.

9. I did not know that he had deceived you.

10. They said they had not heard about the king's arrival.

11. We threatened to attack them as they were returning home.

12. Men say that the citizens are very rich.

Exercise 48 [A].

1. They informed the general that hostages would be given by all the states.

2. Our men[1] were told[2] that the enemy had fortified their camp, and were expecting an attack.

3. It was reported that the Gauls were close at hand.

4. The soldiers all declared that they would never leave their leader.

5. You have promised to come to me in the camp.

6. They declared that reinforcements had been seen, and would soon arrive.

7. I know that they promised to come before sunset.

8. They were so terrified that they did not see that the enemy were charging.

9. Ambassadors had told the king that war was finished.

10. They pretended to have told the king about the disaster.

11. Do not pretend to be wiser than your father.

---

1. **Nostri** alone.
2. **certiores facti sunt**. *To inform* = **aliquem certiorem facere** (literally '*to make more sure*'). *I informed him* — **eum certiorem feci**. In the Passive '*to be informed,*' '*to be told,*' '*to hear*' — **certior fieri**. *They will be informed* — **certiores fient**. Remember that **dicor** = *I am said*, never *I am told*.

Exercise 48
state, civitas, -tatis, *f.*
attack, charge, impetus.
charge, impetum facio.
finish, conficio.
leader, dux, ducis.

Exercise 49 [B].

1. It is said[1] that the enemy are at hand.

2. News was brought that the enemy were at hand.

3. He was told that the legions would follow as soon as possible.[2]

4. It is agreed that the traitors were rightly killed.

5. Having been told that the city was taken, we retreated.

6. He promised to give the booty to the soldiers.

7. He said they had never asked him for money.

8. You know that they will not return.

9. The prisoners themselves declared that they were Gauls.

10. They said they were sure that the camp would be taken.

---

1. Do not use **dicitur**. Latin prefers the personal construction, *e.g.* **hostes dicuntur.** . , . Similarly do not use **videtur** for *it seems* where the sentence can be made personal; *e.g. It seems that the ambassadors have returned* = **Legati videntur redisse**.
2. **quam primum. Quam** with a superlative (adj. or adv.) always has this sense; *e.g.* **Quam plurimos milites collegit** (*he collected as many soldiers as possible*). **Quam celerrime progressi sunt** (*they advanced as quickly as possible*).

Exercise 49
as soon as possible, quam primum.
traitor, proditor, -oris, *m.*
rightly, jure.
prisoner, captivus, -i.
legion, legio, -onis, *f.*

Exercise 50 [B].

1. The general perceived that the enemy were about to attack.

2. It was announced by scouts that reinforcements were coming up.

3. They said he had not given them the promised reward.

4. I hope to see you at Rome next year.

5. Having ascertained that the enemy would soon attack them, they began to retreat.

6. Having been told of this disaster they declared that they would retreat.

7. We ourselves noticed that our men wished to yield.

8. Do you not perceive that we are surrounded by the enemy?

9. The messengers tell us that the enemy left their camp two days ago.

10. The ambassadors informed the king that they would give him reinforcements.

Exercise 50
come up, arrive, advenio.
reward, praemium.
surround, cingo, -ere, cinxi, cinctum; circumvenio. ago.

Exercise 51 [A].

An old man used to complain to his wife in these words. He used to say that he went to the fields every day, and returned home in the evening tired with work; but that she sat at home idle. The wife replied that she did not wish to be idle, and promised that she would go to the fields the next day. The husband accordingly stayed at home to prepare the supper, but not being skilled in[1] such things he prepared nothing which they could[2] eat in the evening; and in the morning he said he would rather work and eat than sleep and be hungry. So he went to the fields himself.

1. **peritus** with *Gen.*
2. *Subj.*

Exercise 52 [A].

It was told Philip that the Romans were at hand. Crying out that he had been betrayed he ran out into the forum, and sent some men to throw his treasures[1] into the sea and others to burn the ships. Men who saw him say he was like a madman.[2] He declared that the passes had been purposely abandoned by his generals, and that he would punish the guilty. At the same time he promised to give a large sum of[3] money for every Roman killed in his kingdom.

1. **thesaurus**.
2. *madman* - **furens** (participle).
3. *a large sum of* — **multus**.

Exercise 51	Exercise 52
old man, senex, senis.	**run out**, procurro. *Perf.* -curri *or* -cucurri.
complain, queror, -i, questus.	**pass**, saltus, -us, *m.*; angustiae, *f.pl.*
wife, uxor, -oris.	**purposely**, de industria.
field, ager, -ri, *m.*	**abandon**, relinquo.
sit, sedeo, -ere, sedi, sessum.	**guilty**, nocens, -entis.
supper, cena.	**at the same time**, simul.
be hungry, esurio, 4.	**kingdom**, regnum.
	forum, forum.

Exercise 53 [A].

On hearing that[1] the Roman general had sent 3000 soldiers to besiege the town, the citizens, whose food was already beginning to fail, were greatly alarmed. So they resolved to send ambassadors to the camp to ask for peace. The Romans answered that this would be given when hostages had been surrendered (*abl. abs.*). The Roman general demanded these before night; but the citizens refused[2] to obey the order: they said that they would rather die than accept such a peace. And accordingly the city was blockaded for four months. Then the Romans withdrew to defend their own territories against the Suevi.

1. Translate by "*having been informed that.*"
2. Use **nege** (said they would not ...).

Exercise 54 [B].

At daybreak Leonidas perceived that he had been surrounded by the enemy. Nevertheless, being endowed with great bravery, he resolved to engage in battle and die for his country. Having praised the allies, he sent them all to their homes. Many of the Spartans also he wished to dismiss, but they all said they would never leave their king. At length Leonidas perceived that the enemy were approaching, and drew up his men in line of battle to withstand their attack. They all knew that the enemy's forces were so great that there was no hope of escape; but they fought bravely for many hours, and all to a man were killed.

Exercise 53
besiege, beset, blockade, obsideo, -ere, -sedi, -sessum.
fail, deficio.
greatly, magnopere.
order, jussum.
territories, fines, -ium, m. [finis, *in singular* = **boundary**].
nevertheless, tamen [*usually not first word*].
withdraw, discedo.

Exercise 54
engage in battle, join battle, proelium committo.
dismiss, disband, dimitto.
draw up in line of battle, instruo, -ere, -struxi, -structum.
withstand, sustineo.
line of battle, acies, *f.*, 5.
escape, *n.*, fuga.
all to a man, omnes ad unum.

Exercise 55 [B].

When Romulus had returned to the Campus Martius to review the army, a great storm having arisen suddenly, he was hidden by so thick a cloud that the citizens could not see him. Nor was he afterwards seen by any mortal. But on the following day a young man, by name Proculus Julius, came to Rome, and said that Romulus had appeared to him, and had told him that the gods wished Rome to be the capital of the world. Therefore the Romans perceived that they ought to practise the art of war, and become good soldiers, that all men might know that Romulus had spoken the truth.

Exercise 56 [B].

I have many friends, but of them all I think Caius is the cleverest. Once the brother of Caius was accused on account of some offence, and Caius was compelled to give evidence.[1] The accusers wished to make him angry, so that he might deny what he had already said. But he knew that they desired this, and gave his evidence without anger. At length one of the accusers said, "Go away, my friend: you are a very clever man." Caius replied that he wished that he could say the same of them, but that he had sworn to tell the truth.

1. **testimonium dicere**.

Exercise 55
review an army, recenseo, -ere, -ui.
thick, densus.
cloud, nubes, -is, *f.*
any (*in negative sentences*), ullus.
mortal, mortalis.
by name [called], nomine.
appear, videor.
capital, caput, -itis, *n.*
world, orbis terrarum.
practice, studeo.
art of war, ars milltaris.
speak the truth, vera loquor.

Exercise 56
clever, callidus.
offence, noxa, delictum.
give evidence, testimonium dico.
accuser, accusator.
anger, ira.
make angry, lacesso, -ere, -ivi, -itum.
swear, juro, I.

Exercise 57 [A].
PRICE AND VALUE.

The '**Genitive of Value**' (**tanti, quanti, minoris, minimi, magni, pluris, flocci**, etc.—which are properly *Locatives*) is only to be used of indefinite value with verbs of *estimating* or *valuing*.

If the price is exactly stated the Ablative of Price (which is really an Abl. of Instrument) must be used.

e.g. **Multis talentis emptam domum nihili aestimat.**
A house bought for many talents he values at nothing.

1. How much do you think this horse is worth?

2. I bought this book for four denarii.

3. Do you value liberty highly?

4. I bought this house at a low price, because Caius thought it of no value.

5. This house cost me 5000 sesterces.

6. He will sell the horse for 1500 sesterces.

7. I am selling my farm for a great sum of money.

8. I do not care a straw for wisdom.

9. A slave can buy his freedom for a talent.

10. I think this worth less than that (is worth).

Exercise 57
value, think worth, aestimo, 1.
liberty, libertas.
cheap, worthless, vilis.
at a low price, vili.
at a high price, highly, magni.
of no value, nihili.
cost, stare (*dat.* of person). sesterce, sestertius, -i, *m.*
care a straw for, flocci facio.
slave, servus, -i.
talent, talentum.
virtue, virtus, -tutis, *f.*

Exercise 58 [B].

1. Buy a horse for 1250 sesterces.

2. I value this so greatly that I do not wish to sell it.

3. This house cost them a very great sum of money.

4. They set a very high value on virtue.

5. The victory cost Hannibal many men.

6. For how many talents will you sell this slave?

7. How much do you think the slave is worth?

8. Value money less and virtue more.

9. He bought the farm for 9000 sesterces, but now cares nothing for it.

10. For how much money was he liberated?

Exercise 58
None.

PARTITIVE GENITIVE.

Britannorum fortissimi = Bravest {of *or* among} the Britons,

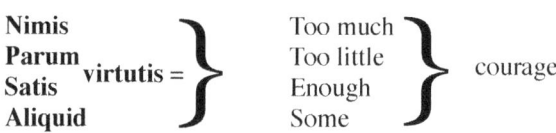

Exercise 59 [A].

1. I know that they waste too much time.

2. He had too little confidence in himself.

3. You both have sufficient boldness.

4. They do this that the State may not suffer any[1] loss.

5. Three thousand of our best soldiers have perished.

6. Some of the citizens wished to surrender, others to resist.

7. Our country, which was once the greatest in the world, still keeps some of its old strength.

8. Most of you[2] have shown more courage than wisdom.

9. I think there is some good in all men.

10. Where in the world do you live?

---

1. **quid**.
2. **Nos** has two genitives—**nostrum** and **nostri**; **vos** has **vestrum** and **vestri**. Use the forms in *-um* for Partitive Genitive, the forms in *-i* for the Objective Genitive.

Exercise 59		
waste time, tempus tero, -ere, trivi, tritum.	**surrender** (*intrans.*), se tradere, dedere; in deditionem venire.	**most**, plerique.
confidence, fiducia.	**strength**, robur, -oris, *n.*	**show (of qualities)**, praesto, -stare, -stiti.
too much, nimis, adv.; nimis, *adj.*	**still**, adhuc.	**where in the world**, ubi gentium.
too little, very little, parum, *adv.*	**keep**, conservo, I.	**live** (= **dwell**), habito, I.
boldness, audacia.	**old (of former times)**, antiquus. (**living** or **lasting long**), vetus, -eris.	
loss, detrimentum.		

Exercise 60 [*B*].

1. Most of our old friends are dead, and some have ceased to be friends.

2. Caesar has always been considered the greatest of the Romans.

3. The Gauls have too much eloquence and too little wisdom.

4. They said that the Helvetii were the greatest nation in the whole of Gaul.

5. So great a storm arose, that the greater part of the ships were lost.

6. Some of us have lost all hope.

7. You, who have some love for your country, ought not to do this.

8. He was the first to march[1] into this part of the country.

9. I do not consider Crassus the greatest man in our country.

10. Send to our help the best of your ships.

1. *He, the first* (adj.), *marched*. So "*he left last*" is **ultimus reliquit**

Exercise 60
eloquence, eloquentia.
nation, gens, gentis, *f*.
lose, amitto.
hope, spes, *f*., 5.
country (*native land*), patria.
country (*district*), regio, fines.
country (*land*), terra.
country (*opp. to town*), rus.
send to help, submitto, *acc.* and *dat.*;
    e.g. copias Caesari submittit.

DATIVE VERBS.
Exercise 61 [A].

1. He promised me wealth, but he has no money himself.

2. He satisfied me, and I think I can trust him again.

3. The enemy spared those who survived the battle.

4. Labienus was put in command of the army by Caesar.

5. A man who is angry with his friends without a cause does himself more harm than them.

6. This does not seem to me to be a place fit for a camp.

7. It is difficult to heal such a disease.

8. My friend Atticus came out of the city to meet me.

9. Having been put in command of a legion, he took part in many battles in Gaul.

10. The cavalry pressed the Gauls hard in their flight.[1]

11. A thousand Gauls threw themselves in our way, and we scarcely held our ground against them,

12. Caesar waged war against the Gauls, but his victories did not please his enemies at Rome.

13. They threatened me with death, but I had not injured them.

---

1. —*flying*. Use Participle.

| **Exercise 61** *The following couples of verbs, one governing Dat. and the other acc., are especially to be noted:* **help, support**, succurro, -ere, -curri, -cursum (*dat.*), subvenio (*dat.*), juvo (*acc.*). **please**, placeo (*dat.*), juvo (*acc.*). | **advise**, suadeo, suasi, suasum (*dat.*), moneo (*acc.*). **command**, impero (*dat.*), jubeo (*acc.*). **hurt, harm**, noceo (*dat.*), laedo, -ere, laesi, laesum (*acc.*). **heal**, medeor (*dat.*), sano, I. (*acc.*). | **marry** (*woman as subject*), nubo, -ere, nupsi, nuptum (*dat.*). (*man as subject*), duco (*acc.*). *The following govern the Dative:* **believe, trust**, credo. **obey**, pareo. | **spare**, parco, -ere, peperci, parsum. **pardon**, ignosco, -ere, -novi, -notum. **envy**, invideo. **to be angry with**, irascor, iratus. **restrain**, tempero, I. **to be devoted to**, studeo. *cont. on next page.* |

Exercise 62 [*B*].

1. Let us declare war immediately against the French.

2. You, who were put in command of the legion, ought to lead us against the enemy.

3. Did your friend marry Claudia?

4. It is the king's pleasure to entrust the command to you.

5. They made war on their countrymen.

6. The judges threatened the prisoners with tortures.

7. Caesar exacted many hostages from the Aedui.

8. The general has sent these troops to our aid.

9. Who does not prefer freedom to slavery?

10. I am unwilling to entrust Caius with this money.

11. Labienus, who was at the head of the sixth legion, resisted the onset of the Gauls.

12. They are much more devoted to agriculture than to war.

---

favour, faveo, favi, fautum.
Also all compounds of sum—
adesse, **to be present at.**
interesse, **to take part in.**
praeesse, **to be in command of.**
deesse, **to fail, to be wanting to.**
superesse, **to survive.**
prodesse (prosum), **to be advantageous, of service to.**
And a large number of verbs compounded with preps, and bene, male, satis, re:

satisfy, satisfacio.
put in command of, praeficio (acc. and dat.); *e.g.* Labienum legioni praefecit.
entrust, committo, acc. and dat.
wage war on, infero bellum.
declare war against, bellum indico.
to press hard upon, insto, institi.
prefer, antepono (acc. and dat.); *e.g.* anteponit rus urbi.

throw in the way of, objicio (acc. and dat.).
threaten, minor, I.; *e.g.* mortem mihi minatur.
hold out against, resist, resisto.
wealth, riches, divitiae.
cause, causa.
disease, morbus, -i, *m.*
meet, obviam eo, *dat.*
enemy (public), hostis. (private), Inimicus.

Exercise 62
French, Galli.
legion, legio.
countrymen (= **fellow-countrymen, fellow-citizens**), cives.
judge, judex, -icis.
torture, cruciatus, us, *m.*
exact from, impero, *acc.* and *dat.*; *e.g.* naves sociis imperat.
slavery, servitus, -tutis, *f.*
agriculture, agricultura.

Exercise 63 [A].

[Exercises 63-70 are intended for revision]

The Greeks valued their liberty so highly that they determined to resist the Persians and never[1] yield to them. Themistocles was put in command of the Greek forces. By his advice the Greeks trusted to their ships, and fought the Persians[2] by sea. The Greek fleet was near the island of Salamis,[3] and most of the leaders wished to withdraw from this place, and leave Athens in the hands of the Persians ; for they valued their own safety more than the city of Athens. Then Themistocles declared that he and the Athenians[4] would sail to Athens with the fleet of two hundred ships. But he was not able to persuade the others.

1. *and . . . not* = **neque**. Never put '**et**' before a negative; *e.g.* do not say '**et nunquam**,' but '**neque unquam**'; do not say '**et nulla navis**,' but '**neque nils navis**.'
2. *Against* the Persians.
3. **Salamis**, *f.*; *Gen.* **Salminis**; *Acc.* **Salmina**.
4. **Athenae, -arum**, *f.*; *Athenian* = **Atheniensis**.

Exercise 63	Exercise 64	Exercise 65
advice, consilium.	**form a plan**, consilium capio *or* ineo.	**fight a battle**, proelium facio.
safety, salus, -utis, *f.*	**secretly**, clam, *adv.*	**suddenly**, subito.
in the hands of, in potestate.	**rout**, fundo, -ere, fudi, fusum.	**take to flight**, terga verto, -ere, verti, versum.
Persians, Persae.		**drive down**, depello.
Athenians, Athenienses.		
the others, the rest, ceteri, reliqui.		
trust, confīdo, -ere, confisus sum, *dat.*		

Exercise 64 [A].

Thereupon[1] Themistocles formed the following[2] plan to save both Athens and the other States of Greece. He sent a messsenger secretly to the king of the Persians to tell him that the Greeks were about to depart. He pointed out that the Persians with their large fleet would easily surround the small forces of the Greeks. There are some who[3] say that by this advice he wished to please the king, and that he put his own safety before the freedom of his country. But the advice was of great service to Greece; for the ships of the Persians hindered one another,[4] and the Greeks routed the enemy.

1. **Quo facto**.
2. *This*.
3. **Sunt qui**, with *Subj*.
4. *One another* here tr. by **se**.

Exercise 65 [A].

In the battle which Caesar fought in that place with the Gauls he lost many of his men. For when he had arrived at the top of a hill, and had begun to fortify a camp, suddenly the enemy made an attack. The Romans, who were not standing in line of battle, at first were unable to resist, and took to flight; but afterwards Caesar sent the tenth legion, which he had with him,[1] to their aid, and at last the Gauls were driven down to the river. Here, however, they again made a stand, and Caesar himself says that they fought very bravely.

1. **secum**.

Exercise 66 [A].

When the king was told of this, he sent an officer[1] with 150 soldiers to take the robbers and bring them to him. On arriving at the place where the robbers were, they found that a very strong camp had been made in a wood, and that all the approaches had been blocked by cutting down trees.[2] At length, however, the place was stormed, and the robbers being taken were put to death: but the king pardoned the leader's son, a boy twelve years old.

1. Here '**centurio**.' The centurion corresponds to the English '*captain*' and also to '*sergeant*.' If a superior officer (*e.g.* colonel) is meant use **tribunus militum**. If the commander of a separate division is meant (a lieutenant-general) use **legatua**.
2. Abl. abs.

Exercise 67 [B].

When the crops began to ripen the general marched through the wood, making use of[1] a guide whom his horsemen had taken prisoner. On his march he sent out scouts to discover the enemy's camp. They having returned informed him that the enemy with their wives and children and a large number of cattle had made a camp in the middle of the marsh, and were awaiting his arrival. When he learnt this he advanced so quickly that he reached their camp at midnight; and such was the bravery of the Romans that few of the Germans escaped in safety.

1. **usus** (utor).

Exercise 66
robber, latro, -onis.
strong (of positions, etc.), firmus.
approach, aditus, -us, *m.*
block, obsideo, -ere, -sedi, -sessum.
cut down, succido, -ere, -cidi, -cisum.
storm, take by storm, expugno, I.

Exercise 67
crop, seges, -etis, *f.*
ripen, maturesco.
ripe, ready (early), maturus.
guide, dux.
horseman, eques, -itis.
take prisoner, capio, captivum facio.
on the march, ex *or* in itinere.

discover, find (find what one is looking for), reperio, -ire, repperi, repertum. (find by chance), invenio. (find out, learn, of facts), cognosco.
children, liberi.
midnight, media nox.
German, Germanus.
in safety, incolumis, *adj.*
cattle, pecus, -oris, *n.*
marsh, palus, -udis, *f.*

Exercises

Exercise 68 [B].

Calenus received a letter from Caesar, who told him that all the harbours and the shore were held by the enemy. On hearing this he recalled all his ships; but one of them, which did not obey his orders, was captured by Bibulus. All the sailors were put to death by the cruel general; he spared neither man nor boy, and hoped by his cruelty to finish the war more quickly. But Calenus pursued his fleet with 40 ships, and defeated him at Oricum three days after the massacre.

Exercise 69 [B].

The kings of England and Germany declared war against Philip,[1] king of France. They felt sure that they would conquer him, on account of the number[2] of their troops, and because they held the French forces in small esteem. Nevertheless he defeated them in a great battle at Bovinium. It was a desperate battle,[3] and all showed the greatest bravery. It was observed that a certain priest had killed great numbers[2] of the enemy. The weapon which he used was an iron club. He had chosen this because he declared that a priest ought not to shed human blood,[4] and by this means his enemies died from the violence of the blow.

---

1. *Philip* = **Philippus**.
2. 'number,' 'numbers,' meaning '*great* numbers,' is always **multitudo**.
3. **atrociter pugnatum est**.
4. *blood of men*.

Exercise 68
letter, litterae, *f. pl.*
hold, occupy, occupo, I.
recall, revoco, I.
order, jussum.
cruel, saevus, crudelis. cruelty, saevitia, crudelitas.
massacre, slaughter, caedes, -is,*f.*
fleet, classis, -is, *f.*

Exercise 69
England, Britannia.
Englishman, Britannus.
France, Gallia.
Frenchman, Gallus.
French (*adj.*), Gallicus.
on account of, ob, propter.
priest, sacerdos, -dotis.
weapon, telum.
iron (adj.), ferreus.
club, clava, fustis, -is, *m.*
by this means, hoc modo.
shed, effundo, -ere, -fudi, -fusum.
blood, sanguis, -inis, *m.*
blow, ictus, -us, *m.*
violence, vis, *f.*

Exercise 70 [B].

The French king himself was the bravest knight in his army. He himself was wounded, and his horse was killed under him; but he rose immediately, and led his men again against the enemy. They charged a squadron of Germans, amongst whom was the emperor himself. The Germans, thinking[1] that their emperor would be taken prisoner, came up to his help, and opened for him a way of escape. Thereupon Philip remarked to his men that they would only see the emperor's back on that day. After the flight of the emperor the French pursued his army, and defeated them with great slaughter.

1. Deponent—**reor**.

Exercise 70
knight, eques, -itis.
wound, vulnero, 1.
charge, impetum facio in, *acc.*
squadron, ala, turma.
emperor, imperator.
open (*a way, etc.*), patefacio.
thereupon, quo facto.
back, tergum.
rise, surgo, -ere, surrexi, surrectum.

Exercise 71
almost, paene, fere.
criminal, guilty, nocens.
majority, major pars.

Exercises

PASSIVE OF INTRANSITIVE VERBS

Rule 9.—Intransitive Verbs cannot be used personally in the Passive, but they can be used impersonally.

e.g. **Pugnatum est diu** = *the battle lasted long.*
Concurritur undique = *men run together from all sides.*

We can often express the same English by an intrans. or by a trans, verb :
e.g. *The Romans are helped* = **succurritur Romanis**, *or* **juvantur Romani**.
I was commanded = **imperatum est mihi, or jussus sum**.
I was advised = **suasum est mihi, or monitus sum**.
N.B.—Remember that all "Dative Verbs" (*i.e.* all verbs that govern the Dative *only*) are Intransitive.

Exercise 71 [A].

1. The rich are envied by the poor.

2. A fierce battle was fought at Cannae.

3. You will not be believed again.

4. You have been advised by many of us.

5. The enemy were resisted for almost three hours.

6. At Rome many criminals are pardoned.

7. You shall be satisfied.

8. I was persuaded by the majority.

9. Many men more ill than you have been healed.

10. Shall such men be favoured among us?

Exercise 72 [B].

1. Is a man believed who has once lied?

2. The work is only hindered by such people.[1]

3. Do not be persuaded by him.

4. Help was brought to the Romans when hard pressed.

5. No man is hurt by advice.

6. They will not be pleased.

7. Orders are given to an army by the general only.

8. What rich man is envied by the wise?

9. Be advised by us.

10. You will be accused and not spared.

---

[1] Here "*such people*" may be expressed by "**tales**" only. Very frequently *people* may be thus omitted or translated by "**ii**" : *e.g. people who lie* = **ii qui mentiuntur**. "**Populus**" is only a people in the political sense, a *nation*.

Exercise 72	Exercise 73
lie, mentior	**arrow**, sagitta.
press hard, premo, -ere, pressi, pressum.	**archer**, sagittarius, -i.
I am hard pressed, laboro, 1.	**hold one's ground**, in loco perstare.

DIRECT COMMAND OR PETITION[1]

Rule 10.

    Second Person.   If positive = Imperative.
                         If negative = (*a*) Ne with Perfect Subj.
                                     (*b*) Imperat. of nolo with Inf.
    First and Third Persons. Present Subj., with **ne** if negative.

EXAMPLES.

Do not buy this horse = { **Hunc equum ne emeris.**
                                   { **Hunc equum noli emere.**
Let us (not) buy this horse = **Hunc equum (ne) emamus.**

When a command is double, and the second part negative, use **neu** or **neve** instead of **neque**, before the second part.

   e.g. **Maneamus in urbe neve discedamus.**
         Let us remain in the city and not depart.

       Ne iratus sis neve me reliqueris.
       Do not be angry or leave me.

Exercise 73 [*A*].

1. Let us escape to the woods.

2. Follow me into the city,

3. Do not try to escape.

4. Let us go to Rome, and let us not remain here.

5. Let them not return to the city.

6. Do not remain at home, nor fear the storm.

7. Do this that you may be praised.

8. Do not give him a sword, but give him a bow and arrows.

9. Do not let us ask our friends for help.

10. Hold your ground, and do not retreat

---

1. This is inserted here for convenience of revision before doing Indirect Command.

Exercise 74

1. Take away this shield.

2. Do not bring cavalry, but bring infantry and archers.

3. Let us try to bring help to our friends.

4. Give me the books which I asked you for.

5. Come to me, and do not be afraid.

6. Do not let us help our enemies or[1] injure our friends.

7. Let them remain where they are.

8. Do not despise the poor.

9. Let us die for our country.

10. Do not let slip this opportunity.

1. In Latin 'nor.' The second half of the sentence is really negative.

Exercise 74
let slip, dimitto.
opportunity, occasio, -onis, *f.*, facultas, -tatis, *f.*
despise, sperno, -ere, sprevi, spretum.

INDIRECT COMMAND AND PETITION

In the sentences "He commands *the building* of a bridge," "He demands *the payment* of the money," the verbs 'commands' and 'demands' govern direct objects. But usually the place of this direct object is taken by a clause ; *e.g.* "He commands *that the bridge be built*," "He demands *that the money be paid*." These clauses are "noun sentences," and are as truly the objects of the principal verbs as the nouns 'building' and 'payment' in the first sentences. These object-sentences after verbs of asking and commanding are what we mean by "Indirect Commands."

Rule 11. Indirect Commands are expressed in Latin by ut (when positive) ne (when negative) with the Subjunctive.

The construction is exactly the same as that of Final Sentences.
Exceptions.—**Jubeo, veto**, take Present Infinitive. Avoid **jubeo . . non**, for which **impero ne** or **veto** must be used. **Neu (neve)** is used for **neque** in Indirect as in Direct Commands and Final Sentences.

EXAMPLES

(a) **Persuadet Rauracis ut una cum Helvetiis proficiscantur.**
He persuades the Rauraci to set out with the Helvetii.

(b) **Pontem, qui erat ad Genavam, jubet rescindi.**
He orders the bridge at Geneva to be broken down.

(c) **Se gladio transfixit ne fame periret neve ab hostibus caperetur.**
He fell on his sword that he might not die of hunger or be taken by the enemy.

Exercise 75 [A].

1. I asked him to follow me into the streets,

2. I beg of you not to let him escape.

3. He ordered Minucius not to attempt a battle.

4. I will persuade them not to leave me here alone.

5. Caesar had encouraged his men to hold their ground.

6. I forbade your asking him for money.

7. I warn you against despising the friendship of such a man.

8. Caesar demanded that the Germans should not cross the Rhine, nor leave their own territories.

9. The Gauls begged Caesar to spare their town.

10. The journey was so long that he told his men to leave the baggage in the town.

11. I have persuaded him to devote himself to his books.

12. Order the vanguard to halt.

Exercise 75
ask, rogo, two accusatives; peto (ab *or* ex.).
pray, beg, oro, I., precor, I.
demand, flagito, I. postulo, I., posco, -ere, poposci.
urge, exhort, encourage, hortor, I., admoneo.
command, impero, I., *dat.*; jubeo, -ere, jussi, jussum, acc.
decree, ordain, edico.
advise, moneo, *acc.*; suadeo, *dat.*
persuade, persuadeo, *dat.*
forbid, veto, -are, -ui, -itum.
street, via.
attempt (*battle*), tempto, I.
friendship, amicitia.
baggage, impedimenta, *n. pl.*
devote oneself to, studeo, *dat.*
halt, consisto, -ere, -stiti.
vanguard, primum agmen.

Exercise 76 [*B*].

1. They have persuaded me to stay at home.

2. Tell your men to follow you.

3. We were asked to bring help to the citizens.

4. I told you not to leave us here alone.

5. They were advised not to leave their lands.

6. I will urge my friends to come to me at Rome.

7. I told the boy not to buy himself a horse.

8. Tell your brother not to cross the river or come into the town.

9. I have ordered the vanguard to halt and wait for reinforcements.

10. He had received such a serious wound that he asked his slave to kill him.

11. They urged their fellow-countrymen not to surrender nor send hostages to the Romans.

12. The people of the town begged Caesar to spare them.

Exercise 76
bring help, auxilium ferre, *dat.*
serious, severe, gravis.

WORDS THAT MAY INTRODUCE STATEMENTS AND COMMANDS

Rule 12.—**The verbs moneo, persuadeo, suadeo, may introduce either an Indirect statement or an Indirect command.** In the former case, of course, they take Acc. with Inf. *e.g.*, in the sentence "*I will persuade him that this journey is dangerous,*" the word "*persuade*" introduces a statement; but in "*I will persuade him to abandon this journey*" it introduces a command.

EXAMPLE

Civitati persuasit ut de finibus suis exirent: perfacile esse totius Galliae imperio potiri.
He persuaded the State to migrate from their territories (Ind. command); *saying that it was easy to become supreme in Gaul* (Ind. statement).

There is a similar ambiguity in the use of the English "*tell,*" which may introduce either statement or command; *e.g.* "*I told him the journey was dangerous,*" and "*I told him to abandon the journey.*"

Exercise 77 [A].

1. He ordered his men[1] to break down the bridge which had been made over[2] the Rhone.

2. He persuaded his men not to retreat, and warned them that the whole country was in the hands[3] of the enemy.

3. Caesar told his men that he was persuaded that the Germans had crossed the Rhine.

4. Cicero set out with the cavalry after telling[4] the infantry to follow him in three days.

5. Our men were advised to advance with great caution, that the enemy might not attack them off their guard.

6. The prisoners begged Caesar to spare their lives, and send them back to their friends.

7. You will never persuade me that Romans will be conquered by barbarians.

8. So great was the determination of the prisoners that no one could compel them to speak.

9. Were you told that our men had been ordered to lay down their arms?

10. Thereupon he dismissed the council, and ordered them not to assemble again.

11. They knew that Caesar had forbidden them to attack the enemy, but in his absence[5] they began to prepare for battle.

---

1. **Sui**.
2. **in**, with Abl.
3. **in potestate**.
4. Abl. Abs. Remember that in this construction *impero* cannot be used. See Rule 9.
5. Abl. Abs.

Exercise 77
break down, rescindo, -ere, -scidi, -scissum.
Rhine, Rhenus, -i, *m.*
cavalry, equites, -um.
infantry, pedites, -um.
caution, carefulness, diligentia.
off one's guard, improvidus, incautus.
send back, remitto.
determination, constantis.
lay down, depono, -ere, -posui, -positum.
council, concilium.
thereupon, deinde, quo facto.
assemble (*intr.*), convenio. (*tr.*) convoco, I.
prepare for battle, arma expedio.

Exercise 78 [B].

1. I have been asked to stand for the consulship.

2. I shall forbid their crossing to this side of the river.

3. I warn you that you will be punished.

4. Caesar exhorted the legion with many prayers not to betray him to the enemy, or throw away their last hope of safety.

5. We have been forbidden to plunder the houses.

6. Orders have been sent us to try again to storm the town.

7. I was advised by Caesar not to trust you, or take you with me.

8. Our men were incited to search for the treasure by the promised reward.

9. Catiline is believed to have ordered Rome to be set on fire.

10. Persuade him that it is dangerous to cross the mountain.

11. Divitiacus tried to persuade the Gauls to remain faithful to Caesar, and not to revolt from him.

Exercise 78
stand for, be a candidate for, peto.
consulship, consulatus, -us, *m.*
to this side of, citra, *acc.*,
last, ultimus.
prayers, preces, f. *pl.*
plunder, spolio, I., diripio, -ere, -ripui, -reptum.
induce, incite, adduco.
treasure, thesaurus, -i, *m.*
dangerous, periculosus.
remain faithful to Caesar, fidem Caesaris sequor.
revolt from, deficio ab.
search for, quaero, -ere, quaesivi, quaesitum, peto, -ere, -ivi, -itum.

Exercise 79 [A].

Cincinnatus lived on the other side of the Tiber on a little farm, which he cultivated with his own hands. The messengers, who had been sent by the senate, found him sitting in the fields. They told him that they had come to inform him that he had been appointed dictator, and asked him to set out with them as soon as possible. Thereupon he bade his wife Racilia bring him his toga, in order that he might not displease the messengers of the senate. When it had been brought, he said he was willing to obey their commands, and would go with them at once.

Exercise 80 [A].

A certain[1] king found one of his slaves sleeping and holding a letter in his hand. He read the letter, in which the boy's mother thanked him because he had sent[2] her money, and begged him to obey his master faithfully. The king put the letter back with gold into the boy's hand, and then told another slave to wake him. At first the boy was frightened, when he saw the gold; but the king told him that good fortune often came to men when sleeping, and bade him give the gold to his mother, and say that the king greatly praised the mother of so good a son.

1. **Quidam**, following its noun.
2. Verb in Plup. Subj.

Exercise 79
on the other side of, ultra, *acc.*
Tiber, Tīberis, -is, *m.*
cultivate, colo, -ere, colui, cultum.
senate, senatus, -us; patres.
appoint, creo, I., facio.
bring (*of things*), fero. (*of persons*), duco.
displease, displiceo, *dat.*
dictator, dictator, -oris.
toga, toga.

Exercise 80
hold, teneo, -ere, -ui, -tum.
letter, litterae, epistola.
read, lego, -ere, legi, lectum.
thank, gratias ago (-ere, egi, actum), *dat.*
faithful, fidelis; *adv.* fideliter.
put back, repono.
wake (*trans.*), excito, I.
at first, primo.
fortune, fortuna.

Exercise 81 [A].

In the evening a spy was caught by the guards at the gate of the town. Being brought to the commander of the garrison he fell down, and besought him with tears to spare him. He said he could persuade many of the besieging army to desert, and promised to assassinate their general. But the commander said he did not wage war in that way; and he ordered the guards to conduct the man to the enemy's camp. At the same time he sent a letter to the general, in which he advised him not to make use of traitors again—for (said he) they are always willing[1] to betray their masters to save their own lives.

---

1. This sentence is an Indirect Statement; but the word for '*said he*' will be omitted in Latin, being understood from '*advised.*'

Exercise 82 [B].

After this battle the Spartan commander sent a messenger to Sparta to tell the citizens that their good fortune had been lost, Mindarus slain, and that the soldiers were dying of starvation. Soon, however, Darius sent his younger son Cyrus to the coast to supply pay to the Spartan sailors. These then attacked the Athenians so suddenly that they easily beat them, and took the whole fleet. At length the Athenians, being compelled by famine, surrendered their city, and became allies of the Spartans.

Exercise 81
at (*near*), ad.
guard, custos, -odis.
commander, praefectus, -i.
garrison, praesidium.
tear, lacrima.
assassinate, trucido, I.
at the same time, simul.
beseech, obsecro, I.

Exercise 82
younger, natu minor.
supply, praebeo.
pay, stipendium.
Spartan, Lacedaemonius.
ally, socius.
famine, starvation, fames, -is, *f.*

Exercise 83 [*B*].

On the next day the English advanced by forced marches with the intention of[1] attacking the French off their guard. But the latter had already learnt by means of[2] spies that the English were advancing, and had taken up their position on the top of a mound. When the English came within range, the archers began to shoot their arrows at the enemy. But the French general told his men not to fire back, but to allow the English to approach the bottom of the mound. When they were a few paces distant, he ordered his men not to wait any longer, but to get ready their arms. Then when the signal was given the French charged with such force that the English were routed and took to flight.

1. **Eo consilio ut**.
2. **per**.

Exercise 84.

The general vainly tried to persuade his men to follow him through the wood. He told them that the enemy had retreated, and that no one would attack them on the march. But they replied that night was approaching, and that many enemies could conceal themselves behind the trees; and they begged him to allow them to pass the night in the camp. But the general would not allow this, but said that he himself would advance at once even with a few men. The rest he advised to return to the city, and tell their friends that they had been unwilling to march against the enemy.

Exercise 83
forced march, magnum iter.
with the intention of, eo consilio ut.
the former... the latter, ille. .. hic.
take up position, consido, -ere, -sedi, -sessum.
mound, tumulus, -i, *m*.
long (*of time*), diu ; comp, diutius.
within range, intra conjectum teli.
shoot, mitto.
fire back, return fire, tela rejicio.
take to flight, se fugae mandare.
wait, maneo, -ere, mansi, mansum.

Exercise 84
vainly, frustra.
behind, pone, *acc*.
even, etiam [vel *used only with superlatives*].
not even, ne...quidem [*with emphatic word* between],
conceal, celo, I.
pass (*of time*), ago.

DATIVE OF PURPOSE, OR PREDICATIVE DATIVE.

Exitio eat aridum mare nautia.
The greedy sea is a destruction to sailors.

Hosti ludibrio esse.
To be a laughing-stock to the enemy.

Auxilio Caesari mittitur.
He is sent to the help of Caesar.

These Datives are never qualified by an epithet, except the simplest of quantity ; *e.g.* **magno** **dedecori esse** = *to be a great disgrace.* They are almost always accompanied by a *Dativus Commodi*, as **nautis, hosti, Caesari** in the above examples.

Exercise 85 [*A*].

1. I shall only be a burden to you.

2. To sound a retreat will serve as a signal for flight.

3. This negligence has brought disgrace upon him.

4. It was to the advantage of the Romans to banish the kings.

5. His punishment was the cause of his death.

6. Let your father's constancy be an example to you always.

7. He sent money to help me while ill.

8. It was to my credit that (*quod*) you got home safely.

9. This will be a great disgrace to you.

10. He ought not to be hated by you.

11. They persuaded him that such a plan would mean destruction to the whole army.

Exercises

Exercise 86 [*B*].

1. Avarice is a great evil to men.

2. This is a great proof of his courage.

3. He left three legions for the protection of the camp.

4. He ordered me to sound the signal for retreat.

5. I think this defeat was a great disgrace to the Romans.

6. Let us try to set a good example to others.

7. I believe this plan will prove the destruction of our army.

8. He was an object of hatred to all good men.

9. It is to your credit to have spared the prisoners.

10. This victory was the salvation of the state.

11. The position itself was a great help to the Gauls.

Exercise 85
Datives of purpose or result of action.
to be a burden to, oneri esse.
to sound a retreat, receptui canere, cecini, cantum.
to be (serve as) a signal, signo esse.
to be a disgrace, to disgrace, dedecori esse.
to be to the advantage of, to benefit, usui esse.
to be the cause of, to cause, causae.
to be an example, exemplo esse.
to help, be a help to, auxilio, subsidio esse.
to be a credit to, laudi esse.
to be hateful to, hated by, odio esse.
to be (*mean***) destruction to**, exitio esse.
to be a protection to, praesidio esse.
to be the salvation of, saluti esse.
to be a proof, indicio esse.
constancy, constantia.
negligence, carelessness, negligentia, I.
only, merely, modo, solum, tantum.

Exercise 86
avarice, avaritia.

ABLATIVES OF ORIGIN, SEPARATION, ASSOCIATION.[1]

(1) **Jove natus** — *Son of Jupiter.*
(2) **Libera nos metu** — *Free us from fear.*
(3) **Divitiis abundat** — *He has plenty of money.*

Exercise 87 [*A*].

1. Having been banished from his country, he said he was freed from her laws.

2. He was descended from kings, but he did not enjoy kingly power himself.

3. The exiles were compelled to depart from their land.

4. The king was persuaded to set free the captives from prison.

5. Not only was he free from fault, but he also deserved praise.

6. Being the son of such a father, all the people obeyed him willingly.

7. He lived so far from the city, that even his friends did not see him often.

8. The slaves could not be persuaded to speak even by tortures.

9. When kings were banished from Rone, the people were full of joy.

10. Men are often injured even by praise.

11. Not only does the island abound in fruits and flowers, but it is inhabited by a race descended from the gods.

[1]. Earlier exercises on the Ablative are given in exercise 42 and 43..

Exercise 87
banish, expello.
free, liber, -era, -erum, (vb.) libero, I.
free from, devoid of, vacuus.
far from, procul.
son of, natus.
descended, prognatus, ortus.
abound, abundo, I.
endowed, praeditus.
full, plenus.
depart from, discedo, excedo.
kingly power, regia potestas, regnum.
exile, exsul, -ulis.
prison, carcer, -is, *m.*; vincula, *n. pl.*
captive, captivus, -i.
fault, blame, culpa.
blame (lib.), culpo, I.
praise, laus, -dis, *f.*
willingly, libenter.
fruit, fructus, -us, *m.*
flower, flos, floris, *m.*
inhabit, incolo, -ere, -ui.
not only...but also, non solum...sed etiam.
race, people, gens, -tis, *f.*

Exercise 88 [B].

1. This victory has freed us from all fear.

2. The camp was pitched on a hill not far from the town.

3. Even good men are not always free from blame.

4. Being descended from a noble race, he tried to set an example to the rest of the citizens.

5. Not only the men, but also the women and children were banished from their country.

6. The soldiers were ordered to desist from the siege.

7. Even safety will not induce me to live far from the city.

8. This land abounds in all kinds of riches.

9. We were compelled not only to depart from the city, but also to give up all our goods.

10. They were begged by all of us to set free the captives from prison.

11. These people were rich both in cattle and money.

12. He left the city in a passion.

Exercise 88
noble, nobilis.
children, liberi.
desist from, desisto, -ere, -stiti.
siege, obsidio, -onis, *f.*
goods, bona, *n. pl.*
angry, in a passion, iratus.

ABLATIVES OF RESPECT AND MANNER.

(1) **Numero superiores** = *Greater in number.*
(2) **Summa diligentia naves armare** = *To fit ships with great care.*

The Ablative of Manner must have an epithet, except in a few words : *e.g.* **jure** (rightly), **injuria** (wrongly), **fraude** (treacherously), **silentio** (in silence), etc. If there is no epithet use **cum**: *e.g.* **cum diligentia naves armare**.

Exercise 89 [A].

1. The troops were few in number, but they fought with great bravery.

2. He replied in a loud voice that he would never yield.

3. They were told that the enemy were advancing in great disorder.

4. Having armed as many men as possible,[1] they charged the enemy with the utmost fury.

5. I have been wrongfully accused of treachery[2] by my private enemies.

6. They said they had been accustomed to live in the fashion of their ancestors.

7. These traitors were rightly put to death with all speed.

8. He is younger than his brother, but excels him in wisdom and talents.

9. You, who are an Englishman by birth, ought to resist bad laws with all your power.

10. I had not even heard that they were inferior to us in numbers.

11. By your leave I shall ask him to come home with me as often as possible.

12. Not even you, he said, will persuade me that Caesar was rightly killed.

---

1. See note to Exercise 49.
2. Gen. of *crime*.

Exercise 90 [B].

1. The Athenians joined battle with the utmost fury.

2. What he has learnt with care he values most highly.

3. They are superior in skill, not in courage.

4. He spoke this with sorrow.

5. In everything else they employ Greek characters.

6. I believe that we ought to act according to the customs of our ancestors.

7. With your leave I will tell the slaves to withdraw.

8. He seems to have been rightly punished.

9. To live in the fashion of rich men seems pleasant to you who are poor.

10. He replied in great anger that his enemy had lied.

11. The consul with a smile said, "Go home and do not come here again."

12. We are inferior to the enemy in numbers, but our men excel others in courage.

Exercise 89
rightly, jure.
wrongly, injuria.
in the fashion of, more.
by your leave, pace tua.
by force, vi; **by force of arms**, vi et armis.
with all one's power, summa vi, pro virili parte.
older, natu major.
younger, natu minor.
in a loud voice, magna voce.
disorder, confusion, tumultus, -us, *m.*
arm, arno, I.
fury, furor, -oris, *m.*
excel, supero, I.
talents, ingenium.
inferior, inferior.
numbers, numerus, -i, *m.* (*only in sing.*).
ancestors, majores.

Exercise 90
care, cura, diligentia.
skill, ars, -tis, *f.*
superior, superior.
be superior, praesto.
sorrow, dolor, -oris, *m.*
characters (= **letters**), litterae.
withdraw, go away, abeo, discedo.
smile, risus, -us, *m.* (*vb.*) subrideo, -ere, -risi, -risum.
here, hic; (of motion), huc.
act, ago, me gero.

Exercise 91 [A]. (*Exercises 91-98 are intended for revision.*)

Numa being dead, Tullus Hostilius was made king. While he was king war arose between the Romans and Albans. In order that the war might be finished without great loss, the kings ordered that three Romans should fight for their fatherland against three Albans, and decide the contest. The fight lasted a long time, but at last two of the Romans were killed, and all three Albans were wounded. The third Roman, whose name was Horatius, pretended to flee, and induced the Albans to pursue him. In following him they were separated, and Horatius, turning round, killed them in turn.

Exercise 92 [A].

Eurystheus then set[1] Hercules the eleventh labour, which was harder than those which we have mentioned above. For he ordered him to take away the golden apples from the gardens of the Hesperides.[2] These were nymphs of remarkable beauty, who lived in a distant land, and some golden apples had been entrusted[3] to them by Juno. Many men had before this tried to take away these apples; but it was a difficult thing to do,[4] for the garden in which the apples were was surrounded by a high wall on all sides. Moreover a dragon,[5] which had a hundred heads, guarded the gate of the garden carefully by day and night.

1. **proponere**.
2. **committere**.
3. **Hesperides, -um**.
4. **factu** (supine).
5. **draco, onis**, *m*.

Exercise 91
loss, damnum.
decide the contest, rem decerno, -ere, -crevi, -cretum.
by name, called, nomine.
separate, sejungo, -ere, -junxi, -junctum.
turn round (*trans.*), converto.
turning round (*intr.*), conversus.
in turn, singuli, *adj.*, in vicem.

Exercise 92
mention above, supra commemoro, 1.
golden, aureus.
apple, malum.
garden, hortus, -i, *m*.
nymph, nympha.
remarkable, mirus, insignis, praeclarus.
beauty, pulcritudo, -inis, *f.*, forma.
distant, longinquus.
surround, cingo, -ere, cinxi, cinctum.
on all sides, ab omnibus partibus, undique.
moreover, praeterea.
guard, custodio.
by day...by night, interdiu...noctu.

Exercise 93 [A].

Hearing that the Belgae were conspiring against the Romans, Caesar determined to go himself without delay to central Gaul with two legions, ordering the rest to follow in a few days. On his arrival the Remi, who live on the borders of Gaul, sent ambassadors to say that they were willing to give hostages, and help the Romans with corn. They said that the rest of the Belgae were under arms, and that the Germans had joined them. On hearing this, Caesar promised to come with all possible speed to the help of the Remi, that having joined their forces they might repel the invasion of the Germans.

Exercise 94 [A].

The Romans, having set out about the third watch, advanced with great caution, for they had been informed that the enemy were close at hand. They advanced until late in the night, and then were told to pitch their camp. In the middle of the night shouts were heard on all sides, and they saw that great forces of the enemy were making an attack. So they took up their arms as quickly as possible to repel the onset. But when the enemy perceived that they had not been able to attack our men off their guard, the signal for retreat was given, and they withdrew.

Exercise 93
conspire, conjuro, 1.
conspiracy, conjuratio, onis. *f.*
delay, mora.
centre, media *or* interior pars.
on his arrival, adventu ejus. [If *he* refers to the subject of sentence say *qui quum advenisset*.]
the rest of, reliqui, ceteri, *adj.*
under arms, armati, in armis.
join, *trans.*, conjungo; *intrans*, se conjungere cum.
invasion, incursio, -onis. *f.*
borders, fines, -ium, *m.*

Exercise 94
about, de, *prep.*
watch, vigilia.
caution, diligentia.
until late in the night, usque ad multam noctem.
take up, sumo, -ere, sumpsi, sumptum.

Exercise 95 [B].

Louis[1] could not at this time besiege Tunis,[2] because he had not received reinforcements from his brother Charles,[3] King of Sicily; and meanwhile his army was attacked by a disease which carried off the greater part of his soldiers in a few days. The king himself was seized with the disease, and felt that he would die of it. But, to sustain the courage of his soldiers, he performed all the duties of a king, and attended in every way to the safety of the camp. But at last he was compelled to remain within his tent, and before long[4] died, after telling his men never to abandon the siege.

1. *Louis* = **Ludovicus**.
2. For *Tunis* use **Carthage**.
3. *Charles* = **Carolus**.
4. *Before long* = **mox**.

Exercise 96 [B].

Nothing had been heard of the army for many months, and the citizens began to think that it had been defeated and all their fellow-countrymen killed. The women used to go every day to the temples, and pray the gods to send them back safely their husbands and sons. At last, when winter was approaching, and all had begun to give up hope, a messenger was seen at a distance who was approaching the city with great speed. The citizens all rushed out to meet him, and implored him to tell them without delay about the army. So tired was the messenger by his journey that at first he could not speak; but at length he said that the army had both won many victories and taken many towns of the enemy, and that the soldiers hoped in a short time to return home with a great quantity of booty and many prisoners.

Exercise 97 [B].

As the people of Veii[1] often made incursions[2] for the sake of plunder, the Romans were scarcely able to defend their own territories. Their soldiers went home to their fields in the spring to sow, and in the autumn to gather the harvest, at which times the Veientines did a great deal of harm to[3] their lands. At last the Fabii promised the Senate that they would be under arms the whole year, and undertake the whole war themselves. The Senate thanked them, and going out from Rome they made a camp near the river Cremera. For a little time they checked the Veientines, but at length they were surrounded, and slaughtered to a man.

1. **Veientes**.
2. Abl. Abs.
3. *Harmed much.*

Exercise 95	Exercise 96	Exercise 97
Sicily, Sicilia.	**husband**, vir, maritus, -i.	**scarcely**, vix.
meanwhile, interea, interim.	**give up hope**, spem abjicio.	**sow**, sero, -ere, sevi, satum.
attack (*of a disease*), afficio, -ere, -feci, -fectum.	**rush out**, effundor, -i, -fusus.	**autumn**, auctumnus, -i, *m*.
carry off (= **destroy**), deleo, -ere, -evi, -etum; conficio.	**to meet**, obviam, *dat*.	**gather**, colligo, -ere, -legi, -lectum.
sustain, **encourage**, confirmo, I.	**win a victory**, victoriam reporto, I., rem prospere gero.	**harvest**, messis, -is, *f*.
attend to, studeo, *dat*.; curo, I., acc.	**temple**, templum.	**undertake**, suspicio.
in every way, omni modo.	**great quantity of**, multus.	**check**, cohibeo.
tent, tabernaculum.		
abandon a siege, raise a siege, obsidionem relinquo, obsidione desisto.		
feel, sentio, -ire, sensi, sensum.		

Exercise 98 [B].

We set out from Moscow[1] about the third watch, so that no disturbance might be excited by our friends. I never expected to see my brothers again. For thirty-three days we marched along a road covered by snow a foot deep. Sometimes one of us fell down, and was unable to move further. Our guards did not try to urge him on, for they knew well that the wolves would have him for[2] their prey before the next day. I now often envy those who were thus left on the road, and prefer death to the evils which daily press upon me. I am compelled to work, but that is the least of my ills: I am compelled to see the sufferings of the women who with us dared everything for the sake of liberty.

1. **Moscova**.
2. **pro**, or simple acc. in apposition.

Exercise 98
disturbance, tumultus, -us, *m.*; motus, -us, *m.*
excite, excito, I.
cover, operio, -ire, -ui, -pertum; (shelter), tego, -ere, -ui, -tectum.
sometimes, nonunquam, interdum.
fall down, delabor, -i, -lapsus.
further, longius, ultra.
urge on, urgeo, ursi.
wolf, lupus, -i, *m.*
press upon, threaten, insto, *dat.*
suffering, dolor, -oris, *m.* [also indignation, resentment].
prey, praeda.

Exercise 99
write, scribo, -ere, scripsi, scriptum.
change, muto, I.

Exercises

GERUNDS AND GERUNDIVES

Distinguish the Gerund and Gerundive.
(1) The Gerund is a Verbal Noun of the Active Voice, corresponding to the English verbal nouns in *-ing*; not to be confused with the Present Participle in *-ing*, which is really an Adjective.
(2) The Gerundive is a Verbal Adjective of the Passive Voice.

<u>Rule 13.</u>—A. The oblique cases of the Gerund are used simply as the cases of a Noun. But the Accusative can only be used governed by a Preposition.

e.g.
Acc.	**natus ad regendum**	= *born to rule.*
Gen.	**cupidus discendi**	= *desirous of learning.*
Dat.	**studuit discendo**	= *he was devoted to learning.*
Abl.	(**in**) **discendo sapientior fio**	= *by learning I become wiser.*

When the Gerund is in the Genitive case or the Ablative without a Preposition it may take a direct object.[1]

e.g.
Gen.	**pacem petendi causa**	= *for the sake of seeking peace.*
Abl.	**scribendo fabulas**	= *in writing stories.*

B. But when the Verbal Noun governs a direct object[2] instead of the Gerund we generally use the Gerundive. This attracts the object into its own case, but agrees with the object in number and gender. This construction is known as "Gerundive Attraction."

e.g.
Acc.	**ad pacem petendam**	= *in order to ask for peace.*
Gen.	**pacis petendae causa**	= *for the sake of asking for peace.*
Dat.	**legibus mutandis studuit**	= *he was eager for changing the laws.*
Abl.	**in scribendis fabulis**	= *in writing stones.*

1. Use the Gerund especially where by using the Gerundive we should get two genitives ending in **-orum** or **-arum** together.
2. The Gerundive being Passive, none but transitive verbs (governing a direct object in the Acc.) can have a Gerundive. But **utendus, potiundus, fruendus**, can be used from **utor, potior, fruor**.

Exercise 99.

The art of writing.

The art of writing letters.

By obeying the laws.

By changing the laws.

For the sake of pleasing our friends.

For the sake of saving our friends.

In order to injure the Gauls.

In order to defeat the Gauls.

The signal for advance.[1]

The signal for striking the camp.

The desire of having riches.

By dying.

For the purpose of preserving the state.

For the purpose of helping the state.

For saving the king.

For serving the king.

1. When the Gerund or Gerundive depend on a substantive, put them in the Genitive Case.

Exercise 100 [A].

1. We have done this for the sake of helping our friends.

2. By teaching others we learn ourselves.

3. By learning letters we are able to enjoy reading.

4. They hastened to Rome for the purpose of defending the city.

5. Are you not desirous of saving your friends?

6. The Romans became great through their desire to obey the laws.

7. The art of ruling others is not easily learnt.

8. For the sake of winning honour we suffer much pain.

9. An opportunity has been offered for fighting.

10. This seems a good opportunity for defeating the enemy.

Exercise 100
hasten, propero, 1. festino, 1.
desire, studium, amor, cupido, -inis, *f.*
desirous, anxious, cupidus.
suffer, patior, -i, passus.
reading, lectio, -onis, *f.*
win, adipiscor, -i, adeptus.
honour, honos, -oris, *m.*; fama.
offer an opportunity, facio, potestatem; do occasionem.

Exercise 101 [A].

1. Caesar sent cavalry to bring help to the allies.

2. The officers sent their men to forage in all directions.

3. By obeying the laws we show that we are desirous of preserving our state.

4. He gave his men the signal to advance.

5. The signal was given to advance the standards.

6. The Athenians sent men to Delphi to consult the god.

7. For the sake of pleasing their friends the senate did many disgraceful things.

8. He sent messengers to the Aedui to demand hostages from them.

9. No opportunity was left them for retreating.

10. They are anxious to devote themselves to letters.

Exercise 101
forage, *vb.*, pabulor, I. *n.* pabulum.
consult, consulo, -ere, -sului, -sultum, *acc.*
consult interests of, consulo, *dat.*
disgraceful, turpis.
devote oneself to, studeo, *dat.*
in all directions, passim.

Exercise 102 [B].

1. They were led on by the hope of taking the city.

2. I was induced to do this for the sake of pleasing the soldiers.

3. We were sent to ask for help.

4. They were sent to bring help to the allies.

5. Time is often wasted in writing books.

6. By obeying wise laws the Roman state became great.

7. The people of this city seem anxious to change their laws.

8. Let us not let slip this opportunity of winning a victory.

9. I am anxious to consult your interests.

10. Caesar was anxious to exact hostages from the Gauls.

Exercise 102
lead on, induce, adduco.
waste time, tempus tero.

Exercise 103 [B].

1. Let us not talk of flying, for only by holding our ground shall we conquer.

2. To save his country a man ought always to face death.

3. How many of us are fit for commanding an army?

4. He gave the signal for crossing the river.

5. In our zeal for pursuing the cavalry we advanced too far.[1]

6. For learning one needs[2] talent and a great desire of knowledge.

7. We were sent for to defend the king from harm.

8. A great cause of crime is the desire of having wealth.

9. Officers were ordered to enter the citadel to receive the arms which the enemy had promised to give up.

10. For the sake of filling the ships and sailing at once they bought merchandise at a great price.

11. They are here to ask for pardon.

1. Comparative.
2. *One needs* = **opus est**.

Exercise 103
face, obeo, *acc.*
fit for, aptus ad, idoneus ad.
harm, injury, damnum, incommodum.
send for, arcesso, -ere, -ivi, -itum.
one needs, opus est.
officer, legatus, praefectus.
citadel, arx, arcis, *f.*.
fill, compleo, -ere, -plevi, -pletum.
merchandise, merces, *pl.*
pardon, venia.

SUPINES

Besides the Gerund there is another Noun in Latin called the Supine. It only has two cases—an Acc. in **-um**, and an Abl. in **-u**.

Rule 14.—The Supine in -um can only be used to express purpose after Verbs of motion. It may govern an object.[1]

The Supine in **-u** can only be used after Adjectives,[2] and corresponds to an Infinitive following an Adjective in English, *e.g.* "a question *hard to answer*."

EXAMPLES

Abii dormitum	= *I went away to sleep.*
Venerunt pacem petitum	= *They came to ask for peace.*
Mirabile dictu	= *wonderful to relate.*

Exercise 104 [*A*].

1. It is easy to say, but difficult to do.

2. They say that the city will not easily be captured.

3. Go out to play.

4. Do not always eat what is pleasant to eat.

6. The story is a strange one to tell.

6. Send him to pay the money at once.

7. The general told the officers to send some men to forage.

8. Fire is dangerous to touch.

9. They left Rome to found a new colony.

10. All agree that the city will never be surrendered.

---

1. The Future Infinitive Passive is made up of the Supine with **iri**, so that in the sentence '**Dixerunt nos interfectum iri**,' *interfectum* really governs *nos*, being a supine of purpose after *iri*.
2. Also certain indeclinable nouns used as adjectives, *e.g.* **fas** (right), **nefas** (wrong).

Exercise 105 [B].

1. Aeneas had gone away from the camp to ask for help.

2. I do not believe that the money will be paid.

3. It is not lawful to do this.

4. The mother and wife of Coriolanus were sent to him to ask pardon on behalf of the city.

5. I shall go to bed soon.

6. They often do things disgraceful to relate.

7. I hope the soldiers will be sent home again.

8. The story is easy to tell.

9. Send men to give an answer.

10. He spoke with a voice difficult to hear.

Exercise 104
story, fabula.
strange, mirabilis.
pay, solvo.
found, condo.
colony, colonia.
all agree, constat inter omnes.
play, ludo, -ere, lusi, lusum.

Exercise 105
lawful, fas [*indeclinable*].
go to bed, cubltum eo.
on behalf of, pro, *abl.*

Exercise 106 [A].

Our men saw that they were surrounded on all sides; and no opportunity being left for retreating, they resolved to charge with all their might in the hope of striking terror into the enemy. They knew that they had been brought into these dangers by delaying too long[1] before, and they hoped that by fighting bravely now they would force the enemy to give ground. Therefore, when the signal for advance was given, they ran forward with a loud shout against that part of the line which seemed weakest.[2] The enemy were thrown into such confusion[3] by this unexpected attack that their line was broken at once, and no one resisted our charge.[4]

1. Comparative of **diu**.
2. **tenuis**.
3. *were so disturbed* (**perturbare**)
4. *them charging*.

Exercise 106
strike terror into, inspire with terror, injicio terrorem, *dat.*
bring into danger, in periculum adduco.
give ground, cedo.
unexpected, subitus, inopinatus.
break (a line), inclino, I.

Exercises 115

Exercise 107 [A].

A messenger had been sent to France to ask for help, and to invite French troops to Ireland. Arms and money were promised for the purpose of assisting an Irish army. These were conveyed[1] by a French ship, and a hundred men assembled on the shore to receive the arms which it was going to land.[2] But in a storm two of their boats had been broken, and in repairing them time was wasted.[3] Meanwhile, to scatter the rebels, a troop of horse had been sent out from Cork, at the sight of whom[4] the rebels fled in all directions; and to effect their own escape the French sailors threw the arms overboard[5]; they lie sunk[6] in the harbour to this day.

1. *convey by sea* = **transportare**.
2. **expositura erat.**
3. Use Historic Present.
4. Abl. Abs.
5. **e navi projicere.**
6. **submenus.**

Exercise 107
invite, invito, I.
Ireland, Hibernia.
Irish (*adj.*), Hibernicus.
scatter, dispergo, -ere, -si, -sum, trans. (For intrans. use the Passive.)
rebel, rebellis.
troop (*of horse*), turma.
effect escape, salutem fuga petere.

Exercise 108 [B].

The French general was unwilling to attack us at close quarters, because his troops were inexperienced in battle, and he thought they would fight best (when) sheltered[1] by ramparts. Moreover, three years before his troops had been unable to resist the English hand-to-hand, but having been withdrawn into the town, had defended the walls obstinately. The recollection of that time and the desire to prolong the war induced him to remain where he was. However, in order to give the Belgians[2] an opportunity of deserting us, he sent out troops of cavalry as far as our outposts. But for fear of this we employed no Belgians as sentinels. For throughout the whole year we were expecting every day they would desert us.

1. **tectus** = *covered*. in the sense of *sheltered*; **opertus** = *covered*, in the sense of *hidden*.
2. **Belgae**.

Exercise 108
at close quarters, hand to hand, comminus, *adv.*
at a distance, eminus.
inexperienced, imperitus, *gen.*
withdraw, deduco, trans.
obstinate, pertinax.
obstinately, obstinate.
obstinacy, pertinacia.
recollection, memoria.
prolong, produco, duco.
desert, desgro (-ere, -ui, -tum), transfugio.
desert (= **revolt from**), deficio ab.
deserter, transfuga, perfuga.
as far as, usque ad.
outposts, stationes, *f.*
for fear of this, hoc timore (lit. **through this fear**).
as, pro, *abl.*
sentinels, custodes, vigiliae.

Exercise 109 [B].

The Athenians hoped that a Spartan army would march into Boeotia, and had taken no measures[1] to save their families and property. Therefore they saw with the utmost fear and dismay that the barbarians were advancing with all their forces for the sake of attacking their city. It was evident that in six days Xerxes would be at Athens, and this seemed a very short time for removing the population of a whole city. But they knew that it was of the greatest importance[2] to them to accomplish this, and before his arrival they had safely removed all who were willing to leave their homes. Some were taken to Aegina, others to Troezen;[3] but many could not be induced to proceed farther than Salamis.[4]

1. 'had done nothing.'
2. **Maximi interesse** = to be of the greatest importance.
3. **Troezen**, *Gen.* **Troezenis** *f.*
4. **Salamis**, *Gen.* **Salaminis**, *Acc.* **Salamina** *f.*

Exercise 109
it concerns, *interest*, refert.
These take a Genitive of the person concerned. But instead of the Gen. of pronouns they take mea, tua, *etc. They may also be qualified by a Gen. of value or neuter adjective:*
e.g.{ maximi interest, multum interest} = *it is of the greatest importance.*
They can be followed both by infinitive and indirect question.

family, household, familia.
property, bona, *n. pl.*
evident, manifestus.
remove, transfero.
population, populus, multitudo.
accomplish, efficio.
safely, tuto.
dismay, pavor, -oris, *m.*

DIRECT QUESTIONS

Rule 15. Direct Questions may be asked without any special Interrogative word, but they are frequently introduced

(a) by Interrogative Pronouns or Adverbs, such as **quis**, *who?* **quando**,[2] *when?* **ubi**, *where?*

(b) by Interrogative Particles. These Particles are in Single Questions **-ne** (enclitic), **nonno** (expecting answer "*yes*"), **num** (expecting answer "*no*"); in Double Questions **utrum ... an, -ne ... an, utrum ... annon**.

EXAMPLES.

(a) **Caesarne** ad castra advenit?
Has Caesar reached the camp?

(b) **Nonne** Caesar ad castra advenit?
Has not Caesar reached the camp? Surely Caesar has reached the camp?

(c) **Num** Caesar ad castra advenit?
Caesar has not reached the camp, has he?[3]

(d) **Utrum** Caesar (or Caesarne) ad castra advenit annon?
Has Caesar reached the camp or not?

[N.B.—Do not append the **-ne** to an unemphatic word.]

---

1. This rule is inserted here for convenience of revision before doing Indirect Questions.
2. *When* in questions is never **quum** but **quando**. Notice also that *where* is often used in English for *whither*, and in this sense must be translated by **quo**.
3. Notice the form of the English. "Has he?" "is he?" "isn't he?" etc., is only our way of showing what answer we expect, and is fully represented in Latin by the **nonne** or **num** at the beginning of the sentence.

Exercise 110 [A].

1. Did you say that you would come?

2. Were you or your brother the first to arrive?

3. What sort of country do you live in?

4. Surely you do not hope to see him again?

5. Where have you come from? Where are you going to? Where have you decided to live?

6. Do you not believe that this loss will increase the panic?

7. How many books have you?

8. How often have you seen him, and when do you expect him to return?

9. Have you determined to accept these terms or not?

10. How great is the army of the enemy, and who commands it?

11. What plan have you formed now?

Exercise 110
Interrogative words.
who? what? quis, quid (*adj.* qui, quae, quod). Also quisnam.
which of two? uter, -tra, -trum.
of what sort? qualis.
how great? quantus.
how many? quot.
how often? quoties.
how? (with *adj.* and *adv.*) quam.
how? (= **in what manner?**) quomodo, quemadmodum.
how long? quamdiu.
why? cur, quare, quamobrem.
when? quando.
where? ubi, qua.
whence? where from? unde.
whither? where to? quo.
increase, *trans.*, augeo, -ere, auxi, auctum. *intrans.*, cresco, -ere, crevi, cretum.
regard as, habeo, duco.
cunning, *n.* sollertia. *adj.* sollers.
panic, pavor.
terms, conditiones.
worthy, dignus.

Exercise 111 [B].

1. Is it easier to command or to obey?

2. Have you seen the horse which I gave your brother?

3. How many times have you been to France?

4. Surely you do not think me worthy of blame?

5. They did not ask you to go to Rome, did they?

6. How large is the house in which you live?

7. Which of these two books do you prefer?

8. Why do you prefer England to France?

9. What plan have you formed now?

10. How great is the army of the enemy, and who commands it?

11. Where did you buy this horse? Where did you send the letter? Where did these ships come from?

Exercises

INDIRECT QUESTIONS

In the sentence " He asked *what I was doing*" the clause '*what I was doing*' is really the object of the verb 'asked.' In the sentence "*What he is doing* is uncertain" the clause '*what he is doing*' is really the subject of 'is.' When a direct question becomes thus the subject or object of a verb we call it an Indirect Question.

<u>Rule 16.</u>—**A clause expressing an Indirect Question in Latin always has its verb in the Subjunctive.**

The principal verb may be any such word as ask, know, doubt, consider, tell, etc.

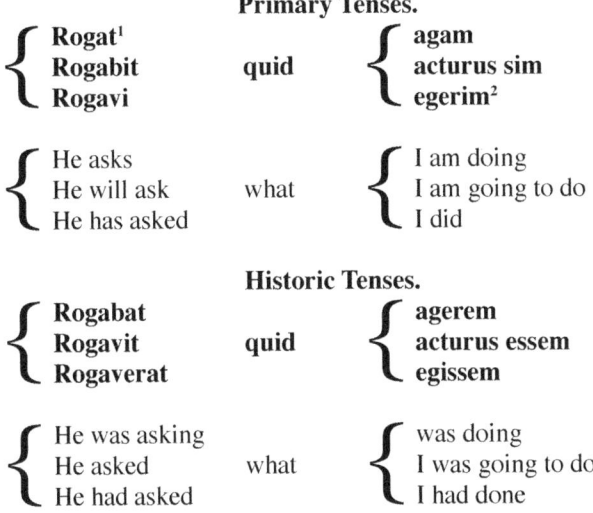

In the above examples it will be noticed that we supply a **Future Subjunctive** by what is called the periphrastic conjugation, *i.e.*, the Fut. Participle with **sim** in Primary, **essem** in Historic sequence.

e.g. **Nescio quando venturi sint**
I do not know when they will come.

Nesciebam quando venturi essent
I did not know when they would come.

The interrogative particles are the same as in direct questions (whether single or double). But in indirect questions **num** does not necessarily expect the answer '*no*,' and **necne** must be used for **annon**. "If" meaning "*whether*" introducing a question must never be translated **si**, but in single questions by **num**, in double by **num ... an** or **utrum ... an**. "When" in questions is **quando**, never **quum**.

---

1. The Imperative is a Primary tense—

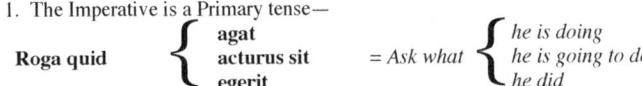

2. The Perfect represents a completed action. Therefore use the Perf. Subj. when the governing verb is primary and the dependent verb relates to an action completed in past time,
   e.g.— **Nescio quomodo mortuus sit** = *I do not know how he died.*

Exercise 112 [A].

1. Tell me why you did that.

2. We have not been told when reinforcements will arrive.

3. It was doubtful if they would arrive before night.

4. We did not know where our friends had gone, nor where we should find them.

5. It is uncertain whether we shall see him again.

6. I was not told whether I ought to remain or go away.

7. Tell me where you have come from.

8. I do not know how I ought to do this.

9. Have you heard what plan the general has formed?

10. I was told how bravely our men had fought.

Exercise 112
Words introducing indirect questions.
ask, rogo; interrogo ; quaero, -ere, quaesivi, quaesitum (ex).
know, scio.
not to know, nescio.
it is doubtful, incertum, dubium est.
to be doubtful, to doubt, dubito, I.
to ascertain, cognosco.
to deliberate, consult, delibero, I., consulo.
to consider, cogito, I., reputo, I.
to be of importance, make a difference, interest, refert. (See *Voc.* 109.)
it matters a great deal, multum *or* magni interest.

Exercise 113 [A].

1. I have not heard when he arrived.

2. It is doubtful whether we ought to do this or not.

3. I do not know if he told the truth.

4. It is hard to say whether this was done on purpose or not.

5. I was not told how I ought to answer.

6. I cannot say how often I have been asked to come.

7. Nobody seems to know how great the enemies' forces were.

8. It was doubtful how many soldiers would arrive.

9. We had not been told what sort of man he was.

10. Can you tell me if he was rightly punished?

Exercise 113
on purpose, de industria.

Exercise 114 [B].

1. Nobody knows whether he said that or not.

2. Have you heard which of the two was elected consul?

3. The soldiers did not know what plan the general had formed.

4. He said he did not know if Crassus had been put in command of the army.

5. It is uncertain how many men he is in command of, and where he has taken up his position.

6. We asked them who they were, where they lived, where they came from, and where they were now going.

7. I cannot tell you when they have promised to come.

8. It is doubtful how he is able to do such things.

9. We, who are old, understand how happy are the young.

10. I do not know whether you deserve praise or blame.

Exercise 114
old, senex, -is.
happy, felix, beatus.
understand, intellego, -ere, -lexi, -lectum.
young, juvenis.

Exercise 115 [B].

1. He wants to know what I am going to do tomorrow.

2. It matters a great deal[1] whether they intend to send out cavalry or infantry.

3. We did not know whether the enemy were going to attack in the evening or late in the night.

4. It was doubtful what news the messenger would bring.

5. Let us ask if one regiment will be enough.

6. When the enemy would cross the river was quite uncertain.

7. Tell me if your father is dead.

8. It makes a great difference whether he bought the horse at a low price or not.

9. Have you heard if he has been persuaded to return?

10. It is uncertain whether he will hinder us more than he will help us.

---

1. **maximi interest.**

Exercise 115
tomorrow, cras.
intend, in animo habeo.
late at night, multa nocte.
what news? quid novi?
regiment, cohors, -ortis, *f.*
quite, admodum.

Exercise 116 [A].

N.B.—Abstract nouns should generally be translated by concrete expressions;

e.g.— What is the *character* (nature) of the island!	=	**Qualis est insula?**
What is the *size* of the island?	=	**Quanta est insula?**
What are the *numbers* of the enemy!	=	**Quot sunt hostes?**
Their *decision* is	=	**constituerunt.**

What is your { reason for doing this! / intention (object) in doing this } **Quo consilio id agis!**

1. The general tried to discover the numbers and intentions of the enemy.

2. Have you been able to discover his reason for doing this?

3. Nobody seemed to understand their object in asking for such terms.

4. I almost think we ought to retreat.

5. They had not heard the decision of the king.

6. It was doubtful where our friends were, and when they would come to meet us.

7. I rather think he has been advised to depart.

8. He sent me to discover the nature of the island.

9. It is uncertain where they started from, and when they will reach the city.

Exercise 116
None

Exercise 117 [B].

1. I could not discover his reason for saying that.

2. We cannot find out the size of the enemy's camp.

3. I did not tell him by what road we should march.

4. The generals did not inform the soldiers of their decision.

5. Spies were sent forward to learn what was going on in the enemy's camp.

6. Can you tell me how many miles the town of Veii is distant from Rome?

7. We could not easily discover the numbers of the enemy.

8. Do you know the destination of these travellers?

9. I almost think they have been compelled to retreat.

10. We could not discover their reason for returning home.

Exercise 117
go on, happen, *passive of* ago.
traveller, viator.

Exercise 118 [A].

It is said that a certain prophetess brought nine books to Tarquin,[1] king of Rome, and asked him if he wished to buy them. The king asked for what price she was willing to sell them; to which she replied that she would sell them for three hundred pieces of gold. The woman went away, but afterwards she returned with six books. Tarquin asked where she had left the others, and she replied that she had burnt them, but that she would sell him these for the same price. Tarquin would not buy them, and she again left him. But once more she returned with only three books, and asked whether he was willing to buy these at the same price or not.

1. **Tarquinius.**

Exercise 119 [A].

The king, who wondered why she had returned so often, now asked his senate whether he ought to keep them. They first asked him what sort of books they were, and if the prophetess had shown them to him. The king replied that she had said nothing, but that she had burnt six books out of[1] nine, and now offered three at the same price. It seemed doubtful to the senators what they ought to do, but at last they advised the king to buy the books. Then the woman, having received the money, advised the Romans to keep the books very carefully, and went away.

1. **de.**

Exercise 118
prophet, prophetess, vates, -is
piece (of gold), nummus, -i, *m.*
once more, rursus.
price, pretium.

Exercise 119
wonder, miror.
offer, offero, offerre, obtuli, oblatum.
show, ostendo, -ire, -di, -sum, *or* -turn.

Exercise 120 [A].

The story is told of King Tarquin that he once determined to add new companies[1] to the Roman knights. Attius the augur said it could not be done. Moved by anger the king demanded that he should show by a sign what the gods wished. Attius replied that he would tell the king what he had in his mind. But Tarquin said, " Tell me rather whether that which I have in my mind can be done." " It can be done," said Attius. Then the king bade him cut a whetstone[2] in two, for he said he was thinking of that. Without any delay (so they relate[3]) Attius cleft it with a razor.[4]

1. **centuriae**.
2. **cos, cotis**, *f.*
3. **ut ferunt**.
4. **novacula**.

Exercise 121 [B].

In the following year Cleon was sent to Macedonia to recover the cities which had been taken by the Spartans. He first marched to Amphipolis, and encamped on rising ground near the city. In the meanwhile Brasidas, the Spartan general, who knew what sort of man Cleon was, resolved to deceive him by a trick. He ordered his men not to show themselves on the wall, but to conceal themselves behind the ramparts. Meanwhile he sent out spies to discover how large the forces of Cleon were, and if reinforcements were coming. These men brought back word that the army of the enemy was small, and was not drawn up carefully. Then Brasidas ordered his men to throw open the gates and attack the enemy at once. The Athenians, who did not trust their general, took to flight, and most of them were killed.

Exercise 120
add, addo, -gre, -didi, -ditum.
moved (by anger), commotus.
sign, signum.
rather, potius.
cut in two, discindo, -fere, -scidi, scissum.
augur, augur, -uris.

Exercise 121
following, next, proximus.
recover, *trans.*, recipio.
rising ground, editus locus.
trick, dolus, -i, *m.*
most of them, plerique.
encamp, consido, -ere, -sedi, sessum.

Exercise 122 [B].

The prisoner was brought before the king, who asked him where he had concealed his money. To this the man replied that he had indeed been rich once, but that now all his money had been taken away from him by the soldiers, and that nothing was left. The king asked the soldiers if this was true, but they all declared that they had not taken the gold, and did not know where the prisoner kept it. Then the king said that he would discover by means of tortures who was telling the truth; but the prisoner, being overcome by fear, asked if the king would pardon him when the money was given up.[1] The king promised to do this, whereupon the prisoner said he would show them at once where he had carried the money.

1. abl. abs.

Exercise 123 [B].

I once went to the house of a celebrated man, who had formerly been a friend of mine, to ask if he would help me in a matter which I had in hand.[1] The servant (slave) said he was not at home, but as I had caught sight of my friend, I knew the fellow[2] lied. Some days after the great man[3] came to my house, and I, having no servant,[4] opened the door to him myself. On seeing him I exclaimed, with unmoved countenance, "He is not at home." In astonishment my friend asked whether I was mad. To which I replied, "I believed your servant when he told lies about you. Are you not willing to believe me when I speak about myself?"

1. *undertaken* (**suscipere**).
2. **homo** — often contemptuous.
3. **ille**.
4. *'to whom there was no servant.'*

SUBORDINATE CLAUSES IN INDIRECT STATEMENT, ETC.

Rule 17. All clauses which are subordinate to an indirect statement or command or question have their verbs in the subjunctive.

EXAMPLE.

Ariovistus respondet se non in eas partea Galliae venire audere quas Caesar possideret.
Ariovistus replied that Tie did not dare to come into those parts of Gaul which Caesar held.

Exercise 124 [*A*].

It was the custom of the Falisci to send their children to a schoolmaster to live with him. When the Romans were waging war with the Falisci, this schoolmaster thought that he would please the Romans if he gave them these children as hostages. He therefore purposely led them, without the knowledge of the citizens, to the Roman camp, and offered them to the general. The latter, however, asked him how he had dared to betray children who had been committed to his care, and threatened him with severe punishment. Then he told the children to take such rods as their master was himself accustomed to use, and with these to drive him to the city.

Exercise 122
indeed, quidem.
once, formerly, olim, quondam.
by means of, per.
overcome (*by fear*), perculsus.
whereupon, quo facto.

Exercise 123
celebrated, praeclarus.
catch sight of, conspicio, -ere, - spexi, -spectum; conspicor, I.
some days after, aliquot post diebus.
door, janua.
in astonishment, attonitus.
be mad, furo, -ere (no Perfect), *adj.* insanus, amens.
exclaim, clamo, I.

Exercise 124
custom, mos, moris, *m*.
schoolmaster, magister, -tri.
without the knowledge of.
   Use inscius.
former...latter, ille...hic.
commit to one's care, mando, I., acc. and *dat*.
rod, virga.
such ... as, talis ... qualis.
drive, ago.
severe, gravis.
punishment, poena, supplicium.

Exercise 125 [A].

The news reached[1] Rome that their army had been defeated, and that of the two consuls who were in command one had been killed and the other was a fugitive. At first the whole city was full of panic and grief. But soon the Senate assembled to take measures[2] for the safety of the State. They decreed that those who were able to fight should go with the women and children to the capitol; but they declared that they themselves, who were old men, and unable to bear arms, would remain in the city. The Gauls found these old men sitting in silence, and clothed in their state robes.[3] At first they wondered greatly, but finally they approached the Senators, and a soldier stroked the long beard of one of them with his hand. The Senator, being enraged, struck the man, whereupon the rest of the Gauls slew all the Senators.

1. *to bring news* = **afferre nuntium**.
2. = *consult*.
3. **toga laticlavia**.

Exercise 125
panic, pavor.
in silence, silentio.
decree, decerno, -ere, -crevi, -cretum.
clothe, vestio.
stroke, mulceo, mulsi, mulsum.
beard, barba.
strike, percutio, -ere, -cussi, -cussum.

Exercise 126
visit, viso, -gre, -si, -sum.
unlike, dissimilis.
discuss, dissero, -ere, ui, -tum (de).
fortunate, felix.
happy, beatus.
whoever, whatever, quisquis, quicquid, *or* quicunque, quaecunque, quodcunque.

Exercise 127
piety, duty (natural affection), pietas.
ox, bos, bovis, c.
drag, draw, traho, -ere, traxi, tractum.
cart, carrus, -i, *m*.
both, ambo.
prove, demonstro, I.
liable to, obnoxius, *dat*.
misfortune, res adversae.
honorable (*of things*), honestus, (*of persons*), probus.
indeed, revera.

Exercises

Exercise 126 [*B*].

Solon, the wisest of the Athenians, went once to visit Croesus at Sardis.[1] You have all heard how these two men became friends, and discussed many things together.[2] But the story is worthy of[3] being told again. Croesus considered that that man was most fortunate who had great power and riches, and who could do whatever he wished; and he thought that he himself was such a man. He therefore showed Solon all his gold and silver, and told him how many nations he ruled. He then asked him whom he considered the happiest of mortals. He was sure that Solon would answer that he who ruled the city of Sardis and such a great kingdom was the happiest. But Solon replied that two young men, Cleobis and Biton, were the most happy.

1. **Sardes** pl. Gen. **Sardium. Solon, Solonia.**
2. '**inter se**,' which often translates words like '*together*,' '*mutually*,' '*one another*,' etc.
3. **digna quae**, with subjunctive.

Exercise 127 [*B*].

Croesus said he had never heard of these men, and asked Solon who they were. The latter replied that they were two youths of great piety, whose mother was a priestess. [He said that] when she wished to go to the temple the oxen which used to draw her cart had died, and that her two sons had drawn her there instead of the oxen; that therefore she had prayed to the gods to give them their best gift, and in the night they had both died. By this story Solon wishes to prove that those who are alive must not be accounted[1] happy, since all are liable to misfortune; but that those who have met[2] an honourable death are indeed the happiest.

1. *to be reckoned, thought* — **duci** or **haberi**.
2. **obire**.

IMPERSONAL VERBS.

1. In using **oportet** there is the same difficulty as in using **debeo**. In English we say, "*I ought to have come,*" expressing the Perfect tense in the Infinitive. In Latin the tense must be expressed in the modal verb, not in the following Infinitive; *e.g.* **Debui venire** *or* **oportuit me venire**. There is the same difference in the use of **possum**; *e.g.* **Fotui hoc facere** = *I might have done this.*

2. Remember that **se** refers to the subject of the sentence. An impersonal verb has no subject, and therefore cannot be followed directly by **se**; *e.g.* *He was ashamed* = **eum puduit**. If, however, the impersonal is used in an indirect statement **se** must be used for the third person, because it refers to the subject of the verb of saying; e.g. **Dixit se pudere** = *He said he was ashamed.* See Rule 7.

Exercise 128.

I repented of my crime.

You may go away.

Do you pity the prisoner?

You might have gone away.

They are weary of life.

We are resolved to banish the kings.

He was ashamed of his deed.

It happened that the king was killed.

It becomes us to do this.

It is the lot of all men to die.

You ought to speak.

You ought not to be ashamed of your friend.

You ought to have spoken.

You might have pleased the gods.

It is lawful for us to use arms.

It is our duty to fight.

Do not repent of your deed.

I happened to be present.

Exercise 128
Impersonal Verbs.
A.
me miseret, **I pity**.
me taedet, **I am tired of**.
me pudet, **I am ashamed of**.
me paenitet, **I am sorry for, I repent**.
The above "verbs of feeling" may take a Genitive for a further object; e.g. me paenitet crudelitatis, *I am sorry for my cruelty.*

B.
me decet, **it is becoming to me**.
me oportet, **it is my duty, I ought**.
C.
mihi placet, **I am pleased, it seems good to me, I am resolved**.
mihi licet, **I am allowed, I may**.
mihi accidit, **it happens to me**.
mihi contingit, **it happens to me** (*generally of good fortune*).

All the verbs B and C may be followed by an Infinitive, C may be followed by a Subjunctive. (For interest, refert, *see Voc. 109.)*

Exercise 129 [A],

1. I am sorry for your grief.

2. I am ashamed of my country.

3. It seemed good to the judge to put the prisoner to death.

4. He said he pitied me.

5. I believe you repent of your crime.

6. He replied that he was tired of living in the city.

7. Every man has not the good luck to go to Corinth.

8. You ought to know what you are doing.

9. You ought to have done this of your own accord.

10. It is becoming to children to obey their parents.

11. Do not be ashamed of such a deed.

Exercise 129
of one's own accord, sua sponte.
parent, parens.
deed, factum.

Exercise 130 [B].

1. Do not get tired of living in the country.

2. He said we ought to leave our home.

3. A man who runs away in battle soon repents of his cowardice.

4. We happened to be present at that time.

5. I was sorry for his sufferings.

6. He said he was ashamed of his deed.

7. I do not think you ought to have done that.

8. Do not repent of your kindness to us.

9. It happened that the general was present with his staff.

10. You might have escaped before the battle.

11. Why do you repent of saving the state?

Exercise 130
cowardice, ignavia.
kind, benignus.
kindness, benignitas, benevolentia, beneficium (= act of kindness).
towards (*of feelings*), erga, *acc.*
staff (= officers), legati.

Exercise 131
Words followed by genitive.
remember, memini (sometimes *acc.*).
forget, obliviscor (sometimes *acc.*).
recall, recollect, reminiscor (sometimes *acc.*).
remind, admoneo, *acc.* and *gen.*
accuse, accuso, I., *acc.* and *gen.*
pity, misereor.
mindful, memor.
forgetful, immemor.
ignorant of, inscius, imperitus.
skilled in, peritus.
experienced in, expertus.
anxious to, desirous of, cupidus.
eager for, avidus.
unaccustomed to, insuetus.
recollection, remembrance, memoria.
skill, peritia.
desire, cupido, studium.
knowledge (*of things*), cognitio (*of persons*), acquaintance, consuetudo, -inis, *f.*
belonging to other people, alienus.
address, alloquor, -i, -locutus.
absent, absens.
necessary, necessarius.
past, praetertius.
for the sake of honour, honoris causa.
administer public affairs, rempublicam administro, I.

Exercise 131 [A].
GENITIVE CASE

1. Through fear of death the bravest men forget their courage.

2. He is ignorant of many things which he ought to be skilled in.

3. Looking after[1] other people's affairs is difficult.

4. I pitied them all as they came back from the battle.

5. Skill in addressing his soldiers was necessary for a Roman general.

6. The remembrance of his past life brings one man joy, another pain.

7. Your care for me reminds me of my father.

8. I am anxious to thank you for your kindness, which I shall never forget.

9. He is skilled in every labour which you demand of him.

10. I am sure he will be mindful of us in our absence.

11. Under the emperors Romans were made consuls for the sake of honour, not for the sake of administering public affairs.

12. My knowledge of Caesar made me eager for his friendship.

1. Use the noun **cura**.

Exercise 132 [B].

1. No one will repent of a life well spent.

2. You have a chief mindful of others, forgetful of self.

3. Pity a man suffering undeservedly.[1]

4. He was charged with treachery.

5. His love for his country is more powerful than his fear of death.

6. The best men are fonder of doing than of speaking.

7. Out of pity for the woman he gave up his design.

8. He is unaccustomed to swimming.

9. They were unaccustomed to toil, but despised danger.

10. I hope you will not forget your country through your eagerness to see new things.

11. Caesar's friendship for me I value very highly.

12. These barbarians seem skilled in making bridges.

1. *unworthy things.*

Exercise 132
spend (*life, period of time, etc.*), ago.
treachery, proditio.
powerful, potens.
design, consilium.
give up, abandon, relinquo, *acc.*; desisto, *abl.*
swim, nato, I.

Exercise 133
now, moreover (*continuing a narrative*), autem (second word).
ship of war, longa navis.
several, aliquot, complures.
turn back (*especially with object unaccomplished*), revertor.
proud, superbus.
looks, expression, face, vultus, -us, *m.*
dress, attire, ornatus, -us.
splendid, insignia.
come on board, embark, (in) navem conscendo.
embark (*trans.*), impono (milites, etc.).
land, disembark (*intr.*), egredior e navi; (*trans.*) expono (milites, *etc.*).
by chance, forte, casu.

Exercise 134
need, egeo, indigeo, *abl. or gen.*
he needs money, opus est ei pecunia.
be without, lack, careo, *abl.*
kindly, benigne.
hold on course, cursum tenere.

Exercise 133 [A].

[Exercises 131-140 are for revision.]

Now when they had sailed for several days, it chanced that they caught sight of a ship of war approaching them. Some were afraid, and wished to turn back, but the captain[1] said that he was ashamed to turn back, "For," said he, "brave men ought to meet an enemy boldly, and I do not believe that by flight we shall escape from so large a vessel." As the ship came near they saw that there were on board[2] many soldiers, one of whom, by his proud looks and splendid dress, seemed to be the king. This man called out to them to come on board his ship. And when they had done this he asked them where they came from, and why they had left their homes.

1. **dux**.
2. *to be on board* - **in nave vehi**.

Exercise 134 [A]

On hearing their answer he asked them to sail with him, and promised to give them lands in his country, because they seemed to be good soldiers, and because he pitied them for their misfortunes. But they declared that they wished to discover what fortune the gods would give them in distant regions. Then the king replied that he was sorry for this resolve,[1] but that he would no longer try to persuade them to follow him. He asked them if they needed gold or provisions; and when they said that they had no need of such things, he dismissed them kindly, and held on his course.

1. **consilium**.

Exercise 135 [A],

I have lately with much care found out and written in a book the strange stories which the inhabitants[1] of this district believe. Among other things they believe that a man who throws a garment into the stream which flows near our town will be free from disease for a year. I have asked why they believe this, and they say that a god dwells in the stream; but why the god of a river wants such gifts they do not understand. They also believe that a certain spring which rises outside the town is able to make rich the man who visits it on a certain night in the summer; but on which of all the nights of summer one ought to visit the spring no man can tell, and I have never found a man made rich in this way.

1. **incolae**.

Exercise 136 [A].

The gallant Brutus,[1] who had been blockaded for a long time, wished to know when the reinforcements would arrive. Accordingly he sent away two ships, under the command of his lieutenant, with the intention of informing the Roman commander[2] in what great danger he was. But these ships being wrecked, the enemy surrounded them, and asked the lieutenant who they were, and where they came from. On learning that they were Romans, they promised to spare their lives, and be their guides. But when they had led them two miles they surrounded and slew them. The Roman commander, on hearing of this through his scouts, decided not to delay any longer, but to send forward two legions as soon as possible.

1. Lat. "Brutus a very gallant man."
2. *Commander-in-chief* — '**imperator**'; in a general sense, *commander* = '**dux**.' The '**legatus**' is the second in command, properly the general to whom the command of a separate division was assigned.

Exercise 137 [B].

When the king of France was besieging Amsterdam[1] the citizens were greatly terrified, and summoned a council to consider what they ought to do. Most of them said that there was no hope of holding out any longer against the enemy, and advised that the keys of the city should be given up to the king. But they observed that one of the elders was asleep, and had not given his opinion. So they woke him up, and asked him what he advised about giving up the keys. He enquired if the king had demanded them; and when they said that he had not done so, he replied, "Then let us wait at least till[2] he be pleased to ask for them." It is said that these words saved the city.

1. **Amstelodamum**.
2. Use **dum** with Subj.

Exercise 135
lately, nuper.
inhabitant (*of country*), incola. (*of city*), civis. (*of town*), oppidanus.
garment, vestis, -is, *f.*; vestimentum.
stream, rivus, -i. **a certain** (= *Indefinite Article*), quidam.
want, cupio.
flow, fluo.
rise, orior.
outside, extra.
district, regio, -onis, *f.*

Exercise 136
with the intention of, eo consilio ut.
wreck (*of ship*), frango, -ere, fregi, fractum.
to be shipwrecked, ejicior in litus (or litore).

Exercise 137
key, clavis, -is, *f.*
elders, patres.
give an opinion, sententiam fero.
wake, arouse, excito, I.
at least, certe, saltem.

Exercise 138 [B],

The soldier, thus recognized, was soon surrounded by a mob of citizens asking who he was, where he came from, where he was going, for what purpose he was in the town, and why he had not come through the gates, but had climbed over the wall in the night time. In no wise terrified, he replied that neither could he answer so many things at once, nor was it the business of private citizens to know what was his name or what he came for. On which he was dragged with much violence to the magistrates, who questioned him again as to his purposes.[1] As he would not speak, they were deliberating whether they ought to detain him or set him free; but there came up a soldier who pretended to recognize the prisoner, and asked whether he had not been seen in the rebels' camp.

1. See head of Exercise 116.

Exercise 139 [B],

A boy and his sister were once found by the inhabitants of a village, near the entrance of a cavern. They were in form like other men, but they were different in the colour of their skin, which was tinged with a green colour. No one could understand what they said. When they were brought to the house of a certain knight they wept bitterly.[1] Food being set before them they refused to touch it, though it was clear that they were tormented by great hunger. At length, when some beans[2] were brought into the house, they asked by signs that these should be given them. They fed on these with great delight, and for a long time would eat no other food. The boy, however, was always languid[3] and sad, and died in a short time.

1. shed (**fundo**) many tears.
2. **fabae**.
3. **languidus**.

Exercise 140 [B],

The girl, however, becoming accustomed[1] to various kinds of food[2] at length lost that green colour. For many years she remained with the knight to whom she and her brother had first been brought. Being frequently asked about her country, she declared that the inhabitants were of a green colour, and that they saw no sun, but enjoyed such a light as we see after sunset. Being asked how she came into this country, she replied that as they were following their flocks they came to a certain cavern, where they heard a delightful[3] sound of bells.[4] Led on by this they wandered for a long time through the cavern, and at last reached its mouth. When they came out of it they said they were stupefied by the excessive heat of the sun, and were thus caught by the inhabitants of the village.

1. **assuefactus ad**.
2. **omne genus cibi**.
3. **jucundus**.
4. **tintinnabulum**.

Exercise 138
recognise, agnosco, -ere, -novi, -nitum.
mob, turba, multitude,
in no wise, haudquaquam.
drag, traho.
magistrate, magistratus, -us.
detain, retineo.

Exercise 139
sister, soror.
village, vicus.
entrance, os (oris), *n.*, ostium, aditus, -us, *m.*
cavern, spelunca.
limb, membrum.
form, forma, figura.
colour, color.
skin, cutis, -is, *f.*
tinge, tingo, -ere, tinxi, tinctum.
green, viridis.
set before, offero, propono.
touch, tango, -ere, tetigi, tactum.
torment, torture, crucio, I.
sad, gloomy, tristis.
tear, lacrima.

Exercise 140
accustomed to, assuetus ad, assuefactus ad.
healthy, sanus.
light, lux, lucis, *f.*.
flock, grex, gregis, *m.*
sound, sonus, -i, *m.*; sonitus, -us, *m.*
wander, vagor, I.
stupefied, stiupefactus.
excessive, nimius.
heat, calor.
thus, sic, hoc modo.

RELATIVE WITH THE SUBJUNCTIVE

Rule 18. A relative with the subjunctive may express many adverbial meanings, especially a Purpose or a Consequence.

This is the regular way of expressing a *Purpose*—

(1) When the subject of the subordinate sentence is the same as the subject or object of the Principal Verb.

(2) When the subordinate clause contains a comparative, in which case quo (the abl. of the relative) is regularly used for ut.[1]

A *Consequence* is most often expressed in this way with the phrases **is qui, dignus qui,** and **sunt qui.**

EXAMPLES
Final

Duas legiones reliquit **quae** auxilio duci **possent**.
He left two legions to be brought up as reinforcements.

Nervii murum aedificaverunt **quo facilius** equitatum impedirent.
The Nervii built a wall the more easily to hinder the cavalry.

Consecutive

Non **is** sum **qui** mortis periculo **terrear**.
I am not the man to be frightened by the fear of death.

Dignus erat **qui** rex **fieret**.
He deserved to be made king.

Sunt qui non **habeant**.
There are some who have not (or *some men have not*).

---

[1] We thus have four ways of expressing purpose in Latin, viz. as in the following sentences:
    (1) **Legatos miserunt** *ut pacem peterent* (Rule 2).
    (2) **Legatos miserunt** *qui pacem peterent.*
    (3) **Legatos miserunt** *ad pacem petendam.*
        Legatos miserunt *pads petendae causa* (Rule 13).
    (4) **Legatos mieerunt** *pacem petitum* (Rule 14).
Occasionally also purpose is expressed by the Future Participle ; *e.g.*
        Legatos miserunt *pacem petituros.*

Exercise 141 [A].

1. Caesar has sent out scouts to discover where his reinforcements are.

2. These men are here to give an answer.

3. Hannibal left part of his army to blockade Tarentum.

4. They carried food with them, so that they might march the quicker.

5. I have few men to send.

6. Send cavalry, so that we may the more easily check the enemy.

7. To become wiser, read many books.

8. He promises to send books for me to read.

Exercise 141
check, restrain, cohibeo.

Exercise 142 [B].

1. In order that the flight might be shorter he drew up his line near the camp.

2. I have no one to trust.

3. On the next day men were sent to kill Cicero.

4. There are guards in the streets to restrain the multitude.

5. He went into the country to live more quietly.

6. To make your son better you ought to live better yourself.

7. Caesar set chosen men in the woods to fall on the enemy when fighting.

8. He left Labienus to command the camp.

Exercise 142
short, brevis.
quiet, tranquillus.
set, post, dispono; colloco, I.
chosen, picked, delectus.
fall on, incido, -ere, -cidi, -casum (in).

Exercise 143 [A].

1. He is not a man to rejoice even at his enemy's death.

2. He deserves to be put to death.

3. The consul is doing things that do not benefit the state.

4. Shall I find a soldier brave enough to go with me?

5. There were some who were willing to give Caesar large sums of money.

6. There is no one who could endure such insolence.

7. Does he deserve to receive so great a reward?

8. Is he a man to be trusted with money?

Exercise 143
insolence, arrogantia.

Exercise 144 [B].

1. I am not the man to refuse money to my own brother.

2. Send such troops as can help me.

3. There are men who accuse him of theft.

4. We did not deserve to be put in prison.

5. Men are not easily found who can endure pain patiently.

6. Is he a man to be admitted into my house?

7. There were some who could run faster.

8. The ships are not fit to be launched.

Exercise 144
refuse, recuso, I.
theft, furtum.
put in prison, in vincula conjicio.
admit, admitto.
fit to, dignus qui, *subj.*
launch, deduco.
patiently, aequo animo.

Exercise 145 [A].

1. No one was found to face death for him.

2. I am not the man to shirk danger.

3. They sent five priests to consult the god at Delphi.

4. I will say such things as may persuade him.

5. Five men have to-night entered the camp to announce that the city will be surrendered.

6. Caesar left his baggage at Ravenna in order to reach Rome more quickly.

7. He is worthy of being made a Roman.

8. There are some men who do not desire riches.

9. He led out the tenth legion to attack the enemy in the rear.

10. He drew up his line in this way in order that his forces might appear greater.

Exercise 145
shirk, vito, I., detrecto, I.

Exercise 146 [B].

1. Men were sent by the general to choose a suitable place for a camp.

2. The more easily to cross the river he gave orders for making a bridge.

3. He was not the man to bring his soldiers rashly into danger.

4. Towards evening fresh men arrived to take the place of those who were disabled by wounds.

5. There are some who think that we ought to strike the camp and advance to higher ground.

6. Men who free their country from slavery deserve to be praised by all.

7. A mound was made, and ladders brought up that we might the more easily scale the walls.

8. I am not the sort of man, he said, to wish to avoid danger.

9. Spies were sent to see if the enemy's troops were advancing.

10. There were some who advised the general not to summon a council.

11. These barbarians are not men whom we ought to despise.

12. He placed elephants in front of his line of battle to strike more terror into the enemy.

Exercise 146
suitable, idoneus.
rashly, temere.
towards evening, sub vesperum.
take place of, relieve, succedo, *dat*.
disabled, confectus.
ladder, scala.
scale, ascendo.
elephant, elephantus, -i, *m*.
in front of, pro.
bring up, admoveo.

Exercise 147
prepared to, paratus, *Inf*.
oppose, bar way of, hinder, obsto, obsisto, dat; impedio, *acc*.; prohibeo, *acc*.
build, aedifico, I.
in two days, biduo.
for two days, biduum.
opposite bank, altera ripa.
landing, egressus, -us.
up the river, in adversum flumen, adverso flumine.

Exercise 148
Carthaginian, Poenus (*adj.* Punicus)
cold, frigidus., (*noun*), frigus, -oris, n.
desolate, desertus.
especially, praesertim.
want, inopia.
hardship, labor.
terrible, terribelis.
downwards, deorsum.
rest, se reficere.
encourage, confirmo, I.

Exercises

Exercise 147 [*A*].

Hannibal first crossed the Pyrenees[1] with an army of fifty thousand foot soldiers and nine thousand horse, without any difficulty. No Roman army appeared to hinder his march. He reached the Rhone safely, and found no Romans to oppose him. The Gauls, however, were prepared to bar his way, and Scipio, the Roman general, had arrived at Massilia; so Hannibal determined to cross the river without delay. He ordered such boats as were ready to be brought to him, and trees to be cut down from which to build others. In two days the boats were ready, but the Gauls were drawn up on the opposite bank to prevent the landing. Accordingly Hannibal sent a large number of his men some miles up the river, ordering them to cross and attack the Gauls in the rear upon a given signal.

1. **Pyrenaei**.

Exercise 148 [*B*].

The Carthaginians had now reached the highest point of the mountains; they encamped on a large plateau[1] where they could rest for some days. But it was a cold and desolate place, and not one where they could remain long, especially as winter was approaching. Many had been left behind on the march, overcome with want and hardships; and the cold was terrible to men who came from Spain and Africa. But Hannibal encouraged them, and pointed out that from this place the road led downwards, and that it would soon lead them to a country where they would find friends. "There lies Italy," cried he; "yonder[2] is the way to[3] Rome."

1. **planities**, *f*. 5.
2. **ille**.
3. Use **ducere**.

GERUND AND GERUNDIVE EXPRESSING OBLIGATION

(Translation of "*ought*," "*must*.")

Rule 19.—**The Nominative of both Gerundive and Gerund is used to express obligation. The Gerundive is used with Transitive Verbs, the Gerund with Intransitive Verbs.**

    e.g. Gerundive—**leges mutandae sunt** = *the laws must be changed.*
         Gerund—**succurrendum est amicis** = *we must help our friends.*
         When these statements become *indirect* the Acc. is used in the same sense of obligation.
    e.g. Gerundive — **dixit leges mutandas esse.**
         Gerund — **dixit succurrendum esse amicis**.

Rule 20.—**In this construction the person on whom the obligation lies is expressed by the Dative.** This is often called **Dative of the Agent**. But for the sake of clearness, where there is another Dative, the Agent is expressed by **ab** with the Abl.

    e.g. **Leges nobis mutandae sunt** = *we must change the laws.*
         Legibus a nobis parendum est = *we must obey the laws.*

N.B.—(1) The English words "ought," "must," etc., are often to be translated into Latin by this construction. Remember that the Gerundive is a *Passive* Adjective, and before translating we must turn the English in thought into a Passive form.
    e.g. *We must change the laws* =
         The laws are to-be-changed by us = **Leges nobis mutandae sunt.**

(2) Observe also that the Gerundive can be used with any tense of **sum** according to the sense, and the English translations will be very various, because our words "*must*" and "*ought*" have only one tense.

    e.g. **Leges nobis mutandae erunt** = "We *shall have to* change the laws,
                              (literally, *the laws will be to-be-changed by us*.)

    Leges nobis mutandae erant = We *ought to have changed* the laws.

The Gerund in like manner can be used with any tense.
    e.g. **Legibus a nobis parendum fuit** = We *had* to obey the laws.

Exercise 149 [A].

1. We must set out at once, and you must guard the camp.

2. Caesar had to do everything at the same time.

3. It is agreed by all that the laws must be obeyed.

4. All good citizens must obey the laws.

5. Crassus was ordered to see to the repairing of the fleet.

6. We have undertaken the construction of a bridge over[1] the Rhine.

7. This should not have been done.

8. We must not injure those who are desirous of helping us.

9. Caesar caused a camp to be fortified.

10. They must not be accused of treachery by us.

1. '*in* ' with Abl.

Exercise 149
see to (undertake), the building of a house, curare (suscipere) aedificandam domum.
accuse of, accuso, I. (with Gen. of crime).
treachery, proditio.

Exercise 150 [A].

1. We must not remain here any longer.

2. Let them see to building another bridge.

3. I think we must choose a place for a camp.

4. They will have to return in fifteen days.

5. We must start at once and march until evening.

6. Caesar pointed out that hostages must be surrendered by all the states.

7. We must take measures for the good of the state.

8. Do you think Crassus ought to have done this?

9. He promised to undertake the repairing of the fleet.

10. We have to wait here for reinforcements.

Exercise 150
until (*with nouns*), usque ad.

Exercise 151 [B].

1. We must help the poor.

2. The general decided that he must not delay any longer.

3. We shall have to send forward two legions.

4. Caesar entrusted to Labienus the repairing of the ships.

5. They had to remain a long time where they were.

6. They had to leave their winter quarters in spring.

7. He should not have said that.

8. They promised to see to holding a levy.

9. They did not know where they were to pitch the camp.

10. We must come to the help of our allies.

Exercise 151
delay, moror, I.; cunctor, I.
winter quarters, hiberna, n. *pl.*
hold a levy, delectum (*4th decl.*) habeo.

Exercise 152 [B],

1. We have to cross the sea.

2. We must not delay too long.

3. The soldiers were told to see to fortifying the camp..

4. Crassus ought not to have gone to Asia.

5. All of us must obey the laws.

6. We shall have to leave our country.

7. We were entrusted with holding a levy.

8. They ought to have helped their allies.

9. Hannibal caused his camp to be pitched on the top of a mountain.

10. We should not accuse them of treachery.

Exercise 153 [A],

While the Romans were waging war against the Samnites[1] their general Postumius tried to lead an army into Samnium through a narrow pass. There is in the midst of this pass a broad and open plain, but in order to reach it an army must enter a narrow defile, and afterwards either it must go back by the same way or must get out by a still narrower defile into Samnium. The Romans reached the open plain, but attempting to proceed they could not escape, for meanwhile the Samnites had blocked both the defiles. To escape they had to climb the mountains, and having tried to do this many times in vain they had to fortify a camp where they were.

1. **Samnite** = **Samnis**, Gen. **Samnitis**.

Exercise 154 [B],

Accordingly Postumius sent ambassadors to ask for fair terms. Pontius the Samnite replied that they must give hostages and surrender their arms, and must themselves be sent under the yoke. At length these disgraceful conditions were accepted, and the Romans were allowed to depart. To reach home they had to pass through the country of their Campanian allies, and even ask them for food and clothes. The Roman Senate refused to accept the treaty, and sent back the consul to surrender himself to the Samnites.

Exercise 153
get out, evado, -ere, -si, -sum.
pass, **defile**, saltus, -us, m.; angustiae, fauces, *f.*
narrow, angustus.
in vain, frustra, nequicquam.
both, uterque.
clothes, vestis, -is, *f.*
open, apertus.
plain, campus, -i, m., planities, *f.* 5.
still (= even), etiam.

Exercise 154
fair terms, aequae conditiones.
send under the yoke, sub jugum mitto.
treaty, foedus, -eris, n.
clothes, vestis, -is, *f.*, vestitus, -us, m.

VERBS OF FEARING

Rule 21. Verbs of Fearing have three constructions— (a) Prolate Infinitive. (b) ne with Subjunctive, (c) ne non with Subjunctive.

EXAMPLES.

(a) **Timeo redire.**
I am afraid to return.

(b) **Timeo ne redeat.**
I am afraid that he will[1] return (of his returning).

(c) **Timebam ne non rediret.[2]**
I was afraid he would not return.

Timeo ne non redierit.
I am afraid he has not returned.

Timebam ne non rediisset.
I was afraid he had not returned.

N.B. (*b*) and (*c*) are Final Sentences, Latin preferring to express the *object* or *desire* of the person fearing, while Eng. gives the exact opposite; viz., the thing you wish to *avoid*. Of course (*a*) is only possible when the subject of the two verbs is the same.

[1]. In clauses after verbs of fearing there is no need to express the English Future (*as* in Indirect questions) by the Periphrastic Conjugation (Rule 16). The Present (in Primary sequence) and Imperfect (in Historic sequence) are used for it without causing any ambiguity.
[2]. **Ut** may sometimes take the place of **ne non** (especially after **vereor**).

Exercise 155.

1. I am afraid to do this.

2. I am afraid he will do this.

3. I was afraid you would not do this.

4. I am afraid he is dead.

5. I was afraid he had not seen me.

6. Do not fear to return.

7. Are you afraid of speaking?

8. We were afraid of being seen.

9. I am afraid lest they should see us.

10. I am afraid they will not see us.

11. They were afraid not to tell the truth.

12. I fear that he has lied.

Exercise 156 [A],

1. As they were afraid to follow me, I went away alone.

2. The soldiers were afraid that the enemy would surround them.

3. As the camp was not yet fortified, they were afraid of being attacked by the barbarians.

4. Though[1] he was not afraid to die, he wished to live as long as possible.

5. Fearing that the ships would not be able to keep on their course they returned to the harbour.

6. He was afraid that his plans had been discovered by the enemy.

7. Fearing to advance farther, they took up their position ten miles from the town.

8. Though the city had walls one hundred feet high, the inhabitants feared they could not resist an assault.

9. They were afraid that they would not be able to conceal their departure from their enemies.

10. He was afraid of being betrayed by his own men, and therefore resolved to kill himself.

11. They loved their country so much that for its sake they were not afraid of dying.

12. I am afraid the prisoners have escaped.

1. 'quum' with *Imp. Subj.*

Exercise 156
not yet, nondum.
assault (*on town*), oppugnatio.
departure, profectio.

Exercise 157 [B].

1. You ought not to be afraid to tell the truth.

2. I am afraid that you have not told the truth.

3. Our men were afraid of being surrounded by the enemy.

4. Most men are afraid of dying.

5. I am afraid they will not be able to follow the standards.

6. The general was afraid to give the signal for advance.

7. Were you not afraid that the soldiers would seize and kill your son?

8. Fearing that they would be taken prisoners they fled for refuge into the woods.

9. The general told his men not to be afraid of crossing the river.

10. We were afraid that the city had been taken.

11. I was afraid that we should not reach the camp before sunset.

12. They set out at daybreak, fearing that the enemy might overtake them.

Exercise 157
standards, signa, *n. pl.*.
overtake, assequor, consequor.

Exercise 158 [A].

News having been brought of Caesar's approach, the Arverni, fearing that he would invade their territory, resolved to break down all the bridges over the river. Caesar was very anxious to cross as soon as possible, for he was afraid of being hindered all the summer by this river. He accomplished this by the following trick. He sent forward the greater part of his forces, and the enemy followed these, thinking that the whole army had set out. Thereupon Caesar, who had remained with a few men, ordered them to repair one of the bridges with all speed, fearing that they might not be able to finish the work before the return of the enemy.

Exercise 158
invade, invado, -ere, -vasi, -vasum (in *acc.*).
return, reditus, -us, *m.*

Exercise 159 [B],

A peasant on the point of death[1] summoned his sons, and told them that the end of his life was near. "My sons," he said, "I am not afraid that you will disobey my commands, or forget me when I am dead.[2] I therefore bid you work diligently in my vineyard, for by doing this you will discover great riches." When the old man died, his sons remembered his words, and began to dig up the soil with all their might, hoping to find great riches concealed there. Soon however they were afraid that they had been deceived, for they could find neither gold nor silver; and at first they regretted their labour. But at last they discovered what their father had intended, for by carefully digging up the ground, they made it so fertile that it produced excellent vines.

1. Future Participle.
2. *when I am dead* — use Past Participle.

Exercise 159
peasant, agricola, *m.*
vineyard, vinetum.
dig up, effodio, -ere, -fodi, -fossum.
deceive, decipio, fallo.
fertile, ferttilis.
produce, edo, -ere, edidi, editum.
regret, me paenitet, gen.
vine, vitis, -is, *f.*
excellent, egregius.
disobey, **disregard**, negligo, -ere, -lexi, -lectum.

CAUSAL CLAUSES

A Causal Clause is one which, gives a reason for the statement of the principal cause.

Rule 22.—Causal Clauses have their verb

    (a) in the **Indicative** when the **actual cause** of a fact is given,

    (b) in the **Subjunctive** when only **a suggested reason** is given. But **quum** (since) always takes Subj.

N.B.—Of course the Indicative of a Causal clause becomes Subjunctive if it forms part of an Indirect Statement. See **Rule 17**.

EXAMPLES.

(a) **Tacent quia periculum metuunt.**
They are silent because they fear danger.

(b) **Socrates accusatus est quod juventutem corrumperet.**
Socrates was accused on the ground that he corrupted the youth,
(It is not asserted by the writer that Socrates did corrupt the youth.)

Exercise 160 [*A*],

1. As you have heard this, you ought to announce it to all.

2. Under these circumstances I shall leave the city.

3. This being the case, no one would remain.

4. I am rejoiced that you have decided to come.

5. They declared that they had done this, because it seemed to be for the good of the state.

6. We were told that they had been condemned to death, because they had displeased the king.

7. He must be considered a coward, since he is unwilling to become a soldier.

8. Since night is at hand, let all depart to their tents.

9. In this condition of affairs it was to our interest to withdraw from the meeting.

10. I rejoice that you and the army are safe.

11. They pretended to be glad that we were safe.

12. I pity you greatly, because no one seems to love you.

Exercise 161 [B].

1. The slave was blamed for coming too late.

2. You deserve praise, because you have served your country well.

3. Under these circumstances the general decided to sound the retreat.

4. They were condemned to death for setting fire to the city.

5. I am rejoiced that such men have been condemned to death.

6. He said they ought to be punished, because they had fled from the battle.

7. They were charged with treason, on the ground that they had threatened the king with death.

8. This being the case, we must advance at once.

9. As they have shown themselves brave soldiers, let them receive the promised reward.

10. Our friends declared that they rejoiced that we had returned in safety.

11. Since this is so, you must remain in exile.

12. They were brought to trial on the charge of conspiring against the state.

Exercise 160
because, quod, quia. [Use *quia* for actual cause only, and therefore with *Ind.*, except in Indirect Statement.]
since, quoniam, quando, quum. [*quum* always with *Subj.*]
on the ground that, for the reason that, propterea quod.
this being so, in this state of affairs, quae quum ita sint, essent.
rejoice, be glad, gaudeo, -ere, gavisus (quod).
it is for the good of, ex usu est, usui est, *dat*.
condemn to death, capitis damno, 1.

Exercise 161
late, sero, adv.
sound the retreat, receptui canere.
exile (*person*), exsul, -ulis.
exile (*state*), exsilium.
treason, majestas.

Exercise 162 [A],

The triumph of Camillus, after the fall of Veii, was disliked by the Romans, because he showed too much pride. Amongst other things he was accused of making himself equal to the gods, because he had entered the city in a chariot drawn by four white horses, which were sacred to Jupiter and the Sun. He also made the soldiers still more angry, because he ordered them to return part of the spoils taken at Veii, that he might offer them to the god Apollo. Finally he was accused of having hidden some treasures which he ought to have given up to the people, and was obliged to go into exile.

Exercise 163 [B].

Some Irishmen[1] had been brought to trial on the charge of stirring up a revolution[2] in their country. They asserted that they had done nothing contrary to the law of nations, since the English were oppressing their land, and they themselves were only trying to free her from an unjust dominion.[3] Under these circumstances they declared that they by no means repented of their deed, especially because they had shown that it was not easy to govern Irishmen against their will. These words displeased many who were present; but since the prisoners were young, and had never before been accused of any crime, they were spared.

---

1. **Hiberni**.
2. **seditionem facere** or **novis rebus studere**.
3. **dominatus**.

Exercise 162
triumph, triumphus, -i, *m.*
fall (*of city*), use capio.
be disliked by, displiceo, *dat.*
pride, superbia.
equal, par, paris.
chariot, currus, -us, *m.*
white, albus.
sacred, sacer, -ra, -rum.
Jupiter, Juppiter, Jovis.
finally, postremo, denique.
spoil, spolium.
Apollo, Apollo, -inis.
too much, nimius, nimis (with *gen.*).

Exercise 163
contrary to, contra.
be brought to trial, put on trial, reus sum.
law of nations, international law, jus gentium.
oppress, opprimo, -ere, -pressi, -pressum.
unjust, injustus.
any, *adj.* in negative sentences, ullus.
govern, rego.

Exercise 164 [A]

(*Exercises 164-167 are for Revision.*)

Now when the Delphians[1] knew what great danger they were in, great fear fell upon them. In their terror they consulted the oracle concerning the holy treasures, and enquired if they should bury them in the ground, or carry them away to another country. The god replied that they must leave the treasures untouched, "He was able," he said, "without help to protect his own." So the Delphians, when they received this answer, began to deliberate how to save themselves. First of all they sent their women and children across the gulf into Achaia. After which the greater number of them climbed to the top of Parnassus, and placed their goods in a cave. In this way all the Delphians quitted the city, except sixty men and the prophet.

1. **Delphi**.

Exercise 164
fall on, capio.
oracle, oraculum.
untouched, integer, -ra, -rum.
protect, servo, I.
gulf, sinus, -us, *m*.
except, praeter.
holy, sacer, -cra, -crum.

Exercise 165 [A].

A great plague had broken out[1] in the city, and many of the people,[2] both rich and poor, had perished. A great number of those who survived, who had neither wives nor children, resolved to leave the city and sail away to discover new lands. They pitied those whom they were leaving behind, but they knew that they could not help them. Accordingly they set sail by night, and meeting with a favourable wind, were many miles away from the city before dawn. They did not know to what lands they would come, but they had resolved to sail towards the west.

1. = *arisen*.
2. *People* (= *persons*) should be omitted (as here) or sometimes be translated by it. In the political sense (= *a nation*) it is **populus**. In the sense race or tribe use **gens**, **natio**.

Exercise 166 [B]

The two armies had been gazing at each other a long time.[1] At last an old man came forward, and asked that a warrior from each army should be chosen to fight for his countrymen. Accordingly Sohrab[2] came forward from the one army and Rustum,[2] his father, from the other; but neither[3] of them knew who the other[4] was. For it happened that when Sohrab was born and carried off by the Scythians,[5] his father was absent. At first Sohrab prevailed; for Rustum hurled his spear with such violence that he slipped and fell on the ground. But quickly rising, he dealt[6] his son a deadly wound; for Sohrab had heard Rustum, as he rushed forward, shout out his name, and knowing[7] him to be his father, he did not even move a hand to defend himself.

1. **jamdudum** (imperf. indic.).
2. It is best not to try to turn these names into a Latin shape. In turning a piece into Latin it is often possible to omit the proper names. Where it is not, try to recall some parallel incident in Roman history, and adopt the names from that. Where (as here) this is difficult, it is better to adopt any classical names than to talk of 'Sohrabus' and ' Rustumius.'
3. neuter.
4. **alter**.
5. **Scythae**.
6. **infligere**.
7. **Quum** with Imp. Subj.

Exercise 167 [B].

King James's[1] army was far[2] superior to Monmouth's in numbers, but with such great carelessness did they take up their position on that night that they were almost surprised and destroyed by the rebels. By chance the guides whom Monmouth trusted had not told him that there was a ditch twenty-five feet wide which defended the king's camp in front. Therefore when the rebels were just going to rush forward to attack the ramparts, they were stopped[3] by this trench. The officers ordered their men to throw the waggons into it, but the guards of the other army were now aroused, and their artillery[4] began to play upon[5] the rebels. It is said that Monmouth, having exhorted his men to fight bravely and hold their ground, himself rode out[6] of the fight, hoping to find[7] some place where he might be safe.

1. James has a Latinised form **Jacobus**. But here call him **Octavianus** and call Monmouth **L. Antouius**, who caused an insurrection against Octavianus soon after the battle of Philippi.
2. **longe, multo**.
3. **impedire**.
4. *Artillery* = **tormenta** or **ballistae**.
5. **saxa ingerere in**.
6. **avehi**.
7. *Hoping to*, **si forte** (with Subjunctive).

Exercise 165	Exercise 166	Exercise 167
plague, pestis, pestilentia.	**gaze at**, specto, I.	**carelessness**, negligentis.
survive, supersum.	**warrior**, juvenis.	**surprise**, opprimo.
set sail, navem solvo.	**each of two**, uterque [each army = uterque exercitus].	**in front**, a fronte.
meet with, obtain, nancisor, -i, nactus.	**one...other** (*of two*), alter... alter.	**waggon**, plaustrum.
favourable, secundus.	**choose**, deligo, -ere, -legi, -lectum.	**artillery**, tormenta, *n. pl.*; ballistae.
west, occidens.	**prevail**, supero, I.	
towards, ad.	**spear**, hasta.	
	slip, labor.	
	deadly, mortifer, funestus.	
	rush, ruo, -ere, rui, ruitum.	
	rush forward, proruo.	
	be born, nascor, -i, natus.	
	carry off, abripio, -ere, -ui, -reptum.	

QUIN

Rule 23. — **Quin with Subjunctive is used**

(1) (*a*) after Verbs of doubting and denying ⎧ when these verbs are
    (*b*) ,, ,, hindering and preventing[1] ⎩ preceded by a negative.

In these uses **quin** = **qui-ne**, *by which not*, **qui** being an old Ablative of the Relative.

EXAMPLES.

(*a*) **Non {dubitare *or* negare} debemus quin fuerint ante Homerum poetae.**
We ought not to {doubt or *deny} that there were poets before Homer.*

(*b*) **Nihil me deterrebit quin proficiscar.**
Nothing will prevent my setting out.

Haud multum abfuit quin Ismenias interficeretur.
Ismenias was very near being killed. (There was not much to prevent Ismenias being killed).

Under (1) (*b*) come the important phrases —
    non possum facere quin ...   = *I cannot help ...*
    non potest fieri quin ...   = *It is impossible that ...*
                                                                      not ...
    haud multum abfuit quin (ego) ...   = *I was very near ...*
                                                                  or *I was not far from ...*

(2) In certain phrases where **quin** = **qui-ne**, *who not*, **qui** being Nominative.
    e.g. **Nemo est quin ... nulla navis est quin ...** etc.
    Nullum est aedificium quin collapsum sit.
    There is no building that has not fallen.

N.B. — In all its uses **quin** is preceded by a negative, or virtual negative (*e.g.* **vix**, **aegre**, or a question expecting the answer "*no*," like "*Can anyone prevent ...?*").

---

[1] **Frehibeo, veto** prefer Infinitive.

Exercise 168 [A].

1. There can be no doubt that he did this on purpose.

2. I could not deny that I was guilty.

3. There is no man who does not often do wrong.

4. Do not prevent their setting out.

5. I cannot help writing to you.

6. We had no doubt that he was on our side.

7. It is impossible that the guilty man should escape.

8. I was very near dying of hunger.

9. We must not doubt that he will keep his word.

10. There was no man in the city who had not a son or a brother in the army.

Exercise 168
Verbs and phrases to be followed by **quin**.
non dubito quin.
non est dubium quin.
quis dubitat quin ? (virtual neg.).
fieri non potest quin, **it is impossible that . . . not.**
facere non possum quin, **I cannot help. ...**
minimum abest quin, **be within a very little of** (always impersonal).
nihil praetermitto quin, **leave nothing undone to.**
nemo est quin sciat, **there is nobody who does not know; everybody knows; all the world knows.**
—
do wrong, pecco, I.
be on one's side, faveo, *dat*; ab aliquo stare.
keep word, fidem praesto.

Exercise 169 [B].

1. They do not deny that they desire peace on fair terms.

2. There was no man of noble birth who did not scorn Catiline.[1]

3. They were not far from taking the city by force of arms.

4. I have no doubt that he is already consul.

5. Do not hinder his leaving Rome.

6. He said he had no doubt the news was true.

7. It is impossible for us not to believe him.

8. We cannot doubt that this pleases the multitude.

9. There is no ship that has not been hurt by the storm.

10. I could not help consulting you.

1. Catilina.

Exercise 169
birth, race, genus, -eris, n.
scorn, contemno, -ere, -tempsi, -temptum.
by force of arms, vi et armis.
multitude, plebs, plebis, f.

Exercise 170
Verbs of hindering and preventing, which may be followed by quominus, and when neg. by quin.
hinder, impedio, acc., obsto, dat.
prevent, prohibeo (which prefers Inf.).
deter, deterreo.
refuse, recuso, 1. (also with Inf. in Neg. sentences).
it was due to you that... not, per te stetit quominus.
—
Alps, Alpes, pl.
weigh anchor, ancoras tollo.

QUOMINUS

Rule 24.—**Quominus with Subjunctive is used after verbs of hindering and preventing, whether they are positive or negative.**[1]

Exception.—**Prohibeo, veto**, prefer an Infinitive.

EXAMPLES.

Nihil deterret sapientem quominus reipublicae consulat.
Nothing prevents a philosopher from serving the state.

Per Africanum stetit quominus dimicaretur.
It was due to Africanus that there was no battle.

Exercise 170 [A],

1. It was owing to you that the army was not destroyed.

2. Who hindered you from coming to our help?

3. They were prevented by the snow from crossing the Alps.

4. You ought to have prevented the fleet from weighing anchor.

5. We could not deter the soldiers from charging the enemy.

6. It was due to us that the house was not burnt.

7. We ought to prevent them from attacking us.

8. The soldiers could not be prevented from rushing into the river.

9. I believe it was through me that we were not defeated.

10. I could hardly restrain them from burning the ships.

11. They refused to leave the city.

---

1. **Quomimis** = **quo minus**, and is really a special case of the Relative with the Subj. making a Final sentence.

Exercise 171 [B].

1. It was owing to Horatius that Rome was not taken.

2. The soldiers must be prevented from plundering the town.

3. The general could hardly prevent his men from burning the houses.

4. Let not fear deter you from speaking the truth.

5. You ought to forbid the fleet to set sail.

6. Was it not due to our king that we did not perish?

7. The tribunes were able to prevent laws from being passed.

8. The ambassadors were the cause of peace not being made.

9. By surrendering the city to the enemy, we prevented the inhabitants from dying of hunger.

10. You prevented them by your threats from speaking the truth.

11. Did you not refuse to supply the army with provisions?

Exercise 171
pass a law, legem jubeo.
threat, minae.
destroy, deleo.
supply, praebeo; *acc.* of thing, *dat.* of person.
tribune, tribunus (plebis).

Exercise 172 [A].
QUOMINUS AND QUIN.

1. Every one knows that this ought to be done.

2. We must prevent the enemy from crossing the river.

3. There is no doubt that they ought to have remained.

4. They hesitated to speak, but I had no doubt that they were angry.

5. The city was within a very little of being destroyed.

6. There is no one present who does not know that you are lying.

7. It was due to Themistocles that the Athenians did not leave Salamis.

8. All the world knows that I fought for my country.

9. Do not try to prevent these men from escaping.

10. There is no doubt that they have betrayed us.

11. I cannot help hoping that we shall be saved.

Exercise 172
hesitate, dubito, with *Inf.*
Salamis, Salamis (*acc.* -ina).

Exercise 173 [B].

1. It is impossible that you have not heard this.

2. There is no doubt that there lived brave men before Agamemnon.[1]

3. Who is there so base as not to love his country?

4. It is owing to the gods that we did not die of starvation.

5. Do not refuse to help those who have benefited the state.

6. I had no doubt that they wished to deceive me.

7. Our men could hardly be restrained from making the assault at once.

8. I easily prevented the slaves from reporting this to Caius.

9. There is no doubt that this news will cause great panic to the citizens.

10. It is impossible for us to save the state.

---

1. *Acc.* **Agememnona**.

Exercise 173
make an assault, oppugno, 1.
report, refero; nuntio, 1.
cause panic, pavorem injicio, *dat.*
base, turpis.

Exercise 174
the salvation of. *Cf. Ex. 85.*
again and again, identidem.
with great loss, plurimis amissis, magna strage.
offer a prayer to, invoke, precor, 1.
drown, submergo, -ere, -mersi, -mersum.
contrary to expectation, praeter spem, opinionem.
repulse, repello.

Exercise 175
provoke, lacesso.
ambassador, legatus.
violate, violo, 1.
take part in, interesse, *dat.*
vow, juro, 1.
with the help of the gods, cum dis.
avenge, ulciscor, -i, ultus.
for some time, aliquamdiu.
be amazed, miror, 1.

Exercise 174 [A].

All the world has heard how gallantly Horatius Cocles defended the bridge by which the enemies of Rome hoped to enter the city. First with two companions and afterwards alone he resisted all the attacks made upon him, and prevented the enemy from crossing; and there is no doubt that he was the salvation of the Roman state. Again and again the enemy charged, but were always repulsed with great loss. At last, when the bridge was all but broken by the Romans, his countrymen called to him to come back, and, offering a prayer to the river god, he threw himself into the water. His friends feared that he would be drowned; but contrary to the expectations, both of friends and enemies, he reached the other bank in safety.

Exercise 175 [B].

In this year the Gauls, under the leadership of Brennus, crossed the Alps, and threatened Rome with war. It is said that they were provoked by certain Roman ambassadors, who violated international law by taking part in a battle fought between the Gauls and Etruscans. As the Senate refused to punish the ambassadors, the Gauls vowed with the help of the gods to avenge this wrong, and set out for Rome. At the river Allia they won a great victory over the Romans, nor were they afterwards opposed. They were greatly amazed at[1] no one trying to prevent their entering Rome, and stopped some time outside the walls.

1. **quod**.

Exercise 176 [A].

[Exercises 176-181 are for revision.]

At the time when Russia[1] had as many enemies as neighbours, the king of Sweden laid siege to Novgorod, and the Swedes soon got possession of the city. There is no doubt that this happened through the carelessness of the inhabitants, and there are some who say it was the result of treachery. But there were some who determined to hold out to the last, and among these was a certain priest. He shut himself up in a house with a few friends, who, animated[2] by his courage, refused to surrender, and fired[3] on the enemy. Messengers were sent again and again to command them to surrender, and at last the enemy set fire to the house. But these brave men chose to be burnt in the house rather than to yield, for they had determined not to survive the independence of their country.

---

1. *Russians* = **Scythae**. *Swedes* = **Suevi**. *Novgorod* = **Forum Novum**.
2. **confirmatus**.
3. **tela immittere**. Of course the idea of *fire-arms* can never be reproduced in Latin. *Cannon* must be **tormenta**, *rifles, guns, shot*, etc., must be turned by some phrase with **tela** or **pila**.

Exercise 176
as many as, tot... quot.
neighbour, neighbouring, vicinus.
to the last, ad ultimum, ad extremum.
shut up, claudo, -ere, -si, -sum.
survive, superesse, *dat*.
independence, freedom, libertas.

Exercise 177
greet, saluto, 1.
stretch out, porrigo, -ere, -rexi, -rectum.
despatches, litterae.
read through, perlego, -legi, -lectum.
draw a circle round, circumscribo. rod, virga.

Exercise 178
shed (tears), effundo.
jealousy, invidia.
hatred, odium.
to be most important, maximi interesse (*Voc. 109*).

Exercise 177 [A].

Antiochus greeted the Roman ambassadors on their arrival, and was stretching out his hand to Popilius; but the latter[1] gave him the despatches, and bade him read these first. After reading them through the king said he would consult his friends as to what ought to be done. But Popilius drew a circle round the king with a rod which he was carrying in his hand, and said, "Before you leave this circle[2] give me an answer to take to the Roman Senate." The king at first was on the point of refusing to obey the ambassador; but he knew that it would be to his advantage to keep the friendship of the Roman people, and at last replied that he would do what the Senate wished. Then at last Popilius stretched out his hand to the king as[3] to a friend and ally.

1. **qui tamea.**
2. **priusquam hoc circulo excedas.**
3. **velut.**

Exercise 178 [A].

When ambassadors came to Hannibal in Italy to recall him to Carthage, he received them with great anger, and could hardly refrain from shedding tears. "There is no doubt," he cried, "that it is not the Romans who have conquered me, but my own people through their hatred and jealousy. Take me where you will; it matters little to me where I go, since I have to leave Italy." The ambassadors were now afraid that he would refuse to serve the state any longer, and tried to persuade him that the most important thing was to defend Carthage. But he replied that a city which feared to trust its generals did not deserve to be defended by them.

Exercise 179 [B].

Elated by the rapid departure of the Roman fleet from Africa, the Carthaginians still more rejoiced on hearing of its destruction. They could now boast that they were "friends of the sea, and enemies of all who sailed on it." This being the case the Romans could not prevent them from transferring the war to Sicily, with all the land forces, with 140 elephants, and with a fleet to help the army. They made straight for that island, and, taking the field,[1] prepared to ravage the open country.[2] But the Romans, with unconquerable resolution, undertook[3] the construction of a new fleet, and within three months 220 new vessels had been built, and were ready for action.

1. **copias educere**.
2. **campestres loci**.
3. **suscipere**, followed by Gerundive.

Exercise 180 [B].

The command was entrusted to Xanthippus, who seemed to all to be the man whom they could best trust. A cry was raised for instant battle,[1] for none doubted that they would conquer under the command of Xanthippus. Being thus appointed general, he led his army into the plain, and prepared to give battle to the Romans. He first ordered the elephants to charge the Roman centre, and the cavalry to fall upon the wings on both sides. The Roman horse, who were greatly inferior in numbers, fled without striking a blow,[2] and the elephants, rushing[3] into the foremost ranks of the Roman infantry, laid the enemy low[4] in every direction. Attacked in front by the infantry, on the flanks by the cavalry, and on the rear by the elephants, the majority of the Roman soldiers of the line stood their ground bravely, and died where they were standing.

1. that a battle should be fought at once.
2. **re integra**.
3. **invecti**.
4. **prosternere hostem**.

Exercise 181 [*B*].

Ten years after, Caius, the younger brother of Tiberius, thinking he ought to avenge his brother's death, brought forward laws to upset the whole constitution.[1] The people had not forgotten the death of Tiberius, and all the power of the senators could not prevent their electing Caius tribune of the plebs. But Tiberius had proposed his laws because he pitied the common people; Caius proposed his in order that he might the more easily satisfy his desire for revenge.[2] He was accused also of aiming at kingship. For two years he delivered many speeches before the people, and continued to propose[3] all such laws as might lessen the senate's power, but the most iniquitous of them was that which caused[4] bread to be given to the common people at a very low rate.[5]

1. **evertere rempublicam.**
2. ulciscendi libido.
3. Imperfect.
4. **efficere ut.**
5. **vili** (Abl. of Price).

Exercise 179	Exercise 180	Exercise 181
elated, elatus.	**a cry was raised**, clamatum est.	**bring forward** (*a law*), fero.
departure, discessus, -us, *m.*; profectio.	**reverse**, incommodum.	**common people**, plebs, plebis.
boast, jacto, I.	**give battle to**, proelium committere cum.	**satisfy**, indulgeo, -ere, -si, -tum.
transfer, transfero.	**centre** (*of army*), media acies.	**aim at**, peto.
land forces, terrestres copiae.	**wing**, ala.	**kingship**, regnum, regia potestas.
make straight for, recto cursu peto.	**on both sides**, utrimque.	**deliver a speech before**, orationem habere apud.
ravage, populor, I.; vasto, I.	**foremost ranks**, primi ordines.	**lessen, diminish**, diminuo.
unconquerable, invincible, invictus, indomitus.	**flank**, latus, eris, *n*,	**iniquitous** (**unjust**), iniquus.
	soldier of the line, legionarius miles.	

TEMPORAL CLAUSES

Rule 25. Conjunctions used in a purely temporal sense are followed by the Indicative. But the verb is put in the Subjunctive (a) when it is in Oratio Obliqua, (I) when some other idea than that of time (*e.g.* purpose) is introduced.

N.B.—**Quum** is an exception. Also **dum** in the sense of *while*. For these see Rules 26, 27.

EXAMPLES

(*a*) **Postquam**[1] omnes Belgarum copias ad se venire vidit, ad exercitum properavit.
After he saw that all the forces of the Belgians were coming to him he hastened to join the army.

(*b*) **Caesar priusquam** se hostes ex terrore reciperent in fines Suessionum exercitum duxit.
Before the enemy could recover[2] *from their panic, Caesar led his army into the territories of the Suessiones.*

When the temporal clause refers to Future time the verb will be in the Future (or Fut. Perf.) in Latin, though in English the Present is preferred.

(*c*) Nos **ante** abibimus **quam** tu **redieris** (Fut. Perf.).
We shall go away before you return.

---

1. *The English Pluperfect should be rendered by Latin Perfect after* **postquam**, *and* **simulac**. *But with* **postquam** *the Plup. may be used if the exact interval of time is mentioned.* **Tertio post anno quam veneram** = *three years after I had come.*
2. Implying that Caesar wished to prevent their recovering.

Exercise 182 [A],

1. As soon as they saw us they went away.

2. I knew they would go away as soon as they saw us.

3. After you have heard what has taken place, you will know what you ought to do.

4. He refused to leave before he had seen the general.

5. From the time when we heard of the destruction of the army we gave up all hope of safety.

6. No sooner was the signal given than all the soldiers ran forward together.

7. As often as messengers arrive we all run to the gates.

8. They would not depart until they received their pay.

9. Caesar had embarked all his troops before Pompey could reach Brundisium.

10. Before Pompey reached Brundisium Caesar had embarked all his troops.

Exercise 182
before, antequam, priusquam.
after, postquam.
N.B. Ante, prius, post, may be separated from quam by the principal verb and other words. See the last example,

until, dum, donec, quoad.
whilst, as long as, donec, quoad.
as soon as, simulac.
as often as, quoties.
since, from the time when, ex quo tempore.

Exercise 183 [A],

1. We were defeated almost before battle was joined.

2. The Gauls attacked the camp before our men could man the walls.

3. After landing the soldiers burnt their fleet.

4. We were informed that the general had dismissed his men after giving them their pay.

5. A crowd assembled before I could reach the temple.

6. No sooner had the king appeared, than all the citizens raised a shout.

7. When you return you will hear what has taken place.

8. Advance the standards, my men, before the enemy catch sight of us.

9. They waited in the road until the king had passed.

10. We must remain here until our friends arrive.

Exercise 183
man, compleo.
raise a shout, clamorem tollo.
advance standards, signa fero.
pass, praetereo.

Exercise 184 [B].

1. I will come to you when I have finished this work.

2. As soon as I had finished the work I left the city.

3. The camp was attacked by the enemy before we could take up arms.

4. Caesar addressed his men before leaving winter quarters.

5. It was announced that the cavalry had been sent forward before the scouts had returned.

6. Wait at Rome until you receive another letter.

7. They decided not to leave Rome till they had received our letters.

8. No sooner was war proclaimed, than the general took the field.

9. The prisoners escaped into the woods before the soldiers could overtake them.

10. Our men advanced in close order until they saw that the enemy were retreating.

Exercise 184
finish, complete, perflicio.
address, contionor apud.
take the field, exercitum educo.
in close order, confertus, conferto agmine.

Exercise 185 [B].

1. Horatius stood firm until the bridge was broken down.

2. I will leave the army as soon as the new consul arrives.

3. Cicero refused to go to a province after he resigned his consulship.

4. I will be here as soon as you call me.

5. He refused to leave the army till the new consul arrived.

6. After Pompey had fled from the field, his men scattered immediately.

7. You must not embark before I give you leave.

8. He shall not be accused till he himself is in Rome.

9. The consul said P. Scipio should not be accused before he had returned to Rome.

10. Milo was in the senate till it adjourned.

Exercise 185
stand firm, resisto.
province, provincia.
resign the consulship, abire (se abdicare) consulate.
field (*of battle*), acies.
give leave, jubeo.
adjourn, be dismissed, dimittor.

Exercise 186
armament, classis.
prevail upon, persuadeo.
result (*n.*), eventus.
result (*vb.*) evenio.
unfortunate, infelix.
fall into confusion, perturbor, I.
with one another, inter se.
darkness, tenebrae.
reduce, redigo

Exercise 187
feign, simulo.
south, meridies, -ei, *m.*
despair, spem abjicio.
feast, epulor, I.
drink, bibo, -ere, bibi.
win the day, vinco.
feign, simulo, I.
entice, elicio, -ere, -cui, -citum.
havoc, strages, -is, *f.*
pierce, transfigo,-ere,-fixi, fixum.

Exercise 186 [A].

As soon as Demosthenes arrived with his armament before Syracuse, and joined[1] the army of Nicias, the siege was carried on with renewed vigour.[2] At first Nicias' want of energy[3] prevented even Demosthenes from making a direct[4] assault. But at length Nicias was persuaded to allow his men to assault the city in the night time. This attack had an unfortunate result. The Athenians, before they reached the walls of the Achradina, fell into confusion, and were not far from fighting with one another in the darkness. Demosthenes was obliged to sound a retreat. After this Nicias' counsel again prevailed, and they determined to reduce the city by famine.

1. *Intr.* **se conjungere cum.**
2. the city was besieged more keenly.
3. *want of energy* = **inertia**.
4. **directus.**

Exercise 187 [B].

As soon as news reached him of William's[1] landing, Harold hastened southward by forced marches. Flushed[2] by their recent success, his men did not despair of victory, and spent the night before the battle in feasting and drinking. The battle was stubbornly contested[3] all day, and evening was approaching before it was clear which side[4] would win the day. At length, by feigning retreat, William enticed the enemy from their position, and the Norman cavalry made[5] great havoc in the ranks of the Saxon foot. But not until they saw their king fall, pierced through the eye by an arrow, did the Saxons take to flight. After his death they were routed, and fled in all directions.

1. The Latin forms are **Gulielmus, Haraldus, Narmanni, Saxones.**
2. **elati.**
3. **ancipiti proelio dimicatur.**
4. **utri.**
5. **edere.**

Quum

Rule 26. **Quum** (= *when*) in Primary tenses takes Indicative.
in Historic ,, ,, Subjunctive.

(= *since*)
(= *although*) } always Subjunctive.

EXAMPLES.

(a) Quum **potero** reddam.
I will pay it back when I can.

(b) Quae quum **cognoscerent**, se recipere in animo habebant.
when
since } *they learnt this, they intended to retreat.*
although

Exceptions.—**Quum** (=when) may take Historic tenses of the Indicative in certain cases—

(1) When the clauses are inverted, *i.e.* when the **quum** clause really contains the principal statement.
e.g. **Jam ver appetebat quum Hannibal ex hibernis movit.**
Spring was already approaching when Hannibal moved from his winter quarters.

N.B.—If not inverted, this would be "*Hannibal moved from his quarters when spring was approaching*" (**quum ver appeteret**).

(2) When **quum** *is frequentative, i.e. is equal to* **quoties**, *as often as, whenever.* [In this sense use Perfect and Pluperfect.]
e.g. **Quum consul abfuerat, seditiosi erant.**
They were mutinous whenever the consul was absent.

(3) When **quum** *is equal to* **quamdiu**, *as long as, or* **ex quo tempore**, *since.*
e.g. **Quum consul aberat turn seditiosi erant.**
They were mutinous as long as the consul was away.

Exercise 188 [A].

1. When spring returns we shall leave winter quarters.

2. Though they knew they would be killed, they advanced.

3. They were already approaching the city when news was brought that reinforcements had arrived.

4. Not knowing what was to be done, they decided to wait for the messengers.

5. I always lived in the country whenever I was able.

6. Knowing, as they did, that there was no hope of safety, they resolved to die bravely.

7. When you return, you will find the city changed.

8. We had scarcely begun our march, when we were ordered to halt.

9. Having approached the city, we halted.

10. Believing that they could hold out, they refused to surrender.

Exercise 188
NONE.

Exercise 189 [B],

1. We will come to meet you when you arrive.

2. Hoping to save the lives of his men the general gave the signal for retreat.

3. We were at Veil all the time that you were at Rome.

4. They refused to surrender, although they knew they would be conquered.

5. The citizens were almost dead of starvation, when relief arrived.

6. Knowing that the enemy were at hand, we tried to find out when they would attack us.

7. A signal was given whenever a ship approached.

8. Believing, as you do, that there is no hope of safety, why do you remain any longer?

9. When they came to Athens, they found their friends.

10. Since you think that I have deceived you, why do you not employ another messenger?

Exercise 189
relief, auxĭlium.

DUM

Rule 27. **Dum** (= while[1]) **may take Present Indicative, even of Past Time and in Oratio Obligua.**
(= provided that, if only = **dummodo**) **always Subjunctive.**
(= until) **follows ordinary rule of Temporal Conjunctions** (Rule 25).

Dum arma conquiruntur circiter hominum millia sex ad Rhenum contenderunt.
While the arms were being searched for about 6000 made off for the Rhine.

Oderint dum **metuant**.
Let them hate provided that they fear.

Dum reliquae naves convenirent ad horam nonam exspectavit.
To allow the rest of the ships to assemble, he waited till the ninth hour.

Mansit dum judices rejecti sunt.
He waited till the judges were rejected.

---

1. But when '*while*' can be turned by '*as long as*,' **dum** may take any tense of the Indicative, like **quamdiu**, etc. *See Rule 25. e.g.* **Haec feci dum licuit** = *I did this while (as long as) I was allowed.*
   The difference is that in this case the time of the action of the principal verb and the time of the action of the '**dum**' verb are contemporaneous, *i.e.* begin and end together.

Exercise 190 [A],

1. While they were cutting down the wood the enemy came upon them.

2. If only he is accused, without doubt he will be cast into prison.

3. The enemy quietly surrounded us while we were sleeping.

4. Till Camillus be recalled we shall not prosper.[1]

5. As long as the kings ruled in Rome no one enjoyed liberty.

6. None of the enemy were seen while they crossed the hill.

7. They refused to treat for peace until the deserters were given up.

8. We concealed ourselves until they had crossed the river.

9. While you stay I shall stay.

10. Minucius promised that while the dictator was away he would not join battle.

---

1. rem prospere gerere.

Exercise 190
come upon, incido in.
cut down, succido, -ere, -cidi, -cisum.
without doubt, sine dubio.
quietly, unobserved, clam.
recall, revoco, 1.
prosper, rem gero prospere.
treat for, ago de.

Exercise 191 [B].

1. While we were wasting time the Gauls caught us up.

2. He was kept in prison until the king should return victorious.

3. While the conspirators gathered round Caesar, Antonius was led aside by Trebonius.

4. Do not ask him while he is angry.

6. Provided he reaches Rome in time, he will stand for the consulship.

6. Milo said he had stayed in the senate till it was dismissed.

7. While these were holding their conference the Gauls were seen to be stealthily advancing.

8. Deserters kept coming in till Manlius' army was very small.

9. We shall conquer if only we can entice them to battle.

10. He refused to fight till reinforcements came.

Exercise 191
keep, detain, retineo.
victorious, victor.
conspirator, conjuratus.
gather round, cingo.
in time, ad tempus, tempori.
hold a conference, colloquor.
stealthily, furtim.
lead aside, deduco.

QUUM AND DUM.

Exercise 192 [A],

1. It was decided not to leave winter quarters till spring was approaching.

2. They knew that they could defend the town, provided that provisions did not run short.

3. While provisions held out they resisted all attacks.

4. They were compelled to raise the siege until fresh forces arrived.

5. They were both harassed by the enemy, and were also afraid that their own men would desert.

6. Men generally[1] show themselves brave when danger threatens their country.

7. When I hear what has taken place I will write to you.

8. They were ordered to remain in the camp until the enemy gave them an opportunity of joining battle.

9. We must retreat, he said, especially as the enemy have received fresh forces.

10. No one left his post while the battle lasted.

11. If only the allies can hold out a little[2] longer, we shall be able to renew the fight.

12. The soldiers refused to leave their posts, although the signal for retreat had been given.

---

1. **vulgo, plerumque.**
2. **paullo.**

Exercise 193 [B],

1. While the consul was absent the danger was increasing.

2. Since the enemy were only two miles distant, we were not allowed to wander out of camp.

3. He took it ill when I asked him to repay the money I had given him.

4. When the priests had returned without accomplishing anything, the Romans sent the women to appease Coriolanus.

5. Although Pompeius took part only in the end of the war, he obtained more glory from it than Crassus.

6. The majority advised him to engage while the troops were still fresh.

7. When our messenger has returned we shall understand better what the enemy intend to do.

8. When men are assembled in great numbers they fall easily into riot.

9. Although I am anxious for peace, I am annoyed at this fresh insult.

10. If only they give up their arms, we shall come to an agreement.

11. When the war is finished the tribune will bring Caesar to trial.[1]

12. It was about noon when the Senate assembled.

---

1. *Bring to trial* = **reum aliquem facere**, or **nomeii alicujus deferre**.

Exercise 192	**Exercise 193**	
raise a siege, desistere obsidione.	**wander**, vagor, I.; erro, I.	**credit**, laus, -dis, *f.*
run short, fail, deficio.	**be annoyed at, taken ill**, aegre fero.	**fresh**, integer.
hold out (*of provisions*), suppeto.	**repay**, reddo.	**riot**, tumultus, us, *m.*
harass, lacesso.	**without accomplishing anything**, re infecta.	**insult**, injuria, contumelia.
renew, redintegro, I.; renovo, I.	**appease**, paco, I.	**come to an agreement**, consentio, -ire, sensi, -sensum.
	take part in, interesse. Cf. Ex. 61.	**noon**, meridies.
		bring to trial, reum facio.

Exercise 194 [A].

Both Demosthenes and the common soldiers were greatly disheartened at this defeat, though Nicias seemed almost to have expected it. He now proposed that the siege should be abandoned, since the gods refused[1] their assistance, and they repeatedly met with disaster. But while they were still disputing[2] the Syracusans took away from them their last means of flight. In several engagements in the harbour they destroyed the whole Athenian fleet. Now all were eager to retreat, while it was still possible, towards their allies in the western part of the island. But the superstition[3] of Nicias deterred them from setting out till the new moon had risen; and meanwhile deserters had betrayed their plans to the Syracusans, who blocked the pass by which alone they could hope to reach the interior.

1. **denegare.**
2. **de re discepatur.**
3. **nimia religio.**

Exercise 194
disheartened, metu commotus.
defeat, clades, is, *f.*; incommodum.
propose, censeo, -ere, censui [*acc.* and *inf.* or *subj.*].
meet with, patior, -i, passus.
still, adhuc.
possible, translate by facio *or* fieri potest.
western part, pars quae ad occasum solis spectat.
interior, pars interior.

Exercise 195 [A].

At length, on the day appointed, they marched several miles until they came to the fatal pass. When they found this beset by the enemy, and all their attacks made no impression,[1] they first tried to discover some other path by which they could ascend the mountains; then, almost in despair, they determined to make a dash[2] for the coast, for this purpose dividing their forces into two divisions. Demosthenes was speedily overtaken and surrounded. Nicias met the enemy while crossing a river on the sixth day after he had left Syracuse. But, since his men had found no water to drink for many hours, they could not be restrained from rushing into the water, even when it was red with the blood of their comrades. All order being thus lost,[3] Nicias surrendered at discretion.[4] He and Demosthenes, being condemned to death, died by poison; the rest of the Athenians were kept in the stone quarries[5] at Syracuse.

1. *effected nothing*.
2. **per medios hostes perrumpere**.
3. **confusis signis et ordinibus**.
4. **nullis conditionibus latis**.
5. **lautumiae**.

Exercise 195
appoint, constituo.
fatal, funestus.
in despair, re *or* salute desperata; spe abjecta.
for this purpose, ad hoc.
in two divisions, bipartito.
red, ruber, -bra, -brum.
poison, venenum.
Syracuse, Syracusae.

Exercise 196 [A],

After surmounting all these obstacles, and so signally defeating the Gauls, Hannibal was all but destroyed, not in open fight, but by ambuscade. He had almost reached the top of the Alps, when some old men came to him in the guise of envoys. The misfortunes of others, they said, had been a warning to them, and they preferred to make trial of the friendship rather than the might of the Carthaginians, and were ready to do whatever he wished. Hannibal, considering that he must not rashly either trust or slight[1] them, accepted them as guides, but followed with his army in fighting order.[2] The moment[3] they entered a narrow pass, the enemy sprang out of their ambuscade on all sides, and assailed him both in front and in rear, both from a distance and at close quarters.

1. **aspernari**.
2. *'prepared for battle'*
3. *'as soon as.'*

Exercise 197 [A].

When the Athenians had attempted without success to capture the island of Sphacteria, an assembly was called to discuss what steps should be taken. At this assembly Cleon, who was only a private citizen, and wholly inexperienced in war, declared that they would never be able to take the island while they employed such generals. "Under my command," he said, " I am sure that the enemy would not resist[1] us for twenty days." There is no doubt that he said this only to slight the other generals; but the Athenians at once assigned to him the control of the campaign, and he set out at once for the seat of war. Here, aided by fortune, he accomplished what he had undertaken, contrary to the expectations of all, and within twenty days returned to Athens in triumph.

1. **Non fore ut hostes resistant.** This periphrasis is used to express the Fut. Inf. of Verbs that have no Fut. Inf. The same periphrasis may be used for the Fut. Inf. Passive of any Verb; *e.g.* **sperant fore ut urbs capiatur**.

Exercise 198 [B],

It was already dawning when the general gave the signal, promising a great reward to the first man who[1] climbed the walls. No one indeed resisted them as they entered the city, where the walls had been broken down, or climbed the walls by ladders. As soon as the shouting showed that the city had been taken the Asiatics all left their posts, and sought refuge in the citadel. The general allowed his men to plunder the town, partly because he was incensed with the inhabitants, and partly because the soldiers had hitherto always been restrained from plundering captured cities, and he wished them at last to have some reward for their valour. He was indeed accused of having done it to satisfy a grudge.

---

1. In such phrases the Superlative must be transferred to the Relative clause—'*the man who first. . .*' So for '*he sent the most faithful slave he had,*' the Latin idiom is, '*he sent the slave whom he had the most faithful.*' Also '*the only man who*' — '*the man who alone*' (**solus** or **unus**).

Exercise 196
obstacle, difficultas.
surmount, supero, I.
so signally, tanta strage.
ambuscade, insidiae. In the last sentence use ex insidiis invadere.
open fight, pitched battle, justum proelium, acies.
in the guise of, more.
warning, exemplo esse. *Cf. Ex. 85.*
make trial of, experior.
considering, calculating, ratus (reor).
rashly, temere, inconsulte.
slight, aspernor, I.
narrow, angustus, artus.

Exercise 197
without success, to no purpose, frustra, nequicquam.
private citizen, privatus.
wholly, altogether [with neg. and virtual neg.], omnino.
seat of war, sedes belli.
assign, attribuo. f
control of campaign, chief command, totius belli summa, summa imperii.
in triumph, victor. [Triumphus = the triumphal procession of a Roman general.]

Exercise 198
dawn, illucescit, illuxit.
breakdown, proruo.
seek refuge in, fly for refuge to, confugio ad.
incensed with, iratus, *dat.*
partly, partim.
hitherto, adhuc.
grudge, resentment, invidia.

Exercise 199 [B],

A certain man dreamed that he saw an egg hanging from the top of his bed; and when he had been the next day to consult a friend what the meaning of this dream might be, the friend told him that he would find a great quantity of gold hidden under his bed. After he had been digging for several hours he found a large quantity of gold surrounded with silver. Therefore he sent his friend a small part of the silver. The man, being vexed that he had received so small a reward, sent a messenger to ask whether he could not give him part of the yolk[1] of the egg; for (he said) inasmuch as the gold was covered with silver, the god had intended to show him the gold by the yolk and the silver by the rest.[2] But for my part I am not persuaded that this story is true.

1. **vitellus**.
2. **reliqua para**.

Exercise 200 [B].

This man, although he had been banished from his country on a false charge, did not cease, as often as opportunity was offered, to help her to the best of his ability. He was not the man to put his own prosperity before that of[1] the State; and he used to say that when his countrymen needed him they would recall him; till that time should arrive he was willing to remain in exile. Soon an occasion was offered him to show his devotion. A conspiracy was formed by some desperate men, who killed the chief magistrates, and assumed supreme power. In this crisis the citizens remembered the exile, and sent messengers to ask him to come to their help. He forgot all the wrongs which he had suffered, and by his arrival brought safety to the State which had treated[2] him so unjustly.

1. Omit '*that of*' in Latin.
2. '*used.*'

Exercise 201 [B].

Rutilius was not fit to be made governor of a province. On his departure from Asia, while visiting Ephesus, a city whose inhabitants worship Diana, he had robbed the temple of that goddess. And he did many other such things as would offend all Romans of the old character. And as often as he committed a theft he had a jest to justify[1] it by. He said he always took readily the little golden cups which the statues of gods held in their outstretched hands. And when his companions asked him whether he did not expect some day to be punished, he said the gods would not punish a man who, after praying to them for benefits, took the first gift which they offered him. When he was old he did just the same things as[2] he had done when a young man. When on the point of death he said, "One thing I have been repenting for a long time[3] — that I did not take the golden cloak which Jupiter wears in his temple in Messenia. I could have given him a woollen one for it."

1. excusare.
2. eadem quae.
3. **Jampridem, jamdudum** take the Present for the English Perfect, the Imperfect for English Pluperfect. '**Jampridem miror**' = '*I have long been wondering.*' '**Jampridem mirabar**' = '*I had been for a, long time wondering.*'

Exercise 199
dream, *vb.* somnio, I.; somnio video [— to see in a dream].
dream, *n.* somnium.
egg, ovum.
hang, *intr.* pendeo.
hang, *trans*, suspendo.
mean, **indicate**, significo, I.
bed, cubile, *n.*
dig, fodio.
I for my part, equidem [use only with ist pers. sing.].
be vexed, aegre *or* moleste fero.

Exercise 200
charge, crimen, -inis, *n.*
prosperity advantage, commodum.
to the belt of his ability, pro virili parte.
devotion, studium.
desperate, perditus.
assume, usurpo, I.
supreme power, summa imperii.
crisis, discrimen.
wrong, injuria.

Exercise 201
fit to, aptus, dignus qui (a consecutive clause).
governor of a province, proconsul.
worship, colo.
rob, spolio, I.; diripio.
offend, displiceo, *dat.*
character, mores, *pl.*
commit, admitto.
theft, furtum.
thief, fur, furis, *m.*
jest, jocus, -i, *m.*

justify, excuso, I.
cup, poculum.
statue, statua.
stretch out, extendo, porrigo.
benefit, beneficium.
now for a long time, jampridem, jamdudum.
cloak, pallium.
military cloak, sagum.
wear, *pass. of* induo, vestio.
woollen, laneus.
wool, lana.

CONDITIONAL SENTENCES

Rule 28.

A. **Open Conditions**, *i.e.* those in which we assume the condition without implying anything as to its fulfilment.
  INDICATIVE in both clauses.
Any tense possible according to the sense.

> **Si hoc facis, peccas.**
> *If you do this you do wrong.*

> **Si hoc {facies *or* feceris} peccabis.**
> *If you do this (Fut.) you will do wrong.*

> **Si hoc fecisti peccavisti.**
> *If you did this you did wrong.*

B. Conditions in which it is implied that the fulfilment of the condition is improbable but possible.
  PRESENT (or PERFECT) SUBJUNCTIVE in both clauses.

> **Si hoc facias, pecces.**
> *If you {did or were to do} this you would do wrong*

C. **Impossible Conditions**, *i.e.* those in which it is implied that the fulfilment of the condition is impossible.
  (1) Relating to **Present** time, or to continuous action in **Past** time.
  IMPERFECT SUBJUNCTIVE in both clauses.

> **Si hoc faceres, peccares.**
> *If you were doing this, you would be doing wrong.* (implying "*But you are not doing it.*")
> or, *If you had been doing this you would have been doing wrong.*

  (2) Relating to **Past** time.
  PLUPERFECT SUBJUNCTIVE in both clauses.

> **Si hoc fecisses, peccavisses.**
> *If you had done this, you would have done wrong.*
>   (implying "*But you did not do it.*")

The tense and mood are generally the same in the protasis (*i.e.* the *if* clause) and the apodosis (*i.e.* the conclusion). But in C the condition may obviously relate to *past* time and so be Pluperfect, while the conclusion relates to *present* time and is therefore Imperfect.[1]

> *e.g.* **Si hoc fecisses, nunc felix esses.**
> *If you had done this you would now be happy.*

The apodosis need not always be a statement, but may be a command or wish, *e.g.* **Ne veneris nisi jussero. Moriar si me facti poenitet.**

The English Present is often used for what is really a Future action. In Latin the Future or Fut. Perf. must always be used in these cases, e.g. **Si id feceris (or facies) peccabis** = *If you do this you will do wrong!*

FURTHER EXAMPLES OF CONDITIONALS

A. **Parvi sunt foris arma nisi est consilium domi.**
  Arms are worth little abroad unless there is wisdom at home.

  Si te hic offendero, moriere.
  If I meet you here, you shall die.

  Non si tibi ante profuit, semper proderit.
  If it helped you before it will not help you always.

B. **Nonne sapiens, si fame conficiatur, abstulerit cibum alteri?**
  Would not a wise man, if he were being starved, take food from another?

---

[1]. Moreover, in Impossible Conditions, if the verb of the apodosis is **possum, debeo, oportet**, or a gerundive (or any verb expressing *obligation* or *possibility*), it is regularly put in the Indicative.
  e.g. **Si patriam perdidisset interficiendus erat.**
    If he had betrayed his country he should have been put to death.

C. **Non pacem peterem nisi utilem crederem.**
I should not be asking for peace if I did not think it advantageous.

Si Camillus tale fecisset, non nobis exemplo esset.
Had Camillus done such a thing, he would not be an example to us.

Exercise 202 [A].

1. If you are able to do this, you ought to do it at once.

2. If I could do this, I would do it at once.

3. They always gave money to the poor, if they seemed to need it.

4. If the prisoners escape, we shall be punished.

5. If I thought you needed my advice, I would try to help you.

6. If they had started at once, they would have caught the enemy off their guard.

7. I should not be here now if I had listened to the advice of my friends.

8. Do not leave your home unless I bid you.

9. If they were asked for help, they gave it readily.

10. If they had been asked for, help, they ought to have given it readily.

11. They were always willing to help us, if we deserved help.

Exercise 203 [B].

1. Never promise if you cannot keep your word.

2. If once[1] we reach the camp, we shall be safe.

3. If the river were not so deep, we might have crossed it on foot.

4. They would have shown themselves more prudent if they had landed their forces immediately.

5. You would be wrong if you thought that I did this on purpose.

6. If a man cannot restrain his temper, he is a burden to his friends.

7. Whether he praises or blames you, you know that you have acted rightly.

8. If reinforcements had come, the enemy would have been compelled to raise the siege.

9. If they take up arms against their country, they will deserve to be condemned to death.

10. If he saw a man suffering wrongfully, he always tried to help him.

11. If only we had kept silence, we should not now be suffering such misfortunes.

1. Expressed by Fut. Perf.

Exercise 203
on foot, pedibus.
restrain, moderor, 1., *dat.*
prudent, prudens.

Exercise 204 [A.]

1. If he had not mocked me I should perhaps have forgiven him.

2. They may hate me if only they fear me.

3. If Caesar had thrown a bridge over the Rhine, the Germans could easily have been subdued.

4. If we attack the enemy at once, there is no doubt that we shall conquer them.

5. If he were my own brother I should condemn him none the less.

6. Had not Publius Scipio promised to accompany him, the war would never have been entrusted to Lucius Scipio.

7. But for the imposition of a tribute, the Macedonians would be more prosperous now than under their own kings.

8. If a man has wronged me, I take my revenge on him by law, not by violence.

9. When once Italy is reached, I will lead you straight to Rome.

10. Unless a man uses bribery, it is of no advantage to him to stand for the consulship.

11. Whether you go to Rome or remain here,[1] I shall not leave the city.

---

1. *Whether ... or ...* in double Conditions **sen ... sen (sive)**.
   Whether ... or ... in double Questions **utrum ... an ...**

Exercise 204
mock, irrideo, *dat.*
throw bridge over, pontem facio in, *abl.*
straight, recto itinere, dIrecto.
subdue, subigo, in potestatem redigo.
none the less, nihilommus.
tribute, tributum, vectigal,-alis, *n.*
impose, impono.
prosperous, felix.
wrong, injuriam facio, *dat.*
revenge oneself on, poenas sumo de; ulciscor, *acc.*
bribery, ambitus, -us, *m.*
it is no advantage, minime prodest.

Exercise 205 [B].

1. Poets starve at Rome unless rich men relieve them.

2. If we march straight to Rome we shall feast tonight in the Capitol.

3. In former times if a man showed himself capable of ruling he was generally elected consul.

4. Whether this news is true or false, we must remain where we are.

5. I should certainly have brought you the news in time had I been able.

6. If the enemy make an attack at once, I am afraid we shall not be able to resist them.

7. Were I to make such a request of you, you would be rightly angry.

8. When once you return home you will find many friends.

9. If I had never been poor I should not now enjoy my riches.

10. If Gracchus aimed at royal power he was rightly put to death.

Exercise 205
poet, poeta.
relieve, sublevo, 1.
capitol, capitolium.
in former times, antiquitus.
capable of, aptus ad.
false, falsus.
certainly, certo, sine dubio.
starve, fame pereo.

Exercise 206 [A].

1. We will take the place of the front rank if they are cut down.

2. If I were on the spot I should know what ought to be done.

3. Unless you remind him, he will have forgotten in three days.

4. Were he able to be present, he would certainly now be speaking for this bill.

5. If he should be present tomorrow, he would speak for this bill.

6. If Fabius had had more influence in the state, Varro would never have been elected consul.

7. If he does anything contrary to the law, punish him.

8. If a man does anything contrary to the law, he must be punished.

9. He would be arrested if anyone caught sight of him.

10. He would be in prison now if only we could have arrested him.

Exercise 206
take place of, succedo, *dat.*
cut down, occido.
front rank, prima acies.
remind, admoneo.
bill, rogatio.
influence, auctoritas.
have influence, valeo.
arrest, comprehendo, -ere, -di, -sum.

Exercise 207 [B].

1. If they have conspired against the state, they deserve to be punished.

2. If they had not conspired, they would still be living in the city.

3. If once you reach the shore, you will be able to embark.

4. Had you listened to my advice, you would have kept your riches.

5. If they repent of their crime, they will be forgiven.

6. Unless you spare this man, you will be an object of hatred to all.

7. If he had consulted his own interests, he would not have lost the friendship of Caesar.

8. If we were to send help to the Carthaginians, we should incur the anger of the Romans.

9. If they come to see you, tell them to wait until I arrive.

10. You must use your riches well, if you wish to be happy.

11. You ought to have done this whether you wished to or not.

Exercise 207
object of hatred. (*See Ex. 85.*)
incur, subeo.

Exercises

Exercise 208 [A]

"Fellow soldiers, we have lost many brave men through treachery, and have been abandoned by our friends. But we must not lose heart; and if we cannot conquer, let us choose rather to perish gloriously, than to fall into the hands of barbarians, who will inflict upon us the greatest miseries. If our ancestors had not been willing to encounter the vast forces of the Persians, Greece would now be in the hands of the barbarians. If we show ourselves worthy of them, we too shall benefit our country. The gods, the avengers of perjury, will be favourable to us, and seeing that they are offended by the violation of treaties, they will also follow us to battle, and combat for us."

Exercise 209 [B].

The general delivered this speech before his men: " You see how great the forces of the enemy are, and how impregnable their position is. If we attack them we shall without doubt suffer a severe defeat. But if, on the contrary, they were to leave their position and attack us, we should have good hopes of victory, for they have to cross a deep river and climb a steep hill, before they can reach our lines." By these words the general with difficulty persuaded his men to remain within their fortifications; and his advice was the salvation of the army. For if the Romans had attacked the enemy, who were superior to them both in numbers and position, they would undoubtedly have been conquered.

Exercise 208
lose heart, despero, animum demitto.
fall into hands of, in potestatem, venire.
gloriously, (cum) summa laude.
inflict ... on someone, aliquem afficere, *abl*.
avenger, ultor.
perjury, laesa fides.
be favourable to, faveo, *dat.*; sto ab aliquo.
violate, violo, I.
be offended at, aegre fero.
misery, suffering, dolor.

Exercise 209
impregnable, inexpugnabilis.
steep, praeruptus.
lines, munitiones, mummenta.
siege works, opera, *n. f.*

Exercise 210 [A],

After the death of Tib. Gracchus, C. Blosius showed his friendship for him in a marvellous way. For the senate decreed that all who had taken part with[1] Gracchus should be punished. Blosius, when accused before the consuls, excused himself on the ground of his friendship[2] for Gracchus. "Whether my judges condemn me," said he, "or whether they acquit me, I shall still always rejoice that I was the friend of Gracchus. If you, consuls, should bid me save my life by accusing Gracchus, I would not so save it. If I must die, let me die loyal to my friends." The two consuls hesitated. At last one of them asked Blosius, "If Gracchus had ordered you to set fire to the temple of Jupiter would you have done it?" To which Blosius replied, "Gracchus would not have ordered it."

1. **consentire cum.**
2. **amicitiae excusatione uti.**

Exercise 210
marvellous, mirus.
before the consuls, apud consules.
condemn, condemno, I.; damno, I.
acquit, absolve.
loyal, fidelis.

Exercise 211 [B],

On receiving news of the approach of Fairfax, the governor of Raglan Castle called together his men, and spoke as follows : " If all were going well I should not conceive it to be my duty to consult the men whom I command. But since the enemy are already upon us, and we have not collected[1] sufficient provisions, if there should be any here faint-hearted, or any that careth not to fight to the death in his Majesty's cause, let him depart, and be not burdensome to us in the siege. If I am able I will set[2] him safe on the Welsh[3] side of the river." If the king himself had addressed them the men could not have shown more zeal than they did on hearing this speech, and if there was any there desirous of going he did not dare to confess it.

1. **frumentum comparare.**
2. **exponere.**
3. **Celticus.**

Exercise 211
go well, proficio.
fainthearted, timidus.
to the death, usque ad mortem.
burdensome (*cf. Ex. 85*), molestus.
speech, oratio.
confess, confiteor.
side (*of river*), ripa.

PRONOUNS AND ADVERBS

TRANSLATION OF 'ANY.'

Quisquam (adj. **ullus**) to be used when 'any' is *exclusive*; *i.e.* with negatives and sentences virtually negative. Sentences are virtually negative (1) when they contain **vix, aegre, sine**, (2) when they are questions expecting the answer 'no,' (3) when they are comparative, "he was taller than *any* of his friends."

Quivis, Quilibet to be used when 'any' is *inclusive*; *i.e.* when it means *anybody you like*, or *everybody*. means *anybody you like*, or *everybody*.

Quis (adj. **qui**) only used after **si, nisi, num, ne** (and after **quo, quanto**, with comparatives).

Aliquis only when *someone* may be substituted for anyone in the English without altering the sense.

TRANSLATION OF 'SOME.'

Aliquis and **Quispiam** are the ordinary words.
    aliquis should be used for '*somebody*,' when it means '*a person of consequence*.'

Quidam = *a certain man*, almost the Eng. Indefinite Article. As a rule it *follows* its noun.

Nescio quis = *some one or other*, no definite person indicated.

Alii .. alii = *some . . . others*.

Nonnulli = *some, of number*, opposed to *none*, and often implying *a considerable number*.

Aliquot = *some, of number*.

EXAMPLES

Quivis de virtute loquitur, **vix quisquam** virtutem praestat.
Everyone talks about virtue, scarcely anyone practises it.

Si quid cognovisti, loquere.
If you have learnt anything, speak.

Forsitan dicat **aliquis** . . .
Perhaps some one may say.

Hic **nescio quis** loquitur.
There is someone or other talking here.

Other Pronouns

Quisquis, whoever (adj. **quicunque**).
Ecquis? Interrog. and Indef. combined, — '*anyone at all*'?
Quisnam? = the Interrog. **quis**.
Quisque, each man.
    Its commonest uses are with superlatives and ordinals; *e.g.* **optimus quisque** (*all the best men*), **decimus quisque** (*every tenth man*, or *one in ten*), and in combination with **suus** or **ipse** ; *e.g.* **suam quisque salutem petit** (*each man seeks his own safety*).

Adverbs

Unquam (*ever*) and **usquam** (*anywhere*) can only be used according to the rule of **quisquam** ; *i.e.* with negatives and virtual negatives.

Quo (*anywhither*), **quando** (*at any time*), in the same way correspond to **quis**.
    e.g.   **Si quando peccaveris, ne celaveris unquam**.
         If ever you sin, never conceal it.
         Contrast — **Ne semper celaveris** =
         Do not be concealing it.

Alicubi (*somewhere*), **aliquando** (*some time, once upon a time*), **aliquantum** (*some quantity*), **aliquamdiu** (*for some time*), correspond to **aliquis**. The syllable **ali** always corresponds to the Eng. *some*, and these words must not be used for the Eng. *any*, except when it stands for *some*.

Nonnunquam (*sometimes*) corresponds to **nonnulli**.

Exercise 212 [A].

1. If all the best men have perished, who is left to rule the state?

2. If he ever saw his men suffering hardships, he tried to help them himself.

3. The order was given that each man should see to his own safety.

4. It is of the utmost importance to us to find out if anyone has been here during our absence.

5. The horse has been lost for a long time, and no one can find it anywhere.

6. He said that no one had ever persuaded him to take bribes.

7. If the city is taken, I do not suppose the enemy will spare any of the citizens.

8. Having remained within their lines for some time, our men at last sallied out against the enemy.

9. A philosopher has said that fire is the origin of all things.

10. There is no doubt that a considerable number of the enemy are trying to attack us in the rear.

Exercise 212
suffer hardship, laboro.
bribe, pecunia.
philosopher, philosophus.
origin, origo, -inis, *f*.

Exercise 213 [B].

1. On my return I was told that someone had come to see me.

2. I returned as quickly as possible, but could not find anyone in my house.

3. Did anyone ask you what ought to be done?

4. If anyone were to say that there was no hope, he would be killed by the citizens.

5. I am willing to send anyone at all to find out what is going on.

6. Someone or another has said that a long life is the greatest misfortune.

7. For some time it was asserted that all our best troops were lost.

8. There is no doubt that they perished, but their bodies have never been found anywhere.

9. When I return to Rome I shall find out if anyone has bought my house.

10. An order was given that whoever plundered the houses should be put to death.

Exercise 213
in my house, apud me.
misfortune, malum.

Exercise 214
fugitive, fugitivus.
imagine, reor, duco.
really, revera.
rest, reliqua pars.

Exercise 215
ignorance, inscientia.
responsible for, auctor.
main road, via, certum iter.
unmolested, incolumis.
on equal terms, aequo Marte, aequa contentione.
cliff, rapes, -is, *f.*

Exercises

Exercise 214 [A].
[Exercises 214-222 are for revision.]

If after so great a victory the Gauls had immediately pursued the fugitives, Rome would certainly have been taken, so astonished and terrified were the citizens at the return of those who had escaped from the battle. The Gauls, however, not imagining the victory to be so great as it really was, gave way[1] to feasting and plundering the camp. Accordingly numbers, who wished to leave the city, had opportunity to escape, while those who remained were able to make preparations for defending the city. The latter, quitting the rest of the city, retired to the Capitol, which they fortified by strong ramparts; for they knew that if the Gauls attacked them they would need all their strength.

1. **se delere**, dat.

Exercise 215 [A],

There can be little doubt that the guides, whether through treachery or ignorance, were mainly responsible for the disaster. If the army had marched by the main road they would have arrived unmolested, and could have joined battle on the following day on equal terms. But following a shorter way across the fields, they found the road blocked on one side by a marsh, and on the other by cliffs. Then the general called together his officers, and said, "If we advance we shall run the risk of[1] being surprised by the enemy; on the other hand, if[2] we retreat we shall perhaps arrive too late. Had we only kept to the main road, we should already be approaching the city." No one replied at once, and before any plan could be determined the cry was raised that the enemy were upon them.

1. Use '**in periculum adduci ut.**'
2. **Sin** = '*but if*' (introducing a second and contrary condition). '*If not*,' '*otherwise*,' without a verb = **si minus.**

Exercise 216 [A].

A young Spartan, named Isadas, distinguished himself[1] particularly in this action. He had neither armour nor clothes upon his body, and he held a spear in one hand and a sword in the other. In this condition[2] he quitted his home with the utmost eagerness, and was the first to enter the battle. He dealt mortal[3] wounds at every blow, and overthrew all who opposed him without receiving any hurt himself.[4] Whether the enemy were dismayed at so strange a sight, or whether the gods preserved him on account of his extraordinary valour, it is certain that no man ever accomplished such marvellous deeds. It is said that after the battle the Ephori decreed him a crown for his valour, but fined him a thousand drachmae for having exposed himself to so great a danger without arms.

1. **eniteo**.
2. *thus armed*.
3. **mortifer**
4. **ipse incolumis**.

Exercise 217 [A].

On the very day on which the Senate was deliberating whether they ought to summon back to Rome the Master of the Horse, news was brought that he had led out the troops which had been left in the camp, and in a battle with the Samnites had suffered a great disaster. The Dictator would not even wait to learn what the Senate determined, but hurried back to the camp. The Master of the Horse, summoned before the tribunal,[1] was asked why he, to whose care the safety of the Roman people had been entrusted, had without the orders of the Dictator led into battle the legions which he had been ordered to keep within the camp. The only reply he could make was[2] that he had thought he ought to use the legions which he commanded for the good of the Roman people whenever an opportunity offered.[3]

1. **tribunal** (*n.*)
2. 'he could only answer this.'
3. '*was given.*'

Exercise 218 [A],

An Indian[1] chief was taken prisoner by the Spaniards, and because he was a man of influence[2] among the tribes they cut off his hands, with the intention of disabling him[3] from fighting any more against them. But he, returning home eager to avenge this wrong, incited his countrymen not to let the Spaniards think their accustomed valour had forsaken them. And when they saw the cruelty which the Spaniards had practised[4] towards him and others his companions, they burnt their homes, to prevent anyone's wishing to return, and fell upon the Spanish settlement, with minds made up either to drive the Spaniards out of the town or to perish themselves in battle. While the battle was being fought the maimed chieftain himself carried arrows in his mouth with which to supply the combatants.

1. **Indicus** (*subst.* **Indus**).
2. Use '**pollere**.'
3. '*that he might not be able.*'
4. '*used.*'

Exercise 216
named, by name, nomine.
particularly, praeter omnes.
overthrow, sterno.
sight, spectaculum.
extraordinary, egregius.
crown, corona.
fine, mulcto aliquem, *abl.*
expose oneself to, se objicere, *dat.*, occurro, *dat.*
eagerness, studium.
dismayed, perterritus, pavore perculsus.
marvellous, mirus.

Exercise 217
master of the horse, magister equitum.
without the orders of, injussu.

Exercise 218
cut off, deseco.
accustomed, solitus.
settlement, colonia.
with minds made up, obstinatis, animis.
maimed, saucius.

Exercise 219 [B].

The Romans, when they heard of the disaster which had befallen Regulus, fitted out a large fleet for the rescue of the survivors; while the Carthaginians, rightly judging that the resolution of the Romans would not be broken by one calamity, also began to build a new fleet to protect them from another invasion. But in vain did they endeavour to reduce Clypea before the Romans could reach it. The small garrison, with surprising courage, repelled all attacks, and held out till the ensuing summer, when the Roman fleet arrived. A naval battle took place off the Hermaean promontory. The Romans gained the day, and took on board the defenders of Clypea who had so well earned their safety.

Exercise 220 [B].

Hanno was now entrusted with the command. If he had followed[1] the example of Hamilcar, the Romans would without doubt have been defeated. But before he had held the command long he proved himself entirely unworthy of confidence. If ever he won a partial success,[2] he was unable to make use of it; and after having won, as he thought, a complete victory, he allowed his camp to be surprised and taken. Under these circumstances the Carthaginians once more offered Hamilcar the command, although they could not expect a man whom they had treated so unjustly before to come to their help. But Hamilcar, still placing his country before all else, consented to take the command. By his strict discipline, by his energy, and by his great influence with the Numidian chiefs, he defeated the enemy in a pitched battle, and recovered a considerable number of cities which had revolted.

1. *used.*
2. **ex parte rem prospere gerere.**

Exercise 221 [B].

When Ulysses was cast upon[1] the island of Phaeacia, he was treated with all the hospitality which in those days strangers used everywhere to receive. Nausicaa, the king's daughter, was the first person who met him, and she conducted him to her father's palace. The best raiment which the maidens had woven was bestowed upon him; and he enjoyed the most sumptuous feast which his hosts could provide. On the next day games were held, and he was asked to join in[2] them, an honour which he at first refused. But afterwards, stung by the insults of the king's son, the only man who forgot his duty to a guest, he showed that his strength was almost as great now as when he fought against Troy, and he surpassed the Phaeacians[3] in their own sports.

1. **ejectus in.**
2. **intercesse.**
3. **Phaeacea.**

Exercise 219
fit out, instruo.
rescue, reduco.
survivor, superstes, -itis, *or* verb superesse.
break, frango.
reduce, redigo.
naval, navalis.
off, prep. contra.
promontory, promontorium.
take on board, in navem excipio.
defender, defensor.
earn, mereo, mereor.

Exercise 220
hold a command, imperium obtineo.
prove oneself, se praebere.
confidence, trust, fides,
complete, certus, manlifestus.
treat, utor.
place before, prefer, antepono *Cf. Ex. 61.*
consent, volo.
strict, severus.
discipline, disciplina.
energy, studium.
influence with, auctoritas apud.
pitched battle, justum proelium.
recover, recipio.

Exercise 221
treat, afficio.
hospitality, hospitium.
host, guest, hospes.
everywhere, ubique.
raiment, vestis, -is, *f.*
weave, texo, -ere, texui, textum.
sumptuous, magnificus, lautus.
hold games, ludos celebro, I.
stung, commotus, lacessitus.
provide, praebeo.
bestow, dono, I.
surpass, supero, I.
sports, ludi.

Exercise 222 [B].

If ever a man[1] deserved to be well treated[2] by his fellow citizens it was Tib. Gracchus. Son of a father who had pacified Spain (a work[3] in which a whole series of consuls had failed), and connected by birth with both the conquerors of Africa,[4] he might have easily claimed the first place in the state, if he had been willing to obey the laws without[5] trying to change them. But he had to journey through Etruria to his first province, Spain, and that country, then desolate, devoid of freemen, cultivated by slaves, made such an impression[6] on him that he determined to find a remedy if he perished in the attempt. All the best men of Rome favoured the laws he proposed, and had not a tribune stood in the way he would have accomplished his work with the goodwill of most, if not all.[7]

1. Translate 'Tib. Gracchus, if any other, was worthy,' etc.
2. **beneficiis afficere**.
3. 'That which (**id quod**) *many other consuls had relinquished without success*' (**re infecta**).
4. **uterque Africanus**.
5. 'and had not' = **nec**.
6. **commovere**.
7. **ne dicam omnea**.

CONCESSIVE CLAUSES

<u>**Rule 29**</u>. **Concessive Clauses have their verb (a) in the Indicative when what is conceded is allowed to be a fact; (b) in the Subjunctive if it is only conceded as a hypothesis for argument's sake.**

Quamvis, licet, quum, ut are only to be used with Subjunctive.

Quanquam is only to be used with Indicative.

Etsi, etiamsi, tametsi may be used with either according to meaning.

EXAMPLES.

(*a*) Romani **quanquam** fessi **erant** procedunt.
The Romans advanced in spite of being tired.

Cur nolint, **etiamsi tacent**, satis dicunt.
Though they are silent they show clearly why they are unwilling.

(*b*) Quod turpe est, id, **quamvis occultetur**, tamen honestum fieri nullo modo potest.
What is base cannot be made honourable, however much it be disguised.

Rectum est, **etiamsi** nobis indigna **audiamus**, iracundiam repellere.
It is right to restrain our passions, even though we should hear things that we resent (things unworthy of us).

Exercise 223 [A].

1. Although they were not convicted of treason, they inflicted great injury on the state.

2. Even if you denied this, no one would believe you.

3. However[1] great the numbers of the enemy may be, we must not despair.

4. Knowing, as they did, that their plans were discovered, they still pretended to be innocent.

5. I am willing that you should do this, though I should not have done it myself.

6. Although the general had won many successes, he was disliked by his troops.

7. I am resolved to tell the truth even if my enemies threaten me with death.

8. Although Caesar had already borrowed[2] immense sums, men still trusted him.

9. Although he had deceived me five times, I should still[3] have trusted him.

10. I should be quite contented even if I had to go into exile for a little time.

1. **quamvis**.
2. **mutuari**.
3. **nihilo minus**, *or* **nihilo secius**

Exercise 222	Exercise 223
pacify, paco, 1.	**convict of treason**, damno majestatis.
connected by birth, cognatus, natu conjunctus.	**inflict injury**, injuriam inferre, *dat*.
claim, usurpo, 1.	**innocent**, insons, -tis.
first place, principatus, -us, *m*.	**quite**, satis.
devoid of, nudatus, vacuus.	
remedy, remedium.	
attempt, conatus, *or* use verb.	
with the good will of. Use appro bare.	
Spain, Hispania.	

Exercise 224 [A].

1. Though he were to offer me a great price, I should not sell the farm.

2. We must get to Rome today, however[1] many obstacles hinder us.

3. Though I know very well he is guilty, I shall do my best to acquit him.

4. Great though his army may be, he will not risk all on one battle.

5. Even if he were chieftain of all Gaul, I would not spare him.

6. Though he was the richest man in all this county[2] he gave little money to the poor.

7. Though the gods are on our side, we shall need the sword.

8. Though they were my best legions, I should send them back to Pompey.

9. Caesar sent back the two legions Pompey had sent him, though they were the best he had.

10. However great my peril was, I should not try to avoid it in such a cause.

1. **quamvis**.
2. **regio**.

Exercise 224
to do one's best to, id agere ut.
risk, periclitor, 1.

Exercise 225 [B].

1. Anyone can remain silent, even if he is angry.

2. They had resolved to remain silent, however many tortures might be inflicted upon them.

3. They held out for some time, although they knew that there was no hope of safety.

4. Believing, as I do,[1] that you wish to serve me, yet I cannot accept your help.

5. I should never believe you, although you bound yourself by an oath.

6. At this crisis the allies deserted, though they had promised to remain faithful.

7. We shall still be soldiers, even if the army is disbanded.

8. The battle raged fiercely for a long time, although we were greatly inferior to the enemy in numbers.

9. You ought not to say such things in the presence of others, however true you may believe them to be.

10. Although he tried to conceal his indignation, there is no doubt that he was annoyed at this.

---

1. = *Although I believe*.

> **Exercise 225**
> **remain silent**, taceo.
> **bind** (*by oath*), obstringo.
> **in the presence of**, coram.
> **oath**, jusjurandum.
> **disband**, dimitto.
> **indignation**, ira, dolor.

Exercise 226 [B].

1. Although they had long been living in a foreign land, they observed the customs of their ancestors.

2. They refused to do this, though it was to their own advantage.

3. We will not yield to the enemy, however large their forces may be.

4. Although they were inferior to the enemy in numbers, they held their ground resolutely.

5. Clever as he was, he could not deceive us.

6. I cannot trust him, in spite of his promising to keep his word.

7. Although they were so poor, we could not offer them help.

8. Great as a general's power may be, he is always responsible to the government.

9. Even should they be brought to trial, they would without doubt be acquitted.

10. They were led out to execution,[1] in spite of the general's promise to spare their lives.

1. **ad necem**.

Exercise 226
foreign, externus.
observe customs, institutis uti.
be responsible, *translate by "I must give an account,"* rationem reddo.
government, magistratus, ei qui rempublicam administrant.
resolutely, obstinate, summa constantia.

Exercise 227 [A],

Although Lucullus had won many successes, he was unable to bring the war with Mithridates to a close. The king, after defeating Triarius in a pitched battle at Zela, had retreated to the mountains, satisfied with his success, and Lucullus gave orders for pursuit. But however desirous he might himself be of capturing the king, he found his men unwilling to follow him. Most of them had been absent from Italy for nearly twenty years, and since Lucullus had taken the command, they had suffered great hardships. Lucullus, though a good general, had none of that geniality which wins the affection of soldiers, and moreover he had been living in great luxury, though his soldiers often suffered from want. The result was that the army agreed to defend Pontus from Mithridates, but positively refused to undertake a new campaign.[1]

1. *war.*

Exercise 227
bring to a close, conficio.
satisfied, contentus.
geniality, comitas.
win affection, studium conciliare.
luxury, luxus, -us, *m.*
want, inopia.
the result is that, evenit ut.
positively, absolutely (*with negative words*), omnino.
undertake, suscipio.

Exercise 228 [A],

Though the army opposed to Caesar had been much more numerous he would nevertheless have come out of this campaign victorious. The discipline and experience of his soldiers were such that, although fortune might be adverse, they never lost heart. This appeared especially in the war round Dyrrhachium. Though the lines which they had constructed with so much trouble were assailed and the defenders driven out of them, there was no panic, nor did the soldiers scatter in flight in all directions over the country; but those who survived the defeat kept together, and retreated[1] along the road which led into the mountains. Next day Caesar had again an army, which, though[2] diminished, was prepared to face all dangers manfully.

1. *retreated in close order.*
2. Of the Concessive Conjunctions **quamvis** is most frequently used where the verb is omitted.

Exercise 229 [B].

However men may differ as to Napoleon's character, there can be no doubt that he acquired a wonderful influence over[1] his soldiers. If they sometimes grumbled at his orders in private,[2] yet, when he led them to battle, there was not a man who was not ready to risk his life for him. They did this,[3] although it was evident that he for his part never tried to spare the lives of his men, but was resolved to crush the enemy, however great the losses on his own side[4] might be. Thus it happened that France came off victorious in so many conflicts, although she was opposed by many powerful enemies at the same time.

1. **apud**.
2. say '*secretly.*'
3.. Translate '**idque**' (omitting '*they did*').
4. *of his own men.*

Exercises

Exercise 230 [B].

The determination of the Athenians remained unshaken, in spite of the desertion of so many of the Greek States. They readily granted to the Spartans the supreme command of the forces by sea as well as by land, although they themselves furnished two-thirds of the entire fleet. The great Themistocles tried to inspire the other Greeks with some of the enthusiasm which he had aroused in the Athenians. Had he not displayed as much wisdom as valour, the cause of Greek freedom would have been lost. By his advice the confederates[1] bound themselves to resist to the death, and in case of success[2] to consecrate to the Delphian god a tenth part of the property of all Grecian states which had surrendered to the Persians of their own accord.

1. *allies.*
2. *if things happened well.*

Exercise 228	Exercise 229	Exercise 230
diminish, diminuo, *trans.*	**differ**, inter se differre.	**unshaken**, immotus.
more numerous, major.	**grumble at**, queror de, aegre fero.	**readily**, libenter.
come out, prove, evado, -ere, -is, -sum.	**risk one's life**, periculum capitis subire.	**two-thirds**, duae partes.
experience, usus, -us, *m.*, peritia.	**crush**, oppugno; profligo, I.	**inspire**, injicio aliquid alicui.
in close order, conferto agmine.	**acquire**, acquiro, nanciscor.	**enthusiasm**, studium.
face, obeo, *acc.*		**the cause was lost**. Use actum est de.
adverse, adversus, iniquus.		**display**, praesto.
trouble, labor.		**consecrate**, voveo.
		desert, deficio.
		grant, do, mando, I., trado.

COMPARATIVE CLAUSES

Rule 30. When the Comparative Clause is meant to state an actual fact its verb is in the Indicative; but when it is a purely imaginary comparison the verb is in the Subjunctive.

In the first case the commonest words of comparison used are: **sicut** (*just as*), **perinde ac** (*exactly as*), **aeque ac** (*as much as*), **aliter ac** (*otherwise than*), **alius ac** (*different from*), **idem ac** (*the same as*).

In the second case the commonest are : **velut, quasi, tanquam** (*si*).

EXAMPLES.

Poenas dedit **sicut meritus est**.
He was punished as he deserved.

Absentis Ariovisti crudelitatem **quasi** coram **adesset** horrebant.
They dreaded the cruelty of Ariovistus in his absence just as if he had been present.

Virtus **eadem** in homine **ac** deo **est**.
Virtue is the same in man as in God.

Exercise 231 [A].

1. He behaved just as if he were mad.

2. He was rewarded just as he deserved.

3. He fought as if the safety of the State depended on him alone.

4. I foresaw it all, just as it happened.

5. As you thought, his only object was[1] to deceive us.

6. He governs the State, not as circumstances demand, but as if he were setting an example to the rest of mankind.

7. He is not quite so devoted to us as you think.

8. His performance does not agree with his promise.

9. While[2] I value my own safety a great deal, I value that of the State a great deal more.

10. I envy you as being free from all cares of State.

11. As might be expected[3] in such times, it was long doubtful which side would conquer.

12. As often happens, he was tired of his task before he had finished it.

---

1. **id solum egit ut.**
2. Contrast the clauses by **ut ... ita**, or by **quum ... tum**. These should often be used for *both ... and* or *not only ... but also*, where one sentence is to be emphasised more than the other.
3. '**ut**' only. Cf. **satis impavidus ut in re trepida**, '*keeping presence of mind as much as could be expected in such a panic.*'

Exercise 232 [B].

1. They rushed into the river as if they were mad.

2. Our men have been defeated, just as I foretold.

3. It is our duty to treat others just as we wish them to treat us.

4. It was observed that he often turned round as if someone were pursuing him.

5. Considering their difficult position,[1] they acted as wisely as they could.

6. Seeing is a different thing from believing.

7. There is no doubt that we have less leisure than our ancestors.

8. Their actions were not always in accordance with their promises.

9. They joined battle as if they had no fear of defeat.

10. The Greeks were not distinguished by the same virtues as the Romans.

11. He threw himself into the river, as if he really wished to save his enemy.

12. As was to be expected at such a crisis,[1] the general was the only man who remained unmoved.

---

1. **ut in tanto discrimine.**

Exercise 231
behave, se gerere.
reward, praemio afficio.
depend on, ponitur in.
foresee, provIdeo.
his object was, id egit ut.
be devoted to, studeo, *dat*.
affairs of state, res publicae.
set an example. (*See Ex. 85.*)

Exercise 232
rush into, irruo in.
foretell, praedico.
leisure, otium.
distinguished, insignis.

Exercise 233 [A].

At the battle of Zama Hannibal showed the same resolution and the same skill in drawing up his line as he had shown fourteen years before at the battle of Cannae. But fortune was against him, and he went into the battle as if he himself knew it. The elephants, which before had often been a source of safety to the Carthaginians, now frightened by the shouting of the Romans, turned upon their own army, and threw the first line into confusion. The mercenaries formed[1] the first line and, as they fell back, the Carthaginians, drawn up in the second line, would not admit them through their ranks, and even charged them as if they were the enemy. This was not contrary to Hannibal's expectations. He ordered the third line, his veterans brought from Italy, to charge and drive the disorderly rabble off the field. Then at length the battle with the Romans was renewed.

1. **consistere in.**

Exercise 233
at the battle of Zama, pugna Zamae facta.
mercenaries, mercenarii milites.
contrary to expectation, praeter spem, opinionem.
veteran, veteranus.
disorderly, tumultuarius.
rabble, turba.

Exercise 234
show presence of mind, impavidus esse, se intrepide gerere.
explain, expono, edo.
cry, clamor.
groan, gemitus, -us.
undergo sentence, poenam subeo.
crowd round, circumfundor, *dat.*
sufferings, mala, *n. pl.*

Exercise 235
consider, delibero de.
silent, tacitus.
Egypt, Aegyptus, -i, *f.*
empire, imperium.

Exercise 234 [A].

The messengers, as they had been commanded, informed the people that in three days they must leave their homes and depart to another place. These at first made no answer, as if they did not understand what was demanded of them. But the chieftain, who under the circumstances showed great presence of mind, asked the messengers to explain more clearly the reason for this demand. The latter replied that they were only acting in accordance with the orders they had received. Then from the whole village arose loud cries and groans, as if they had undergone sentence of death; and one and all crowded around the messengers, with as much fury and indignation as they could have shown if those men had themselves been responsible for their sufferings.

Exercise 235 [B].

Antiochus had invaded Egypt at the beginning of spring. But it happened just as some of his followers had foretold. As soon as he approached Alexandria a Roman ambassador, Popillius, met him, and handed him a letter from the Senate. The king read it, and replied that he would call his friends to a council and consider it; but Popillius with his staff drew a line round[1] the king, and bade him not move from the spot before he had given him an answer. Nor did he reply to any of the questions which the king asked him, but stood silent as if he did not hear; until the king, frightened by the ambassador's boldness, promised to do what the Senate decreed. In like manner, wherever Romans went, they acted as if to them belonged the empire of the world.

1. **circumscribere**.

Exercise 236 [B].

On hearing that he had been proscribed by Antony, Cicero fled for refuge to his villa,[1] which was close by the sea, and got on board a ship with the intention of crossing over into Macedonia. He put out several times, but was driven back by adverse winds, and at last returned to his villa, declaring that he would die in the country which he had so often saved. He went to bed, and slept well considering his critical position. His slaves, however, as if foreseeing his danger, aroused him, and placing him in a litter carried him through the woods towards the sea. He was soon overtaken by the soldiers, who had been sent in pursuit of him; and when they came up he forbade his slaves to offer any resistance, and stretching his neck out of the litter bade the soldiers complete their work.

1. **villa.**

Exercise 236
proscribe, proscribo.
put out to sea, evehor (in altum).
adverse, adversus.
litter, lectica.
stretch out, porrigo.
neck, cervices, *f. plu.*
drive back, repello.
considering his critical position, ut in tanto discrimine.

ORATIO OBLIQUA

Rule 31. In Latin it is much commoner than in English to report a long speech not in the exact words of the speaker, but in the Indirect form, or **Oratio Obliqua**. Each clause in this will be either an Indirect Statement, or an Indirect Command, or an Indirect Question, or a clause dependent on one of these; and the mood and tense must be determined by the rules already given.

But observe—
(1) The Oratio Obliqua being continuous, the verb of "saying" which introduces it is not to be repeated before each clause, and a verb of command or questioning may be understood from one of saying and *vice versa*.

(2) Where a command comes in the middle of Oratio Obliqua the **ut** is not expressed, though if it is a prohibition the **ne** must be expressed.

(3) Questions in Oratio Obliqua may be expressed by the Infinitive when they are asked for rhetorical purposes, and not to obtain an answer, and are practically equivalent to negative statements. Questions which in the direct form are in the 1st or 3rd Person are generally rhetorical.

> *e.g.* the following are rhetorical questions:
> "*Am I a coward that I should fly without striking a blow?*"
> "*Is freedom a possession to be lightly esteemed?* " (**Num libertatem parvi aestimandam esse?**)

(4) All pronouns representing the 1st and 2nd Persons must be changed into the 3rd Person.
> *e.g.* **ego, meus, nos, noster, become se, suus.**[1]
> **tu, tuus, vos, vester, become ille, illius, is, ejus, etc.**
> **hic and iste become ille and is.**

Adverbs require similar changes:
> **hodie becomes illo die.**
> **hic becomes ibi.**
> **nunc becomes jam or tune.**

The following example will illustrate these points:

" *The general asked his men why they hesitated, and urged them to advance at once. He reminded them that everything depended on their bravery, and declared that if they shirked the battle they would disgrace him and their country. Was it credible, he demanded, that he was addressing the same men who had so often defeated the enemy?*"

" **Imperator suos interrogavit cur haesitarent: statim progrederentur, omnia enim in illorum virtute esse posita; quodsi pugnam detrectassent illos dedecori fore et sibi et patriae. Num credibile esse se eosdem adloqui qui hostem toties vicissent?**"

Notice here that the English verbs "*urged,*" "*reminded,*" "*declared,*" "*demanded,*" are all understood in Latin from the one introductory word "**interrogavit**"; that the command "**progrederentur**" is expressed without the **ut**; and that the Infinitive "**esse**" represents a rhetorical question.

Notice also that the Pluperfect "**detrectassent**" stands for the Future Perfect of the Direct Speech.

---

1. Se and suus represent either the speaker alone or the speaker and the people addressed, where the speaker identifies himself with them.

Oratio Recta.

Quod si veteria contumeliae oblivisci *vellem*, num etiam recentium injuriarum, quod me invito iter per provinciam per vim *tentavistis*, memoriam deponere *possum*?

Oratio Obliqua.

His Caesar ita respondit: Quod si veteris contumeliae oblivisci *vellet*, num etiam recentium injuriarum, quod se invito iter per provinciam per vim *tentavissent*, memoriam deponere *posse*?

But if I were willing to forget the old insult, can I also put aside the memory of more recent wrongs, inasmuch as against my will you forced a way through the Roman province?

N.B. Here, as the form of the conditional *si vellet* shows, the infinitive posse implies negation, and the question is rhetorical

O. R.

Ariovistus me consule cupidissime populi Romani amicitiam *appetiit*: cur *hunc* tam temere quisquam ab officio discessurum *judicat*? Mihi quidem *persuadetur*, cognitis *meis* postulatis, eum neque *meam* neque populi Romani gratiam repudiaturum. Quod si furore atque amentia impulsus bellum *intulerit*, quid tandem *veremini*? aut cur de *nostra* virtute aut de *mea* diligentia *desperatis*?

O. O.

Dixit—*Ariovistum se* consule cupidissime populi Romani amicitiam *appetisse*: cur ilium tam temere quisquam ab officio discessurum *judicaret*? Sibi quidem *persuaderi*, cognitis *suis* postulatis, eum neque suam neque populi Romani gratiam repudiaturum. Quod si furore atque amentia impulsus bellum *intulisset*, quid tandem *vererentur*? aut cur de *sua* virtute aut de *ipsius* diligentia *desperarent*?

During my consulship Ariovistus most earnestly coveted the friendship of the Roman people. Why does anyone suppose that he will so hastily cast off his allegiance? For my part I am convinced that when he is acquainted with my demands he will not slight either my favour or that of the Roman people. But if under the impulse of rage and madness he does wage war upon us, why, I ask, are you afraid? or why do you doubt either our courage or my diligence?

O.R.

Si pacem populus Romanus cum Helvetiis *faciet*, in eam partem *ibunt* atque ibi *erunt* Helvetii ubi eos *constituisti*; sin bello persequi *perseverabis*, *reminiscere* veteris incommodi populi Romani. Quod improviso unum pagum *adortus es* cum ii, qui flumen *transierant*, suis auxilium ferre non possent, ne ob *hanc* rem *tuae* magnopere virtuti *tribueris* neve *nos despexeris*.

O.O.

Is ita cum Caesare egit: si pacem populus Romanus cum Helvetiis *faceret*, in eam partem *ituros* atque ibi *futures* Helvetios, ubi eos *Caesar constituisset*; sin bello persequi *perseveraret*, *reminisceretur* veteris incommodi populi Romani. Quod improvise unum pagum *adortus esset* cum ii, qui flumen *transiissent*, suis auxilium ferre non possent, ne ob *eam* rem *suae* magnopere virtuti *tribueret*, neve *se ipsos despiceret*.

If the people of Rome make peace with the Helvetii, the Helvetii will go to that part of the country which you have assigned to them, and will remain there. But should you persist in harrying them with war—remember the former disaster which befell the Roman people. As to the fact of your having fallen unexpectedly upon a single canton, when those who had crossed the river could not bring help to their friends, do not on this account think too highly of your own valour, or treat us with scorn.

Exercise 237 [A],
Put into Oratio Obliqua after a verb in a Historic tense:

1. Deliver up to me the hostages I demanded.

2. Why did they refuse to follow him?

3. I do not wish to betray these men who are under my protection.

4. Do you suppose that you alone know this?

5. If you do this, all men will praise you.

6. If they had followed us, they would have reached[1] the city in safety.

7. Let us advance to attack the enemy.

8. Follow me, fellow soldiers, and we shall easily overcome the enemy.

9. We ought not always to consult our own interests.

10. They were prevented by a storm from reaching the harbour.

11. Today we have won a great victory.

1. **perventuros fuisse**. The Future Participle with **fuisse** always represents the English *would have ...* in Indirect Statement.

Exercise 237
be under protection, fidem sequor.

Exercise 238 [B].

1. Why did you persuade the allies to revolt?

2. Let us depart at once, and never return to this place.

3. I told you before what the result of the battle would be.

4. Give me what I asked you for, and I will depart.

5. When do you suppose that the reinforcements, for which we are waiting, will arrive?

6. We have stormed the walls, but the citadel is not in our hands.

7. Friends, let us not despair of safety.

8. You ought to have sent us help more quickly.

9. Was he mad to say such things?

10. If this is true, I refuse to help you any longer.

11. Unless help had arrived, all the citizens would have died of starvation.

Exercise 239 [A],

Put into Oratio Obliqua after a verb in a Historic tense:

1. Why have you invaded my country?

2. Return to your own country.

3. The Carthaginians attacked us and 700 of their own men, 200 of ours were killed.

4. Let us not forgot the wrongs of our allies, but avenge them speedily.

5. You have shown today more valour than they.

6. When we return to Rome we will enquire into this.

7. I cannot help you now. If you come tomorrow I will consider what I can do.

8. Three days ago we could have left the camp, now we are compelled to stay here whether we will or not.

9. Camillus, your fellow-citizens beg and pray you to return and save the state.

10. If you stay in my house you will certainly be attacked by these men.

Exercise 239
enquire, hold enquiry about, quaestionem habeo de.
wrong, injuria.

Exercise 240 [B].

1. Where can we stay tonight?

2. I am not sure that I shall reach you in time.

3. The two legions which I had I have sent to Pompey.

4. Here there is no safety either for me or for you.

5. If he kept his word he would be here now.

6. Let us all remember that liberty depends for us on this one battle.

7. Never give away your money to a man you do not know.

8. It is not easy, my friend, to think of the interests of[1] your fellow-citizens and at the same time of your own.

9. Is my friend to be neglected because he is away?

10. Why should I humour a man who was my father's freedman?

1. **consulere**, *dat.*

Exercise 240
humour, morem gero, *dat.*
freedman, libertus, -i.

Exercise 241 [A].

Labienus was the next to speak, and he expressed contempt for Caesar's forces. They must not imagine, he said, that this was the army which conquered Gaul and Germany. He was present himself at the battles fought in those countries, and was not rashly stating facts beyond his knowledge.[1] A very small fraction of that army survived. Many had been destroyed by pestilence, many had gone home. Had they not heard that regiments had been manufactured[2] at Brundisium out of the wounded that had been left behind? The forces which they saw before them were raw recruits, and most of them came from colonies beyond the Po. Moreover the flower of the army had perished in the two engagements at Dyrrhachium. He himself finally would swear never to return to the camp unless victorious; let all the rest follow his example.

1. *which he had not ascertained.*
2. *made.*

Exercise 241
regiment, cohors.
(raw) recruit, tiro, -onis.
Po, Padus, -i, *m.*
flower (*of army*), robur, -oris, *n.*

Exercise 242 [A].

According to the historian Livy,[1] Appius declared to the assembled Senate that he wished he was deaf so that he might not hear the disgraceful counsels which were that day dishonouring the Roman name. He greatly regretted, he said, their change of temper; it was very different from the temper of former days. Whither had their pride and courage fled? Had they not once boasted that they would have opposed Alexander himself if in the period of their youth he had dared to invade Italy? Let them not now deliver up to Lucanians and wretched Greeks[2] what their fathers had won by the sword.

1. **Apud Livium scriptum invenimus**.
2. **Graeculus**, the diminutive expressing contempt.

Exercise 243 [A].

The terms of peace, heavy though they were, were only such as they expected under the circumstances;[1] and Hannibal dragged down with his own hands from the rostrum an orator who was recommending the continuance of the war. The people were indignant with Hannibal for thus infringing upon their liberty of speech; but Hannibal replied that they must forgive him if, after serving thirty-six years in the camp, he had forgotten the manners of the forum. Livy relates that the terms agreed upon by Scipio and the Carthaginian government were then referred to the Senate at Rome, and were accepted by them, both because they felt that they were sufficiently severe, and also because they feared that if they rejected them the Carthaginians would renew the war.

1. **in tali re**.

Exercise 244 [A],

The general then summoned a council of war and spoke thus: (*Or. Obl.*) "We must now decide whether it is to our advantage to hold our position or to retreat while we still have the opportunity. The reinforcements, which we have so long expected, have not arrived; and for my part I believe we are no match for the enemy. But I know we can trust the courage and endurance of our men, and if it is your wish, I am prepared to hold out as long as possible. Tell me plainly your opinion, for I shall do nothing without your approval." When the general had finished his speech, many different opinions were expressed; but at length it was decided that, considering the numbers of the enemy, it would be wiser to retreat and not to run the risk of a severe defeat.

Exercise 242
deaf, surdus, auribus captus.
dishonour, disgrace, dedecoro, I; dedecori esse.
regret, deploro, I.
change, muto, I.
temper, animus.
former days, tempus prius, superius.

Exercise 243
drag down, detraho.
orator, orator.
continue a war, bellum duco, produco.
infringe upon, deminuo.
serve as soldier, stipendia mereo (stipendium = soldier's pay).
agree upon, fix, constituo,
refer, refero.
reject, rejicio, respuo.
be indignant with, irascor, *dat*.

Exercise 244
endurance, patientia.
plainly, aperte, plane,
approval, consensus, -us, *m*.
opinion, sententia.
express, edo, fero.
run risk of, periculum subeo.

Exercise 245 [A],

Caesar, when the report of the Senate's action reached him, addressed his soldiers. He told them what the Senate had done, and why they had done it. "For nine years he and his army had served their country loyally, and had won many victories. They had driven the Germans over the Rhine; they had made Gaul a Roman province; and the Senate had now broken the laws of the state, and had deposed the tribunes because they spoke in his defence. They had declared that the state was in danger, and had called Italy to arms, when he himself had in no wise injured them." The soldiers whom Pompey supposed disaffected, declared with one consent that they would follow their commander and the tribunes. In all the army only one officer proved false.

Exercise 246 [A].

When Sulla had overcome his enemies and assumed supreme power, he assembled the senate and demanded with the utmost eagerness that Caius Marius should at once be declared an enemy to the state. No one dared to oppose him until Scaevola, on being questioned, refused to express an opinion. When, however, Sulla repeatedly asked him in a threatening voice to give his opinion, at length he replied, (*Or. Obl.*) "You may show me the troops of soldiers with which you have surrounded the senate house; you may threaten me with death again and again; but you will never compel me to say that Marius, by whom the Roman state was saved, is an enemy to Rome."

Exercise 247 [A].

There are men in our times who seem to desire not only to change the laws (which[1] perhaps would be a laudable desire [2]), but to upset the whole state.[3] I was listening to one such yesterday as he addressed a crowd of artisans in the forum. (*or. Obl.*) "Who is it," he asked them, "that oppresses us? Who is it for whom we pile up wealth, while we want ourselves money to buy food? You yourselves can answer (the question), nor is there any need for me to tell you. Our senators have the power to prevent good laws being carried, and M. Crassus buys the consulship every year for himself and his friends. Fellow-citizens,[4] there is only one remedy—let us drive them from the city. Let us teach them by fire and bloodshed how great a wrong they have done to the people."

1. **id quod**.
2. *worthy of praise*
3. **rempublicam evertere**.
4. A Vocative in the middle of a speech will usually be simply omitted in Oratio Obliqua.

Exercise 245	Exercise 246	Exercise 247
depose from tribuneship, abrogare tribunatum, *dat*.	**declare an enemy to the state**, hostem decerno.	**in our times**, his temporibus, nostra aetate.
disaffected, mutinous, seditiosus.	**ask repeatedly**, rogito.	**artisan**, artifex, -icis.
with one consent, consensu.	**threatening**, minax.	**pile up**, congero.
loyal, fidelis.	**senate house**, curia.	**want** (*be without*), careo, *abl*.
prove false, me infidelem praebeo.		**bloodshed**, cruor, -oris, *m*.
		every year, quotannis.
		senators, patres.
		carry (*a law*), fero.

Exercise 248 [A].

Three days after the setting out of the troops from Rome the gloomy intelligence arrived that the enemy, after having utterly routed the Roman army on the 12th of March, were now in possession of the city of Corioli, and all the territory and other property of the allies. (*or. Obl.*) "I am the only man," said the messenger, "who has survived the battle. The enemy, flushed with recent victory, are coming in, and must[1] even now be not more than three miles from the city. So savage is their temper, that I am sure no one, however old and infirm, will be spared." Having heard this the Senate determined at once to send envoys to meet the enemy on their approach, with the intention of suing for peace.

1. Use '**sine dubio**.'

Exercise 249 [B].

He had now won a decisive victory, and it seemed certain that the campaign would shortly be brought to a successful issue, when all his hopes were dashed to the ground[1] by the refusal of his troops to continue the war. They declared that they were worn out with the hardships of the campaign, and that the prospect[2] of bringing the war to an end seemed as distant as ever. Why, they asked, must they leave their country and all that was dear to them and undergo every kind of suffering that their general might win the glory of a barren victory? They asserted that, even if they pursued the enemy, they would be unable to overtake them in their mountain fastnesses, while even the victories which they had already won had been purchased at the cost of much Roman blood.

1. **perdo**.
2. **spes**.

Exercise 250 [B].

The general replied that no one could be more anxious than himself to consult the interests of his men; but he reminded them how foolish it was to lose the advantages of a victory well-nigh assured. They must not think, he said, that he had undertaken this campaign merely in the hope of winning glory for himself. They would share equally with him in the fruits of victory, and if once the enemy were crushed, they might return home enriched with spoils taken from the enemy. He also pointed out that though the enemy were seeking refuge in the mountains, they had not yet reached them, and that if an immediate advance were made, it would be easy to overtake them before they reached a place of safety.

Exercise 248
gloomy, tristis, funestus.
utterly rout, profligo, I.
infirm, infirmus, invalidus.

Exercise 249
decisive, haud anceps.
be brought to a successful issue, prospere evenire.
barren, irritus.
be purchased at cost of, stare, *abl.*
fastness, castellum. dear, carus.

Exercise 250
assured, exploratus.
share with, partior cum.
enriched, auctus.
equally, aeque, pariter.

Exercise 251 [B].
Put into Oratio Obliqua after a Historic tense:

Do not believe what is commonly asserted in the city, that I am seeking the consulship for the sake of a province and the wealth that many of our senators steal from the subject states of Rome. Can you think that I, who was once the dear friend of Cato, am so changed in mind? Indeed, I had rather give up all hope of office than involve myself in such disgrace. I have heard recently that the publicani of Cilicia asked our friend Cicero to give them his legionaries to collect the taxes with. He refused at first, but afterwards was prevailed upon. If they were not Romans the very soldiers would refuse to take part in such cruel work. But let us try to devote ourselves to philosophy, and forget evils which we cannot cure.

Exercise 252 [B].

On this night the king gathered round him his little band of followers, and in a few words said farewell to them. (*Or. Obl.*) "Gentlemen,"[1] he said, "your fortune has so long been linked with mine that the word which I speak tonight nothing but the last necessity forces me to utter. If there were yet a hope, I would still make use of your loyalty and your aid. Do not think that I value these lightly. You are the few who, having enjoyed with me the times of prosperity, refused to desert me in adversity. And for this I thank you. But permit me now to think of your safety, for the sake of which I shall tomorrow give myself up. Why should I destroy you with myself? When the rebels have me in their hands they will perhaps leave you free to escape whither you will."

---

1. Omit the Vocative.

Exercise 253 [B].

Hearing of those immense numbers, Robert Guiscard assembled a council of his principal officers. (*Or. Obl.*) "You behold," said he, "your danger: you see how urgent[1] it is. The hills are covered with arms and standards; and the Emperor of the Greeks is accustomed to wars and triumphs. Union is our only safety.[2] Only bid me, and I am ready at once to yield the command to a worthier leader." The acclamation even of his foes assured him at this perilous moment of their confidence;[3] and he thus continued, (*Or. Obl.*) "Let us trust in the reward of victory, and let us not leave cowards the means[4] of escape. Burn your vessels and your baggage, and give battle on this spot." This resolution was unanimously approved, and Guiscard awaited in battle array the approach of the enemy. Perhaps he was not conscious that on the same ground Caesar and Pompey had formerly disputed the empire of the world.

1. Use verb.
2. *Our safety depends on your union.*
3. *Even his private enemies shouted by their applause that they trusted him.*
4. **locus** or **facultas**

Exercise 251
recently, nuper.
commonly, vulgo.
steal, abripio.
subject (*adj.*), subjectus imperio.
dear friend, conjunctissimus.
office, honores.
involve oneself in, occurro, *dat.*
disgrace, dedecus, -oris, *n.*, ignominia.
tax, vectigal.
philosophy, philosophia.
cure, medeor, *dat.*, sano, I., *acc.*

Exercise 252
followers, comites.
say farewell to, jubeo aliquem valere.
last necessity, ultima necessitas.
loyalty, fides, *f.* 5.
prosperity, res prosperae.
adversity, res adversae.

Exercise 253
principal officers. (*See note on Ex. 66*).
union, consensus.
yield (*trans.*), concedo.
applause, plausus, -us, *m.*
approve, probo, I.
in battle array, acie instructa.
dispute, decerto de.
perilous moment, discrimen.

Exercise 254 [B].
Turn into Oratio Obliqua after a Historic tense:

I might have gone to Spain, where I should have had my brother to share my labours, and Hasdrubal instead of Hannibal for my foe. But hearing as I sailed along the coast of the arrival of the enemy in Gaul, I landed immediately, sent on my cavalry before, and moved my camp up to the Rhone. I am anxious to try whether Carthage in the last[1] twenty years has produced a new race of citizens, or whether these are the same men whom we held so cheap when we let them go from Eryx. Would that this contest were for honour merely, not for very life! But you are fighting for Italy itself, and for your homes; nor is there another army in your rear to bar the enemy's way if you fail[2] to conquer him. Let each one of you consider that the Senate is watching him, and that the fate of Rome depends upon his valour.

1. **his**.
2. Use **nisi**.

Exercise 254
share, take part in, particeps sum (gen.).
sail along, lego, praetervehor.
produce, edo.
hold cheap, parvi facio.
let go, dimitto.
would that, utinam.
  (1) *Present subj. of future time.*
  (2) *Imperfect subj. of present time.*
  (3) *Pluperfect subj. of past time.*
contest, certamen.
watch, specto, 1.

Exercise 255
fully, satis.
weak (*of forces*), exiguus.
reef, saxa, scopuli.
success, successus, -us.
ride, be at anchor, in ancoris stare.
make his way in, se insinuare.
rashness, temeritas.
dash against, allido, -ere, -si, -sum.
opposite to, contra, e regione, gen.
aghast, obstupefactus.

Exercise 256
tumultuous, tumultuosus.
assailant, oppugnator.
fortress, castellum.
thicket, virgultum.
bloody, cruentus.
to be in a blaze, arde
wigwam, casa.

Exercise 255 [A],

Meanwhile the Carthaginians, knowing the weakness of their naval force at Lilyhaeum, and fully conscious that the place would not hold out unless they sent help, resolved to despatch troops at once. Hannibal, son of Hamilcar, was despatched with all haste to Sicily with fifty ships and 10,000 troops. He moved his fleet among the Aegatian islands opposite to Lilybaeum, waiting the moment when he should be able to pass the rocks and reefs that girt the harbour. At length a favourable wind sprang up. He set sail, and, massing his troops on deck to be ready for an engagement, with a boldness that deserved success he made his way safely through the narrow entrance. In the meanwhile the Roman ships remained at anchor close by, the sailors looking on aghast at his rashness, and expecting to see him dashed against the rocks.

Exercise 256 [B].

The fight was fierce and tumultuous. The assailants were repulsed in their first attack, and several of their bravest officers were shot down in the act of storming the fortress sword in hand. The assault was renewed with greater success. The Indians were driven from one post to another. They disputed their ground inch by inch,[1] fighting with the utmost fury. Most of their veterans were cut to pieces, and after a long and bloody battle Philip and Canonchet, with a handful of surviving warriors, retreated from the fort and took refuge in the thickets of the neighbouring forest. The victors set fire to the wigwams and forts; the whole was soon in a blaze; many of the old men, the women, and the children, perished in the flames.

---

1. **pedem gradatim rettulerunt**.

THE ORDER OF WORDS IN THE SIMPLE SENTENCE

1. Normal Order. A word receives most emphasis when placed at the beginning or end of a sentence, therefore in an ordinary Latin sentence place the Subject first and the Predicate last.

N.B.—By the Predicate we do not mean necessarily the *Verb*. When the verb **esse** is used with Adjectives or Participles it need not take the last place.

2. The middle of a simple sentence must be arranged on this principle: Expressions which naturally qualify the subject (generally adjectives or adjectival expressions) must be grouped near the subject, expressions which qualify the predicate (objects, adverbial and prepositional expressions) must be grouped before the verb.

3. Before the subject, however, will naturally come any words which connect with the preceding sentence; *e.g.* relatives, expressions of time, &c. It is exceedingly important to remember that Latin sentences do not usually follow one another without *some* expressed connection. In English we constantly leave the connection to be understood from the general sense.

Thus a Latin simple sentence, in which there is no need to emphasize particular words, will usually be arranged in this order:

        (1) Connecting words.
        (2) Subject.
        (3) Attributes of Subject.
        (4) Objects and Attributes of the Objects.
        (5) Adverbial expressions qualifying Predicate.
        (6) Predicate.

Postero die mane | [1]Servilius consul cum omnibus copiis | flumen quam celerrime transit.
Early next day the consul Servilius with all his forces crosses the river as speedily as possible.

Quibus rebus auditis | dux hostium, vir magna belli peritia | suos ex castello se recipere jubet.
When he heard this news the leader of the enemy, who had gained experience in many wars, ordered his men to leave the fort.

4. Special Emphasis. To emphasise any special word it must be placed out of its usual position. The Predicate is most emphasised by being placed first, the Subject by being placed last or nearly last. Any other word will be emphasised by taking either of these positions. An attribute separated from its noun, or an adverb separated from its verb, is thereby emphasised.

      Habet **senectus magnam auctoritatem.**
      *Old age **certainly has** great influence.*

      Hac clade periit *libertas*.
      It was liberty that perished *in this disaster.*

      Recte **igitur deos esse diximus.**
      We were right in saying *that there are gods.*

      Exempla proponamus illi *optima*.
      Let the examples we set before him lie the best.

In English also we can sometimes emphasise by order; *e.g.* "*A friend I am unwilling to accuse.*" But we more often put the emphatic words in a clause by themselves, as in the last three examples given above. Compare "*It is not often that a rich man envies the poor*" with the Latin "**Haud saepe invidet pauperibns dives,**" where the necessary emphasis on "*not often*" is given by position.

---

[1]. The above sentences are divided by lines into (1) Connecting words, (2) those parts which naturally go with the subject, (3) those that go with the predicate. The connection in thought between two sentences is most frequently one of time or place; *e.g.* **postero die** in the first sentence.

5. Attributes, &c. An Adjective more often follows than precedes its noun, and a slight emphasis is often given by placing it first.

> *e.g.* **Vir bonus ac sapiens.**
> *A good and wise man.*
>
> **Bonum ac sapientem virum fingimus.**
> *It is the good and wise man that we are describing.*

Nouns in apposition generally follow the noun to which they are attached. If they precede it they are thereby emphasised.

> *e.g.* **Lemnos insula** = *the island of Lemnos.*
> **Insula Lemnos** = *the island Lemnos* (as opposed to the *town*).
>
> **Servilius consul** = *the consul Servilius.*
> **Consul Servilius** = *Servilius when consul*, or *as consul.*

Where there is both an attribute and some defining phrase (a case or a prepositional phrase) put the latter between the attribute and the noun.

> *e.g.* **Multa tua erga me beneficia.**
> *Your many kindnesses to me.*
>
> **Filius patri similis.**
> *A son like his father.*

THE COMPOUND SENTENCE

6. The Compound Sentence consists of a Principal Clause and Subordinate Clauses. The Subordinate Clauses all stand in some relation to the principal verb or its subject, being equivalent to nouns, adjectives, or adverbs; and they will for the most part fall into the places that these would have occupied if the sentence had been simple. Compare, for instance, the following sentences:

Simple	Compound
Quibus rebus auditis, Ibororum dux, vir magna belli peritia, collectis omnibus copiis, impediendi causa Eomanos, pontem rescindit.	Quae quum audiisset, Iberorum dux, qui bellorum peritissimus erat quum omnes copias collegisset, ne Eomani celerius advenirent, pontem rescindi jubet.
Hearing this, the Iberian leader, a man of great experience in warfare, collected all his forces, and broke down the bridge in order to delay the Romans.	*When the Iberian leader, who had had great experience in warfare, heard this, he collected all his forces, and ordered the bridge to be broken down, so as to delay the Romans' advance.*

The main principle therefore of the Compound Sentence is that the subordinate parts of the sentence are enclosed between the subject, which must stand near the beginning, and the principal verb, which will most frequently come at the end. The order of clauses will therefore naturally be as follows:

(1) Any clause which connects with the previous sentence.
(2) The subject followed by any attributive clauses which belong to it.
(3) Any clauses which naturally belong to the Predicate—
  (*a*) Adverbial clauses of time, &c.;
  (*b*) Object clauses, such as *Acc.* and *Inf.*, Indirect Questions or Commands.
(4) The Predicate.

Quod cum vidisset dux, quia quid hostis paret nescit, paullum moratur.
Seeing this, the general delayed a little time, because he did not know what the enemy was preparing to do.

Reliquis diebus Caesar, ne qui inermibus militibus impetus fieri posset, onmem eam materiam, quae erat caesa, conversam ad hostem conlocabat.
During the remaining days Caesar piled up facing the enemy all the timber that had been cut, so that no attack might be made on his men when unarmed.

Tanien Senones, quae est civitas imprimis firma et magnae inter Gallos auctoritatis, Cavarinum, quem Caesar apud eos regem constituerat, interficere publico consilio conati, cum ille praesensisset ac profugisset, usque ad fines insecuti regno domoque expulerunt.
Nevertheless the Senones, who are the strongest and most influential tribe among the Gauls, tried to kill Cavarinus, whom Caesar had made king among them, and when he found out the plot and fled, pursued him as far as their boundaries, and drove him from his kingdom and home.

But these principles will be modified by many considerations of (*a*) Emphasis, (*b*) Logical Arrangement, (*c*) Sound. No system of rules can take the place of observation in reading, but the following suggestions may be added.

(*a*) **Emphasis**. As in the Simple Sentence, the beginning and end are emphatic positions, and a subordinate clause may be emphasised by being placed in one of these positions. It often happens that the verb which is grammatically the principal verb is not the important part of the predicate, and in that ease it will not come last. This is especially frequent with the verb of "saying" that introduces Oratio Obliqua, which is not as a rule kept to the end of the sentence.

e.g. **Eo cum de improviso celeriusque omni opinione venisset, Remi, qui proximi Galliae ex Belgis sunt, ad eum legatos miserant qui dicerent se suaque omnia in fidem atque in potestatem populi Romani permittere.**

But Caesar arriving there suddenly and sooner than anyone had expected, the Remi, who are the nearest to Gaul of the Belgian tribes, sent him ambassadors to say that they surrendered themselves and all they possessed to the sway and authority of the Roman people.

In this sentence **miserunt** is the principal verb, and **dicerent** the main verb of the subordinate clause, but neither contains the main statement of the sentence, and therefore neither stands last. The object of the sentence is to give the message of the Remi "**se . . . permittere.**" It is a common mistake of beginners to think they must write "**legatos qui se . . . permittere dicerent miserunt.**"

For the same reason a Purpose Clause or Causal Clause will stand last, if to state the Purpose or Cause is the real object of the sentence; *i.e.* if it is more emphatic than the statement of the Principal Verb.

Compare the following:

> *He said it to frighten me.*
> **Haec dixit ut me terreret.**

> *He threatened me with torture to frighten me.*
> **Ut me terreret cruciatum mihi minabatur.**

In the first sentence to state the purpose is the object of the sentence. In the second the principal verb contains the main idea.

(*b*) **Logical arrangement**. It is generally essential to clearness that the statement of *circumstances* (*e.g.* time, place, etc.) should precede the main statement, and statement of cause precede the statement of the effect. For this reason a Consecutive sentence will almost always come after the verb it depends on, though grammatically subordinate. It also tends to clearness to observe the following:

(1) When the principal verb and subordinate verb have the same subject, do not put the subject, as we do in English, inside the subordinate clause; *e.g.* for "*When Caesar heard this, he returned*," say, "**Caesar, quum haec audiisset, rediit.**"

(2) In translating complicated English sentences into Latin avoid the frequent change of subject which we allow in English. The change of Active for Passive will often obviate difficulty.

(*c*) **Sound**. If we followed universally the rule of enclosing subordinate clauses, we should find three or four verbs sometimes together at the end of the sentence. Avoid this by altering the arrangement of words in one or more of the clauses.

Avoid generally placing together similar terminations (especially **-orum, -arum**). Avoid also a sentence consisting entirely of words of the same length; *e.g.* such a combination as "**Erat quondam pastor quidam Gygis regis.**"

The sound often helps the sense; *e.g.* where the writer wishes to describe a series of events rapidly following one another he may use a series of short sentences, even without conjunctions.

e.g. **Concilium dimittit, Liscum retinet. Quaerit ex solo ea quae in conventu dixerat. Dicit liberius atque audacius. Eadem secreto ab aliis quaerit; reperit esse vera**.

On dismissing the council he detained Liscus and enquired of him privately about those matters that he had mentioned at the meeting. Liscus spoke then more openly and boldly, and by private enquiries from others Caesar found that his statements were true.

7. Pronouns.

(*a*) The Relative always comes first in its clause where possible.

> *e.g. These towns, one of which has 'been burnt.'*
> **Haec oppida, quorum unum incensum est** (never **unum quorum**).

> *Catiline is here, by whose slaves he was kitted.*
> **Adest Catilina cujus ab servis interfectus est** (not **ab cujus servis**).

So **quamobrem, qua de causa, quas inter urbes, &c.**
But if the relative is used substantially, the preposition will precede it as a rule—**inter quos, ex quibus, &c.**

(*b*) Many adjectives (especially superlatives) and words in apposition are attracted into the ablative clause in Latin contrary to English usage.

> *e.g.* *The beautiful city of Corinth, which was destroyed by L. Mummius.*
> **Corinthus quae urbs pulcherrima ab L. Mummio diruta est.**

(*c*) Observe that cases of **se**, **suus**, **ipse**, **quisque** in the same sentence generally stand next one another.

> *e.g.* **Suae quisque fortunae faber.**
> *Each man is the maker of his own fortune*
>
> **Sceleris sui sibi conscius.**
> *Conscious of his guilt.*

SPECIAL VOCABULARIES

N.B. — in these Vocaularies the principle parts of the Irregular Verbs are given where they first occur, but are not as a rule repeated afterwards. Verbs of the First Conjugation are distinguished from verbs of the Third by the mark **I**. Where the construction is not given verbs govern the accusative.

Editor's Note: The Special Vocabularies have been moved to each individual lesson.

Appendix

PREPOSITIONAL PHRASES

Ad.

Gaul lies towards the north.	Gallia vergit ad septemtriones.
A battle fought in the neighbouhood of Cannae.	Pugna ad Cannas[1] facta
About 10,000 soldiers.	Ad decem milia militum.
At a fit time, opportunely.	Ad tempus.
They advanced as far as the gate.	Usque ad portam progressi sunt.
On the right.	Ad dextrum.
All without exception, all to a man.	Omnes ad unum.
Finally, at the extremity.	Ad ultimum, ad extremum.
To speak to the point, to good purpose.	Ad rem loqui.
For the purpose of keeping up hope.	Ad spem servandam.

Apud.

In the writings of Caesar.	Apud Caesarem.
At my house.	Apud me.
Among the Gauls.	Apud Gallos.
A speech delivered before the people.	Oratio apud populum habita.

Secundum.

To march along the banks of a river.	Secundum flumen iter facere.
To live in accordance with nature.	Secundum naturam vivere.

Per.

To ascertain by means of scouts.	Per exploratores cognoscere.
A man loved for his own merits.	Vir per se ipsum amatus.
It was owing to you that we did not cross the river.	Per te stetit quominus flumen transiremus.
I beseech you by the gods.	Te per deos oro (or Per ego te deos oro).

Sub.

To winter under canvas, in tents.	Sub pellibus hiemare.
To halt at the foot of a mountain.	Sub monte consistere.
To send an army under the yoke.	Exercitum sub jugum mittere.
Towards evening.	Sub vesperum.

Praeter.

He led his forces past Caesar's camp.	Praeter Caesaris castra suas copias transduxit
To speak beside the mark.	Praeter rem loqui.
To an extraordinary degree, unnaturally.	Praeter modum.
Beyond hope.	Praeter spem.
Contrary to expectation.	Praeter opinionem.
They have no clothing besides skins.	Nihil vestitus praeter pelles habent.
You do more than all the rest.	Praeter ceteros laboras.

Super.

Beyond all others.	Super omnes.

---

1. Distinguish carefully — **Cannas** = *to* Cannae.
   Cannis = *at* Cannae.
   Ad Cannas = *near* Cannae.

Ab or a.

At a distance of 15 miles.	A milibus passuum quindecim.
In the rear, on the side, &c.	A tergo, a latere.
From sunrise till late in the day.	Ab sole orto usque ad multum diei.
Since the foundation of Rome.	Ab urbe condita.
He was on our side.	A nobis stetit.

Cum.

With the help of the gods.	Cum dis.
To live virtuously.	Cum virtute vivere.
Some were tortured and put to death.	Pars cum cruciatu necabatur.
I have to deal with you.	Tecum mihi res est.
He wrote with care.	Cum diligentia[2] scripsit.

De.

To throw oneself down from a wall.	De muro se dejicere.
About midnight.	De media nocte.
On purpose.	De industria.
Unexpectedly.	De improviso.
We are ruined, it is all up with us.	Actum est de nobis,

Ex or e.

To dismount.	Ex equo desilire.
To fight on foot or on horseback.	Pedibus aut ex equis pugnare.
In the course of a march.	Ex itinere.
Over against the town.	E regione oppidi.
After the consulship of Cotta.	E Cottae consulatu.
A man miserable after being happy.	Homo miser ex beato.
Since (of time).	Ex quo.
None of the barbarians.	Nulli e barbaris.
For the good of Gaul.	Ex usu Gallprum.
In accordance with the treaty.	Ex foedere.
Partly.	Ex parte.
Favourably, as we would wish.	Ex sententia.

Pro.

Caesar led his troops before the camp.	Caesar pro castris suas copias pro duxit.
To be sure.	Pro certo habere.
To state as a fact.	Pro certo ponere.
Considering the size of the population.	Pro multitudine hominum.
With your usual prudence.	Pro tua prudentia.
To the best of one's ability, manfully.	Pro virili parte.
According to time and circumstances.	Pro tempore et pro re.
He was a father to me.	Pro parente mihi fuit.
Proconsul, propraetor.	Pro consule, pro praetore (later as single word—Proconsul).

Prae.

He displayed a dagger.	Prae se pugionem tulit.
I made no secret of having done this.	Hoc me fecisse semper prae me tuli.
They seem cowardly in comparison with the Gauls.	Prae Gallis ignavi videntur.
I do not know where I am for joy.	Prae gaudio nescio ubi sim.

(Only use **prae** in this sense with negatives or **vix**.)

---

2. Or **magna diligentia**. If there is no epithet '**cum**' must generally be used. See Voc. 89.

In

To make a bridge over a river.	Pontem in flumine facere.
To be under arms.	In armis esse.
At present.	In praesenti.
Our safety depends upon you.	Salus nostra in te posita est.
Daily, from day to day (of something increasing).	In dies.
For the future.	In posterum, in futurum.
In turn.	In vicem.

SYNONYMS

About........... (around, of place), **circum, circa**.
(of time or number), **cirtiter**, *adv.* or *prep.*
(of number), **ad**.
(= concerning), **de**.

Again........... (general word), **rursus**.
(a second time), **iterum**.
(again and again), **saepenumero, identidem**.

All............... (general word), **omnis**.
(with superlatives), **quisque**, *e.g.* **optimus quisque**, *all the best.*
(all together, implying connection), **cunctus, universus**; *e.g.* **cunctus senatus**.
(the whole, entire), **totus**, *e.g.* **tota provincia**.

Ask............... (questions), **rogare, interrogare, quaerere (ex)**.
(requests), **rogare, petere (ab), poscere, postulare, orare, flagitare**.
Petere is most frequently used of a request addressed to a superior.
Poscere and **postulare** imply a claim or demand, made as of right.
Orare is 'to beg.' **Flagitare** is used of a vehement or importunate demand.

Bear............. (carry), **ferre, portare, vehere**.
Vehere is most used of conveying by ship, carriage, or animals.
Equo vehi = *to ride*; **nave vehi** = *to sail.* (endure), pati, tolerare, ferre.
Pati is the most general word. **Tolerare** is '*to put up with.*' **Ferre** is '*to bear bravely.*'

Call.............. (summon), **vocare, arcessere**.
(name), **nominare, appellare, vocare**.
(call to, accost, invoke), **appellare**.

Each............. (of any number), **quisque**. (of two), **uterque**.
(one by one, separately), **singuli**; *e.g.* **singulos interrogavit**, *he questioned each separately.*

Fear............. (general word), **timere**.
(often with the idea of respect), **vereri**.
(dread, apprehend future evil), **metuere**.
The nouns **timer, metus** correspond to their verbs. favor is 'panic,' 'trembling with fear.'

Find............. (a thing or person), **invenire, reperire**.
Reperire most often means finding something lost and searched for.
(find out facts), **cognoscere, comperire**.

Follow......... **Sequor** and compounds.
Consequor, assequor = come up with, reach.
Prosequor = escort.
Subsequor = follow close after, come next.

	Persequor = follow up, follow to the end.
Happen	(generally of bad fortune), **accidit**.
	(generally of good fortune), **contingit**.
	(result, happen as result of something else), **evenit**
Kill	(general word), **interficere**.
	(in fighting), **occidere**.
	(especially of hunger, poison, etc.), **necare**.
	(massacre, implying cruelty), **trucidare**.
	(murder), **jugulare**.

Know, Knowledge
    (know mentally, *e.g.* languages, sciences, etc.; know how to do a thing), **scire**.
    (know persons), **novisse**.
    (learn facts), **cognoscere, comperire**.
    (perceive, learn by the senses), **percipere, sentire**.
    (understand), **intellegere**.
    (recognise persons or things known before), **agnoscere**.
    The nouns **scientia** and **cognitio** correspond to **scire** and **cognoscere**;
    knowledge of persons is to be translated by **consuetude**.

Land	(opposed to sea), **terra**.
	(a country, district), **regio, terra.**
	(lands), **agri**, *e.g.* **agros populatus est**.
	(native land), **patria**.
	(ground, soil), **solum**.
Last	(furthest, *i.e.* first or last, of a series, in place or time), **ultimus, extremus**;
	e.g. **extremum oppidum Allobrogum**.
	(utmost, extreme), the same words; *e.g.* **ultimum supplicium**.
	(immediately preceding), **proximus**; *e.g.* **proxima nocte**.
	(latest), **novissimus**; *e.g.* **qui novissimus venit, necatur**.
Lose	(wilfully), **perdere**.
	(lose by carelessness, *etc.*), **amittere**.
	(let slip opportunity, *etc.*), **omittere, dimittere**.
Man	(human being, opp. to animals), **homo**,
	(opp. to women, children, cowards), **vir**.
Mind	(general words), **animus, mens. Animus** is more often used of the emotions,
	mens of the intellect, (talent, intellect), **ingenium**.
More	(comparing qualities or acts), **magis** ; *e.g.* **magis consilio quam virtute**.
	(comparing degree, quantity), **plus** ; *e.g.* **valet salus plus quam libido**.
	(rather, implying preference), **potius**; *e.g.* **consilium potius quam vis postulatur**.
	(usually of time or number), **amplius** ; *e.g.* **amplius horis quattuor**.
New, Old	That which has lasted a long time is **vetus**, and opposed to **recens**, fresh, newly made.
	That which existed in former times is **antiquus**, and opposed to **novus**, new, not having previously existed.
People, Race	(a 'nation' in the political sense), **populus**.
	(a race, a people), **gens**.
	(a tribe, generally of distant, barbarous tribes), **natio**.
	Only use '**genus**' for '*race*' where it means '*family*'; *e.g.* **nobili genere ortus**.
	'*People*' in the sense of '*men generally*' (as in '*men say*') is either omitted, or may be
	translated by **homines**, especially where it means '*mankind generally.*'
Power	(legal, official power), **potestas**.
	(political power, not necessarily due to official position), **potentia**.
	(influence, importance, often personal influence), **auctoritas**.
	(supreme magisterial or kingly power, especially from the military point of view), **imperium**.
	(dominion, sway), **ditio, potestas, imperium**;
	e.g. **in potestate Populi Romani esse**, *to be subject to the Romans.*
	(royal power), **regnum**.

	(tyranny, absolute rule), **dominatus**.
	(physical power, strength), **vires**.
See	(general word), **videre**.
	(catch sight of), **conspicere, conspicari**.
	(discern, see clearly), **perspicere**, *pres.* and *imp.* tenses of **cernere**.
	(gaze at), **spectare, intueri**.
	For '*see*' in the sense of '*understand*' *cf.* '*Know*.'
Show	(display, hold out), **ostendere**.
	(show off, parade), **ostentare**.
	(point out, especially of facts, but also '*to point out a road*,' &c.), **demonstrare**.
	(produce, bring out, show up), **exhibere**.
	(show qualities), **praestare**; *e.g.* **praestare virtutem**, or **se praebere fortem**.
Speak	(say something, express thought), **dicere**.
	(talk), **loqui**.
	(speak to, accost), alloqui, **appellare**.
	(address), **alloqui**.
	(make a speech), **orationem habere**.
Take	(general word), **capere**.
	(take up, assume; *e.g.* **arma**), **sumere**.
	(undertake; *e.g.* **bellum**), **suscipere**.
	(take with the hand or arrest), **comprehendere**.
Want	(be without), **carere**.
	(need), **egere, indigere** (or use **opus esse**).
	(wish for), **velle, cupere**.
	(to be wanting, to fail), **deficere**.
Work	(labour, toil), **labor**.
	('*a work*,' '*works*'; most frequently the result of labour), **opus**; *e.g.* **opera**, military fortifications.

Notice the following Verbs, which in English may be either Transitive or Intransitive.

	TRANSITIVE	INTRANSITIVE
Burn	incendere, urmere	ardere.
Change	mutare	mutari
Collect	colligere, cogere	convenire.
Embark	imponere in navem	consvendere (in navem)
Increase	augere	crescere.
Join	conjungere	se conjungere cum.
Land	exponere in terrain	egredi e nave.
Leave	relinquere	abire, discedere.
Move	movere	se movere.
Return	reddere	redire.
Scatter	dispergere	dispergi.
Surrender	tradere, dedere	se tradere, se dedere.
Trust	mandare, committere	confidere, credere.
Turn	convertere	converti, se convertere.

MILITARY VOCABULARY

The Army. Men and Officers.

legion (*largest number, 6000*), legio.
cohort, regiment (*tenth part of legion*), cohors.
squadron (*of cavalry*), turma, ala (tenth part of turma).
company (of infantry), manipulus (= 200 men).
infantry, pedites, *m. pl.*, peditatus, *m.* 4 (collective).
cavalry, equites, *m. pl.*, equitatus, *m.* 4 (collective).
army in battle order *or* **line**, acies. **in marching order or column**, agmen.
those of military age, juventus (*collective*), qui arma ferre possunt.
light-armed troops (*collective*), levis armatura.
troops ready for battle, expediti.
heavy-armed troops, use legionarii.
archers, sagittarii.
slingers, funditores.
scouts, exploratores, speculators.
recruits, tirones.
veterans, veterani.
reserves, subsidia.
reinforcements, supplementum, novae copiae.
auxiliary forces, auxilia (= **allies and light-armed troops** as opposed to **the legion**).
a large force, magnae (*not* multae), copiae.
a small force, exigua manus.
the flower of the troops, robus militum.
camp followers, calories.
non-commissioned officers (sergeants, *etc.*), centuriones.
captains, *best translated* centuriones.
colonels, *best translated* tribuni militum.
officers, general's staff, legati.
commander of cavalry, praefectus equitum.
general of division, legatus.
commander-in-chief, imperator.
the command-in-chief, summa imperii.
to appoint some one to chief command, summam imperii alicui deferre.
to give some one command of legion, aliquem legioni praeficere.
to be at the head of a legion, legioni praeesse.

Arms.

to take up arms, arma sumere, capere.
to make ready for battle, arma expedire.
to be under arms, in armis esse.
to lay down arms, ab armis discedere.
to throw away arms, arma abjicere.
by force of arms, vi et armis.
missiles, tela.
a shower of missiles, crebra tela, *or* magna vis telorum.
to discharge, shoot, conjicere, mittere.
to return fire, tela rejicere.
within, out of range, intra, extra teli jactum.
to draw a sword, gladium stringere.
to sheath a sword, gladium in vaginam recondere.
artillery (see under *Siege*).
helmet, galea.
shield, scutum.
breastplate, lorica.
sword, gladius.
javelin, pilum.

Enlisting, Serving, Deserting.

to enlist men, conscribere.
to hold a levy, delectum habere.
to take the oath of allegiance, in verba jurare alicujus.
to serve a campaign, stipendia merere.
to serve five years, quina stipendia merere.
to review an army, recensere.
to disband, dimittere.
discharged (*honourably*), emeritus.
to avoid military service, militiam detrectare.
a deserter, perfuga, transfuga.
to desert, transfugere, signa relinquere.
mutiny, seditio.
mutinous, seditiosus.

Camp.

to choose a site for a camp, castra capere:, locum castris (ad castra) idoneum deligere.
to pitch camp, castra ponere, munire.
to strike, castra movere, pro movere (= **advance**), signa convellere.
to leave undefended, castra nudare.
to remain inactive in, castris se tenere, continere.
winter, summer quarters [castra] hiberna, aestiva.
sentinels, vigiliae, custodes, custodiae.
to be on guard, keep watch, excubias (custodias) agere.
watchword, signum, tessera.
pickets, stationes.
rampart, vallum, agger.
to raise a rampart, vallum exstruere, facere.
trench, fossa.
to make a trench, fossam ducere.

The March.

the vanguard, primum agmen.
the rearguard, novissimum agmen, novissimi.
to set out, proficisci.
to march, iter facere, contendere.
forced march, magnum iter.
to advance, progredi, signa movere, signa ferre.
with closed ranks, in order of war, agmine quadrato, confertis ordinibus (*opposed to* solutis ordinibus).
to bring up the rear, agmen claudere.
to build a road, viam muntre.
to have one's passage barred, itinere intercludi.
to stop marching, iter intermittere.
to change one's route, wheel, signa convertere.
to halt, consistere.
to station pickets at intervals, custodias disponere.
to reconnoitre, explorare.
to cut off stragglers, palantes excipere.
to climb hill, superare collem.
to transport an army over a river, exercitum flumen trajicere.
baggage, impedimenta.
baggage animals, jumenta.

Commissariat.

supplies, commeatus (*sing.*).
corn, corn supply, frumentum, res frumentaria.
to forage, pabulari.
to get corn, frumentari.
to cut off the enemy's supplies, hostes commeatu intercludere, prohibere.
to look after corn supplies, rem frumentariam comparare, rei frumentariae providere.
to procure supplies, parare, suppeditare frumentum.
there are supplies in abundance, commeatus suppetit.
abundance of provisions, magna vis commeatus.

War. General Phrases.

to proclaim war, bellum indicere.
to make war upon, bellum inferre.
to wage war, bellum gerere (cum).
to prolong, drag on, bellum ducere.
to begin war, belli initium facere.
to finish war, bellum conflcere, finem belli facere.

Appendix

to renew the war, bellum redintegrare.
to conduct a war, bellum administrare.
to act on the defensive, bellum illatum defendere.
to rebel, revolt, deficere ab.
war materials, apparatus (*sing.*) belli.

Invasion, Inroad.

to make an invasion, inroad, incursionem, excursionem facere.
to ravage with fire and sword, omnia ferro ignique vastare.
to plunder, carry off booty, ferre atque agere praedam. (*N.B.*— ferre *of inanimate things*, agere *of cattle.*)
to lay waste the country, agros vastare.

Conquest.

to subjugate, subigere, in potestatem redigere.
to keep in submission, aliquem in officio continere.
to remain in submission, in officio permanere.
submit, in deditionem venire, *or* in fidem ac potestatem se permittere.

Battle.

(1) GENERAL PHRASES.

to engage, proelium committere, signa conferre.
to fight (*with missiles*) at a distance, eminus (telis, jaculis) pugnare.
at close quarters, hand to hand, comminus pugnare.
on foot, on horseback, pedibus, ex equis pugnare.
a skirmish, leve proelium. a cavalry engagement, proelium equestre.
a battle fought near Cannae, proelium ad Cannas factum.
a pitched battle, justum proelium.
to fight a pitched battle, in acie dimicare, justo proelio contendere.
a drawn battle, aequo Marte (aequis conditionibus) pugnare.
a losing battle, fortuna inclinata pugnare.
a decisive battle, proelio decertare.
the battle lasted till late in the day, pugnatum est usque ad multum diei.
to win, lose a fight, rem bene, male gerere.
an indecisive battle, proelium anceps.
a favourable battle, secundum.
an adverse battle, adversum.
to be superior in numbers, numero praestare, superiores esse.
to be inferior in numbers, numero inferiores esse.

(2) BEFORE THE BATTLE.

to offer battle to the enemy, copiam (potestatem) pugnandi hostibus facere
to provoke to battle, proelio (ad proelium) lacessere, provocare.
to decline battle, proelium detrectare.
to give the signal to engage, signum proelii (committendi-) dare.
to draw up forces in battle order, aciem instruere, copias acie instruere.
to extend the line, deploy, aciem explicare.
to muster, ad signa convenire.
to harangue the men, contionari apud milites, *or use* cohortari.
to encourage, embolden the men, aninos militum confirmare.

(3) DURING THE BATTLE.

to attack, aggredi, adoriri, signa inferre (in),
the enemy in front, adversis hostibus occurrere.
in the rear, hostes aversos (a tergo) aggredi.
to charge, impetum facere in (*for gen. dat. abl. plural use forms of* incursio *instead of* impetus],
at full speed, cursu (in hostes) ferri.
at a gallop, citato equo.
to resist a charge, impetum sustinere.
to come to close quarters, manum conserere, signa conferre cum hoste.
to make an obstinate resistance, hostibus strenue obstare.
to repulse the enemy, hostes pellere, repellere.
the line wavers, acies inclinat, inclinatur.
to form a square, orbem facere.
with close, serried ranks, conferti, conglobati, confertis ordinibus.
to break through the enemy's centre, per medios hostes per rumpere.
to dislodge, dejicere (de).
to renew the struggle, pugnam redintegrare.
to restore the fortunes of the day, proelium restituere.
to send up reserves, subsidia sum mittere (*dat.*).
fresh troops relieve, come to help of the tired men, integri et recentes defatigatis succedunt, subveniunt.
to be hard pressed, premi, laborare.
to leave the ranks, ab signis disce dere.

affairs were in a critical condition, res in summum (extremum) dis crimen adducta erat.

(4) AFTER THE BATTLE

Rout, Retreat, Pursuit.

to abandon position, loco excedere.
to sound the retreat, receptui canere.
to retreat, pedem, signa referre, se recipere.
to rout, randere, fugare.
to utterly defeat, rout, profligare.
utterly routed, fusi fugatique.
to put to flight, in fugam conjicere.
to take to flight, fugae se mandare, terga vertere.
to seek safety in flight, fuga salutem petere,
to fly for refuge, confugere (*ad.*),
headlong flight, fuga effusa.
to pursue, sequi, persequi.
to overtake, assequi, consequi.
to press hard on fugitives, fugientibus instare.
to cut off the enemy's flight, fugientes excipere.
to let escape, hostes e manibus dimittere.
(DEFEAT.)
to inflict defeat upon, cladem inferre (*dat.*).
suffer defeat, cladem accipere.
to cause great slaughter, ingentem caedem edere.
to massacre, trucidare, stragem facere, stragem edere.
to cut up, annihilate, concidere, delere.
to be mortally wounded, vulnus mortiferum accipere.
to inflict a wound upon, vulnus infligere (*dat.*).
weakened, disabled by wounds, valuer ibus confectus.
with great loss, multis amissis, magna strage.
(VICTORY.)
victory, to win, victoriam reportare, hostes proelio vincere.
let slip a sure victory, victoriam exploratam dimittere.
to raise a shout of victory, victoriam conclamare.
the victory cost much blood, victoria multo sanguine stetit.
the victorious army, exercitus victor.
triumphant, *use* victor. (*N.B.* — triumphus *is only used of the triumphal procession allowed by the state to a victorious general.*)
a success, res bene (*or* prospere) gesta.

Siege.

garrison, praesidium.
a town with strong natural position, oppidum natura loci munitum.
commander, governor, praefectus.
to besiege, blockade, invest, obsidere.
to assault, oppugnare.
a siege, obsidio.
assault, oppugnatio.
to take by storm, expugnare, vi capere.
to reduce by starvation, fame domare.
to raise a siege (*of relieving army*), obsidione liberare.
to abandon a siege, obsidionem relinquere, obsidione desistere.
to raise siege works, opera facere.
to be busy with siege works, in opere versari.
to advance pent-houses, shelters, vineas agere.
to apply scaling ladders, scalas admovere.
battering ram, aries.
artillery, cannon, machinae, tormenla, ballistae.
to break through the lines, munitiones perrumpere.
to man the wall, murum cingere, complere.
to break down the gates, portas refringere.
a breach, nearest word ruina muri.
to make a breach, partem muri refringere.
to undermine, muros subruere, cuniculum facere.
to drive defenders from the wall, murum nudare defensoribus.
to make a sally, eruptionem facere, erumpere.
to destroy, rase to ground a town, oppidum evertere, funditus delere.
to plunder, diripere, spoliare.
provisions are running short, res frumentaria (cibus) deficit.
provisions hold out, suppetit commeatus.

Surrender, Terms, Peace.

to capitulate, surrender, se dedere, in deditionem venire.
to give up arms, arma tradere.
to receive the surrender of the enemy, hostes in deditionem accipere.
(to surrender) at discretion, nullis latis conditionibus.
to offer terms of surrender, conditiones ferre.
favourable, hard, terms, aequae, iniquae conditiones.
to treat for peace, agere de pace.
to bring about a peace, pacem componere.
a truce, indutiae.
treaty, foedus. **to make a...**, foedus facere, ferire, icere. **according to a...**, ex foedere.
to grant a man his life, aliquem (incolumem) conservare.
their lives were spared, conservati sunt, *or* venia petentibus data est.
to beg for one's life, mortem deprecari.
to exact hostages from the enemy, obsides hostibus imponere.

Naval.

man of war, navis longa.
merchantman, transport, navis oneraria.
ram, beak, rostrum.
sails and rigging, vela et armamenta.
mast, malus.
admiral, commander, praefectus classis.
rowers, remiges.
helmsman, pilot, gubernator.
to embark (*trans.*), (milites) in navem imponere. (*intrans.*), (in) navem conscendere.
to disembark (*trans.*), (milites) in terram exponere. (intrans.), e nave egredi.
to man a ship, navem complere.
to weigh anchor, set sail, ancoram tollere, (navem) solvere, vela dare.
to ride at anchor, ad ancoram deligari in ancoris stare.
to drop anchor, ancoram jacere.
to sail out to sea, navigare, in altum provehi.
to sail along the coast, oram legere.
to sail with the wind behind, vento secundo provehi.
to round, double a promontory, superare promontorium.
to row, navem remis propellere.
to drift, dejici, deferri.
to bring to land, (navem) appellere.
to make land, portum capere.
to hold on one's course, cursum tenere.
to be shipwrecked, naufragium facere, in litus ejici.
to be wrecked, founder (*of ship*), frangi, deperire.
by land and sea, terra marique.
fleet, have a powerful, navibus plurimum posse.
to equip, (naves, classem) armare, instruere.
launch, deducere.
haul up, subducere.
repair, reficere.
build, construct, aedificare.

NAVAL BATTLE.

the admiral's ship, navis praetoria.
to fight a naval battle, proelium navale facere.
to clear the decks for action, navem expedire.
the fleets charge, classes concurrunt.
grappling irons, manus ferreae, copulae.
to board a ship, in navem transcendere, navem expugnare.
to sink a ship, navem submergere deprimere.
to drive on shore, navem in litus agere.
to ram a ship, navem rostro percutere.

General Vocabulary

This Vocabulary contains all the words given in the Vocabularies to the separate Exercises. It is meant to remind of forgotten words, but not to supply again constructions, genders, etc.

abandon, relinquere.
ability, to the best of his a., pro virli parte.
able, to be, posse.
abound, abundare.
about (number, etc.), circiter, *adv.* (**of, concerning**), de, *prep.*
above, to mention, supra commemorare.
absent, to be, abesse.
accept, accipere.
acclamation, plausus.
accompany, comitari.
accomplish, efficere.
accomplishing anything, without, re infecta.
accord, of their own, sua sponte.
according to (*of writers*), apud, *prep.*
accordingly, so, igitur (*generally second word*); itaque (*first word*).
account, on acount of, ob.
accuse, accusare, insimulare.
accuser, accusator.
accustomed, solitus, assuetus.
    accustomed to, assuetus ad.
    to be, solere.
acquaintance (*with persons*), consuetudo; (with things), cognito.
acquire, acquirere, nancisci.
acquit, absolvere.
across, trans.
act, agere, se gerere.
add, addere.
added, it is, accedit.
address, alloqui, contionari.
adjourn (**be dismissed**), dimitti.
administer public affairs, rempublicam administrare.
admire, mirari.
admit, admittere. (confess), fateri.
adopt a plan, inire *or* capere consilium.
advance, progredi, procedere; signa ferre.
advantage, commodum. **to be to the a. of**, ex usu esse; usui esse.
adverse (**fortune**), adversus, iniquus.
adversity, res adversae.
advice, consilium.
advise, suadere, monere. *See Voc. 61 and Rule 12.*
affection, amor, studium.
afraid, territus. **be afraid**, timere.
after, post, *prep*, and *adv.*; postea, *adv.*; postquam, *conj.*
afterwards, postea or post.
again, rursus. (*a second time*), iterum.
again and again, Identidem, saepenumero.
against one's will, invitus.
aghast, obstupefactus.

ago, abhinc.
agree upon (**terms**), constituere.
agreed, it is, constat.
agreement, come to an, consentire.
agriculture, agricultura, agrorum cultus.
aid, auxilium.
aid, send to the, submittere, subsidio mittere.
aim at, petere.
alive, vivus.
all the best men, optimus quisque.
allow, sinere.
allowed, it is, licet. *Voc. 128.*
ally, socius.
almost, paene, fere, ferme.
alone, solus.
Alps, Alpes, *pl.*
already, jam.
also, etiam.
altogether, omnino (*only neg. sentences*).
always, semper.
amazed, to be, mirari.
ambassador, legatus.
ambuscade, insidiae.
amount, any, quantusvis, *adj.*
ancestors, majores.
anchor, to ride at, stare in ancoris.
    to weigh, ancoras tollere.
    to cast, ancoras jacere.
ancient, antiquus.
    in a. times, antiquitus (*adv.*).
anger, ira.
angry, iratus. **be angry with**, irasci. **make angry**, lacessere.
announce, nuntiare, referre.
annoyed at, to be, aegre ferre.
answer, respondere.
    answer, responsum.
anxious to, cupidus.
anyone. See p. 212.
Apollo, Apollo.
appear, apparere, videri.
appease, placare.
applause, plausus.
apple, malum.
appoint, creare.
appointed day, on the, die constituto.
approach, aditus. **to**, appropinquare.(of time), appetere.
approval, consensus. **approve**, probare.
archer, sagittarius.
arise, cooriri.
arm, armare.
armament (= **fleet**), classis.
arms, anna.
arms, to take up, arma sumere. **under arms**, in armis.
army, exercitus.

arouse, excitare.
arrival, adventus.
arrive, advenire.
arrow, sagitta.
art, ars. **of war**, ars militaris.
artillery, tormenta, *n. pl.*
artisan, artifex.
as if, quasi, tanquam.
ascertain, cognoscere.
ashamed of, to be, pudet.
ask, ask for, rogare, interrogare, quaerere, petere. *See Synonyms.*
ask repeatedly, rogitare.
assail, assault, oppugnare.
assailant, oppugnator.
assassinate, trucidare.
assault (**on town**), oppugnatio.
assemble, *tr.* convocare; *intr.* convenire.
assembly (**public**), contio, concilium.
assert, affirmare.
assign, attribuere.
assist, adjuvare, subvenire.
assume, usurpare.
assured (**of things**), exploratus.
astonished, miratus, attonitus.
at. *See Rule 6.*
at last, tandem.
Athenian, Atheniensis.
Athens, Athenae.
attack (**onset, charge**), impetus (*for gen. dat. abl. plural use forms of* incursio).
    to, aggredi, adoriri, impetum facere in; (**of towns**), oppugnare. (**of disease, etc.**), afficere.
attempt, conari. (**battle**), temptare.
attend to, curare, studere.
attire, ornatus.
augur, augur.
autumn, auctumnus.
avarice, avaritia.
avenge, ulcisci.
avenger, ultor.
avoid, vitare.
await, exspectare.
away, to be, abesse.

B

back, tergum. (adverb), retro.
bad, malus, pravus.
baggage, impedimenta, *n. pl.*
band, manus.
banish, expellere.
bank, ripa.
barbarians, barbari.
barren (**profitless**), irritus.
base, turpis.

battle, proelium, pugna. **line of**, acies.
    pitched, justum proelium; acies. **there was a battle**, pugnatum est.
    fight a battle, proelium facere.
    give battle to, proelium committere-cum.
    draw up in battle array, (in) acie instrute.
bear, ferre.
    (**of burdens**), portare.
    (**endure**), pati.
beard, barba.
beat, caedere.
beautiful, pulcher.
beauty, pulchritudo.
because, quod, quia. See Rule 22.
become, fieri.
becoming, it is, decet.
bed, cubile.
    go to, cubitum ire.
befalls, it, contingit (*generally good luck*); accidit.
before, ante, *prep*.; antequam, priusquam, *conj*. (Rule 25); ante *or* antea, *adv*.
    before long, haud multo post.
beg, orare, precari.
begin, incipere, coepisse.
beginning, initium.
behalf, *on b. of*, pro.
behave, se gergre.
behind, pone.
behold (**catch sight of**), conspicere, conspicari.
behoves, it, oportet.
believe, credere.
belonging to others, alienus.
benefit (*nn*.), beneficium.
    (*vb*.) prodesse, usui esse.
beseech, obsecrare.
beset, besiege, obsidere.
besides, praeterea.
besiege, obsidere.
bestow, donare.
betake oneself, se conferre.
betray, prodere.
between, inter.
bill, rogatio.
bind (*by an oath*, etc.), obstringere.
birth (**race**), genus.
bitterly, vehementer.
blame, culpa.
    to, culpare.
blind, caecus, oculis captus.
block, obstruere.
blockade, obsidere.
blood, sanguis.
bloodshed, caedes, strages.
bloody, cruentus.
blow, ictus.
board, to come on, conscendere navem.
boat, linter.
boast, jactare, prae se ferre.
boastful, to be, gloriari.
body, corpus.
boldness, audacia.
book, liber.
booty, praeda.
borders, fines.

born, to be, nasci.
borrow, in aere alieno esse; aes alienum facere.
both, ambo, uterque.
both . . . and, et . . . et.
bottom, imus.
bow, arcus.
boy, puer.
brave, fortis, validus.
    to show oneself, se praebere fortem.
bravely, fortiter.
bravery, virtus, fortitudo.
bread, panis.
break, frangere.
    (**a law**), violare.
    (**a line**), inclinare.
    down, diruere, rescindere.
    through, perrumpere.
breeze, aura.
bribe (= **money**), pecunia.
bribery, ambitus.
bridge, to throw over a river, pontem in flumine facere.
bring (**of persons**), adducere.
    (**of things, news**), afferre.
    help, auxilium ferre. broad, latus.
brother, frater.
build, aedificare.
burden, onus.
burden, to be a, oneri esse. *Voc. 85*.
burdensome, molestus.
burn, *intr*., ardere.
    tr. (**set fire to**), incendere, urere.
bury, sepelire.
but, sed (first word), autem (second word).
    (= **except**), praeter, *prep*.; nisi, conj.
buy, gmere.

C

calamity, incommodum, calamitas.
calculating (**thinking**), ratus.
call, vocare. *See Synonyms*.
    together, convocare.
    (**by name**), appellare.
camp, castra, *n. pl*.
    to keep in, castris tgnere.
    to pitch a, castra pongre.
    to strike a, castra movere.
capable of, aptus ad.
capital (= **city**), caput.
capitol, capitolium.
captive, captivus.
care for, value. *See p. 72*
care, carefulness, diligentia.
carefully, diligenter.
careless, negligens.
carelessly, negligenter.
carelessness, negligentia.
carry, portare.
    off, auferre, abripere.
    (**of a law**), ferre.
cart, carrus.
Carthage, Carthago.
Carthaginian, Poenus. *adj*., Punicus.
castle, castellum.
Caroline, Catalma.

catch, cape re.
    sight of, conspicere, conspicari.
    up, consequi.
cattle, pgcus.
cause (**be the cause of**), causae esse. *Voc. 85*.
    (**see to**) curare (*Voc. 149*); efficere ut.
caution, diligentia.
cavalry, equitatus, *sing*.; equites, *pl*.
cavern, spelunca.
cease, desinere.
celebrated, praeclarus.
    the celebrated Plato, Plato ille.
centre, media pars.
    (*of line*), media acies.
certain, a certain (= *the Indef. Article*), quidam.
certainly, certo; (**at least**), certe.
chance, by, forte, casu.
change, mutare.
character, mores.
characters (**letters**), litterae.
charge (**accusation**), crimen.
    (**attack**), impetus.
    to, impelum facere in.
chariot, currus.
cheap, vllis.
    to hold, parvi (minimi) facere, aestimare.
check, cohibere.
cheer, to be of good, bono ammo esse.
chieftain, princeps.
children, libgri (sometimes pugri).
choose, deligere.
circumstances, under these, quae quum ita sint, essent.
    under the circumstances, ut in tali re.
citadel, arx.
citizen, civis.
city, urbs.
claim, usurpare.
clear, it is, liquet, manifestum est.
clearly, manifesto, certo.
cleave, discindere.
clever, callidus, sollers.
cliff, rupes.
climb, ascendere.
cloak, pallium.
    (**military**), sagum.
close, claudere.
close order, in, conferto agmme.
close quarters, at, comminus.
clothe, vestire.
clothes, vestis, vestitus.
cloud, nubes.
club, clava, fustis.
coast, ora, litus.
cold, *noun*, frigus. *adj*., frigidus, gelidus.
collect, colligere.
colony, colonia.
colour, color.
come, vgnire.
come out, egredi.
    back, regredi, redire.
    between, intercedere.
    down, descendere.
    to the help of, subvenire.
    off victorious, evadere victor.
    upon, incidere in.

Appendix

command, imperare, jubere. *See Voc. 61 and Rule 11.*
    be in command of, praeesse.
    put into command, praeficere.
    chief command, summa imperii.
commander, praefectus. *See p. 140, note 3.*
commit, admittere.
    (**to one's care**), mandare alicui.
commonly, vulgo, plerumque. *or use* constat.
companion, comes.
compel, cogere.
complain, queri.
complete (victory), certus, haud dubius.
conceal, celare.
concerns, -it, attinet ad, pertinet ad, refert, interest. *See Voc. 109.*
condemn, damnare.
    to death, capitis damnare.
conditions, conditiones.
conduct, ducere. conference, colloquium.
confess, confiteri.
confidence (= **trust**), fides, fiducia.
confusion, tumultus.
    throw into, perturbare.
connected with (by birth), cognatus, conjunctus natu.
conquer, superare, vincere.
conqueror, victor.
consecrate, vovere.
consent, velle.
    with one consent, consensu.
consider, cogitare, reputare, deliberare.
considering, ratus.
conspiracy, conjuratio.
conspirator, conjuratus.
conspire, conjurare.
constancy, constantia.
construct, aedificare.
consul, consul.
consulship, to stand for, consulatum petere.
consult, consulgre, deliberare.
interests of, consiilere. Voc. 61.
content, contentus.
contest, certamen.
continue, producere.
continue to march, iter continuare.
contrary to, contra.
control (of campaign), summa imperii, *or* summa belli administrandi.
convict, condemnare.
Corinth, Corinthus.
corn, frumentum.
cost, stare. *Voc. 57.*
council, concilium.
counsel, consilium.
countenance, vultus.
Country (district), terra, regio. (*only when opposed to* **town**), rus.
    in the, ruri or rure.
    (**native land**), patria.
courage, virtus.
    to show, virtutem praestare.
course, to hold on his, cursum tenere.
cover, operire.
    (**shelter**), tegere.

coward, ignavus.
cowardice, ignavia.
credit, laus.
to be a, laudi esse. *Voc. 85.*
crime, scelus.
criminal, nocens.
crisis, discrimen.
crop, sgges.
cross, transire, transjicere.
crowd, turba, multitud0.
crowd round, circumfundi.
crown, corona.
cruel, saevus, crudelis.
cruelty, saevitia, crudelitas.
crush, profligare.
cry, clamor.
cry out, clamare.
    (**a cry was raised**), clamatum est, clamor sublatus est.
cultivate, colere.
cunning, *nn.*, sollertia; *adj.* sollers,
cup, poculum.
cure, sanare, mederi.
custom, mos.
    according to, more.
customary, solitus.
customs, instituta.
cut down, succidere.
    (**kilt**), occidere.
cut off, desecare.
cut in two, discindere.

D

danger, periculum.
dangerous, periculosus.
dare, audere.
dark, obscurus.
darkness, tenebrae.
dash against (*tr.*), illidere.
daughter, filia.
dawn, prima lux.
    to, illucescere.
day, dies.
    space of two days, biduum.
day, every, quotidie, indies.
    on the appointed, die constituto. **on the following**, postero die, postridie.
deadly wound, mortale vulnus.
deaf, surdus, auribus captus.
dear, carus.
death, mors.
    to the, usque ' ad mortem.
    to condemn to, capitis damnare.
    to face, mortem obire.
debt, aes alienum.
deceive, decipere.
decide, constitute.
    (**contest**), rem decerngre.
decisive, haud anceps.
declare, affirmare.
    war, bellum indice re.
decree, edicere, decernere.
deed, factum.
    (*gen.* **with bad sense**), facinus.
deep, altus.
defeat, clades, incommodum. *vb.*, vincere.
defend, defendere,

defender, defensor.
defile, angustiae, fauces.
delay, mora. cunctari.
deliberate, deliberare, consulgre.
delight (= **joy**), gaudium.
delightful, jucundus.
deliver, tradere.
demand, postulare, flagitare, poscere, imperare. *See Synonyms.*
deny (say not), nggare.
depart, abire, discedere.
    (**change homes**), demigrare.
departure, profectio.
depend on, constare in, poni in.
depose, abrogare imperium (tribunatum) alicui.
deprive, privare.
descended, prognatus, ortus.
desert, (*tr.*) deserere, (*intr.*) transfugere.
    (**revolt from**), deficere ab.
deserter, transfuga, perfuga.
deserve, mgreri, dignus esse. *Rule 18.*
deservedly, merito.
design, consilium.
desire, studium, cupido. cupere.
desirous, cupidus.
desist from, desistere.
desolate, desertus.
despair, spem abjicere.
    in, re, *or* salute desperata.
despatches, litterae.
desperate, perditus.
despise, despicere, spernere, contemnere.
destroy, delere.
destruction, to be, *or* **mean**, exitio esse. *Voc. 85.*
detain, retinere.
deter, deterrere.
determination, constantia.
determine, statute, constitute.
devoid of, vacuus, nudatus.
devoted to, to be, studere.
devotion, studium.
dictator, dictator.
die, mori.
differ, inter se differre.
    greatly from, multum distare ab.
difference, to make a, interesse, referre. *Voc. 109.*
different from, alius ac.
difficult, difficilis.
difficulty, difficultas.
dig up, effodere.
diligence, diligentia.
diligently, diligenter.
diminish, dimmugre.
directions, in all, passim, in omnes partes.
    from all, undique, ex omnibus partibus.
disabled, confectus.
disaffected, seditiosus.
disaster, clades.
disastrous, infelix, funestus.
disband, dimittere.
discipline, disciplina.
discover, invenire, reperire. *See Syn.*, ***find***.
    (**of facts**), cognoscere, comperire.

discretion, at, nullis conditionibus latis, acceptis.
discuss, dissgrere de.
disease, morbus.
disembark (*trans.*), exponere. (*intr.*), e nave egrgdi. *Voc. 131.*
disgrace, dedecus, ignominia.
   to, dedgcori esse. *Voc. 85.*
disgraceful, turpis. **disheartened,** metu commotus.
dishonour, dedecorare. dedecori esse. *Voc. 85.*
disliked, to be, odio esse. *Voc. 85.*
dismay, pavor.
dismayed, pavore perculsus.
dismiss, dimittere.
disobey (an order), negligere.
disorder, tumultus.
disorderly, tumultuarius.
display (a quality), praestare.
displease, displicere.
disposition, mens, indoles.
dispute, decertare de.
   (in conversation), disserere de.
distance, at a, procul, eminus.
distant, longinquus.
   to be, abesse.
distinguished, insignis.
district, regio.
disturb, turbare.
disturbance, tumultus, motus.
ditch, fossa.
divisions, in two, bipertito.
do one's utmost to, id aggre ut.
dominion, imperium. *See Syn.,* **power.**
   (with idea of tyranny), dormnatus.
door, porta, janua.
doubt, dubltare. Rules 16, 23.
   (without), sine dubio.
doubtful, to be, incertum, dubium esse.
downwards, deorsum.
drag, draw, trahere.
draw up, instruere.
dread, formido.
dream, somnium.
   to, somniare, somnio videre.
dress, ornatus.
drink, bibere.
drive, agere.
   out, expellere.
drive down, or away, depellere.
   back, repellere.
drown, submergere.
due, it is due to you, per te stat
duty, officium.
   it is one's, oportet.
dwell in, habitare in, incolere.

E

eager, avidus.
eagerness, studium.
early (in the morning), mane.
   (in good time), mature.
earn, merere.
easily, facile.
east, solis ortus, oriens.
easy, facilis.

eat, edere.
effect, efflcere.
effort, labor, conatus.
egg, ovum.
Egypt, Aegyptus, *f.*
elated, elatus.
elders, patres.
elect, creare.
evidence, testimonium.
elephant, elephantus.
eloquence, eloquentia.
embark (*trans.*), imponere. (*intr.*), (in) navem conscendere. Voc. 131.
emperor, imperator.
empire, imperium.
employ, uti.
encamp, considere, castra ponere.
encourage, hortari, admonere.
end, finis.
   bring to an end, conficere, finire.
endowed, praeditus.
endurance, patientia.
enemy (private), inimicus.
   (public), hostis.
energy, studium.
engage in battle, proelium committere.
engagement, certamen.
England, Britannia.
Englishman, Britannus.
enjoy, frui, uti.
enough (quite), satis.
enquiry, hold an, quaestionem habere de.
enraged, iratus
enter, ingredi, intrare.
enthusiasm, studium, ardor.
entice, elicere.
entrance, os, ostium, aditus.
entrust, committere, mandare.
envoy, legatus.
envy, invidia.
   to, invidere.
equal, par.
   (favourable, *or* **fair|,** aequus.**(of the same age, contemporary|,** aequalis.
   on equal terms, aequo Marte, aequa contentione.
equally, aeque, pariter.
equip, parare.
err, errare.
escape, fuga.
   to, effugere. *especially,* praesertim.
esteem. See Voc. 57.
even, etiam.
   not even, ne . . . quidem.
evening, in the, vesperi.
   towards, sub vesperum.
ever, unquam. See p. 212. (= **always),** semper.
every day, quotidie.
everywhere, ubique.
evidence, to give, testimonium dicere.
evident, manifestus.
evil, malum.
exact from, imperare (*dat.* and *acc.*).
example, to be an, exemplo esse *Voc. 85.*
excessive, nimius.
excel, superare.
excellent, egregius.

except, praeter, prep.; nisi, conj.
excite, excitare.
exclaim, clamare.
exhausted, confectus (labore, etc.).
exhort, hortari, admonere.
exile, exsiliura.
   an, exsul.
expect, exspectare.
expectation, contrary to, praeter spem, opinionem.
expedient, it is, expedit. **expel,** expellere.
experience, peritia.
experienced in, expertus, peritus.
explain, exponere, edere.
explore, explorare.
expose (*trans.*), objicere.
   oneself to, se objicere, occurrere.
express, edere.
extent, to a great, magna ex parte.
eye, oculus.

F

face, vultus.
face death, mortem obire.
fail, deficere.
faint-hearted, timidus.
fair, aequus.
faithful, fidelis.
faithfully, fideliter.
fall, cadere.
   (of a.city), capi.
fall down, delabi.
   into or upon, incidere in.
   to the lot of, continegre.
   See 'befall.'
false, falsus.
falsely, falso.
family, familia.
famine, fames.
far, longe.
too far, longius.
far as, as, usque ad.
far off, procul.
farewell, say, jubere valere.
farm, fundus
farmer, colonus.
fashion of, in the, more.
fastness, castellum.
fatal, funestus.
fate, fortuna, fatum.
fated, fatalis.
father, pater.
fatherland, patria.
fault (blame), culpa.
favour, favere.
favourable (of things), secundus, idoneus.
fear, timor, metus. See Syn.
   to, timere, mgtugre. Rule 21.
   (with idea of respect), vereri.
   through fear of this, hoc timore.
feast, epulae.
   to, epulari.
feed, vesci.
feel, sentire.
feign, simulare.
fellow-citizen, fellow-countryman, civis.
fertile, fertilis.

few, pauci.
field, ager.
   of battle, acies.
   take the, milites educere.
fierce, ferox.
fiercely, ferociter.
fight a battle, proelium facere.
   with, pugnare contra.
   in the army, stipendia merere; *sometimes* merere *alone*.
fighting order, in, acie (instructa).
fill, complere, replere.
finally, denique.
find. See '*discover.*'
fine, mulctare.
finish, conficere.
   (**accomplish**), perficere.
fire, ignis.
   set on, incendere.
   back, tela rejicere.
first, at, primo.
fit out, instruere.
   for, aptus ad, idoneus ad.
   to be, dignusqui. Rule 18.
flame, flamma.
flank, latus.
   on the, ab latere.
fleet, classis.
flight, fuga.
   put to, fundere, fugare.
   take to, terga vertere, se fugae mandare.
flock, grex.
flow, fluere.
flower, flos.
   of army, robur.
flushed (**elated**), elatus, sublatus.
fly, fugere.
follow, sequi (*and compounds*).
following (*of time*), proximus.
follows, as, ita, ad hunc modum.
fond of, cupidus.
food, cibus.
foolish, stultus.
foot, pes.
   on, pedibus.
footsoldier, pedes.
for, nam (*first word*), enim (*second word*).
   for the sake of, pro.
forage, frumentum, pabulum.
   to, frumentari, pabulari.
forbid, vetare.
force, coggre. *vis.* **by force of arms**, vi et armis.
forces, copiae.
   land, copiae terrestres.
foreign, externus.
foresee, providere.
forest, silva.
foretell, praedicere.
forget, oblivisci, immemor esse.
forgive, ignoscere.
form, figura.
   a plan, consflium capere, inire.
former, superior, prior.
   the former . . . the latter, ille ... hic.
formerly, antea.

formidable, gravis, metuendus.
fortifications, mummenta.
fortify, munire.
fortress, castellum.
fortunate, felix.
fortunately, feliciter, prospere.
fortune, fortuna.
   (**generally bad**), casus.
forum, forum.
found, condere.
fountain, fons.
France, Gallia.
free, liber.
   from, vacuus, expers.
   to free, liberare.
freedman, libertus.
freedom, libertas.
French, Gallicus.
Frenchman, Gallus.
frequently, saepe.
fresh, integer.
   (**recent**), recens.
friend, amicus.
friendship, amicitia.
frighten, terrere.
front, in, a fronte.
fruit, fructus.
fugitive, profugus.
   (*gen. of* **slaves**), fugitivus.
full, plenus.
furnish, praebere.
further, longius, ultra.
fury, furor.

G

gallant, fortis.
Gallic, Gallicus.
game, ludus.
hold games, ludos celebrare.
garden, hortus.
garment, vestimentum, vestis.
garrison, praesidium.
gate, porta.
gather, colligere.
Gaul, Gallia.
Gaul, a, Gallus.
gaze at, spectare, intueri.
general, dux. *See p. 140, note 3.*
   commander-in-chief, imperator.
   general's tent, praetorium.
generally, vulgo.
geniality, comitas.
German, Germanus.
get out of (**escape**), evadere.
gift, donum, munus.
give, dare.
   up, tradere, dedere.
   ground, cedere loco.
give up hope, spem abjicere.
give opportunity, dare occasionem, facere potestatem. *Voc. 100.*
glad, to be, gaudere. *Rule 22.*
gladly, libenter.
gloomy, tristis.
glory, gloria, decus.
gloriously, summa laude.

go, ire, se conferre.
   away, discedere, abire.
   back, regredi, redire.
   out, egredi.
   well, prospere evenire.
god, deus.
going on, to be, *pass. of* agere.
gold, aurum.
golden, aureus.
good for, to be, prodesse. ex usu esse *or* usui esse.
goods, bona, *n. pl.*
govern, regere, admlnistrare.
government, *the*, ii qui reipublicae praesunt, ii qui renipublicam admministrant, magistratus.
governor, of a province, proconsul.
grant, dare, mandare, tradere.
greatly, magnopere.
greet, salutare.
Greece, Graecia.
Greek, Graecus.
   language, lingua Graeca.
green, viridis.
grief, dolor.
groan, gemitus.
ground, humus, terra.
   to hold one's, in loco perstare (*sometimes translate by* resistere *or* sustinere).
grudge, invidia, dolor.
grumble, queri.
guard, custos.
   off one's, improvidus, incautus.
   to, custodire.
guest, hospes.
guide, dux.
guilty, nocens.
guise of, in the, *more*, pro.
gulf (**bay**), sinus.

H

halt, consistere.
hand, manus.
in hands of, in potestate.
to be at, adesse.
hang, *tran.*, suspendere. *intran.*, pendere.
happens, it, accidit.
happy, felix, beatus.
harass, lacessere.
harbour, portus.
hard, difficilis.
hardly, vix, aegre.
hardship, labor.
harm, malum, damnum.
harvest, messis.
hasten, properare, festinare.
hateful to, to be hated by, odio esse. *Voc. 85.*
hatred, odium.
havoc, strages.
head, caput.
heal, mederi, sanare. *Voc. 61.*
healthy (**of persons**), sanus, validus.
   (**of places**), saluber.
hear, audire.

heat, calor.
heavy, gravis.
height, altitudo.
helmet, galea.
help, auxilium.
   to, juvare, succurrere, subvenire.
   to be a, auxilio, subsideo esse.
here, hic.
   (**implying motion**), huc.
hesitate, diibltare.
hide, celare, condere.
high, altus.
higher, superior.
highway, via.
hill, collis.
hinder, impedire, obstare.
historian, scriptor rerum.
hitherto, adhuc.
hold, tgnere.
hold out (**of supplies**), suppetere. (= resist), resistere.
   on one's course, cursum tgnere.
   one's ground, resistere, in loco perstare.
   (**occupy**), occupare.
hold command, imperium obtinere.
hold cheap, parvi, minimi aestimare.
holy, sacer.
home, domus. *See p. 53.*
homes, penates
   (**household gods**), *or* foci (**hearths**).
honour, honor.
honour, for the sake of, honoris causa.
honourable (**of persons**), probus.
   (**of things**), honestus.
hope, spes.
   to, sperare.
   give up, spem abjicere.
horse, equus.
horse-soldier, eques.
hospitality, hospitium.
host, hospes.
hostage, obses.
hour, hora.
house, domus, or pl. of aedes.
household, familia.
how, quam.
   (**in what manner?**), quomodo, quemadmodum.
   great? quantus.
   long? quamdiu.
   many? quot, *indecl. adj.*
   often? quoties.
however, tamen.
humour, morem gerere.
hunger, fames.
hungry, to be, esurire.
hurl, jacere, injicere.
hurry, festinare, properare.
hurt, laedere, nocere. *Voc. 61.*
husband, vir, maritus.

I

idle, ignavus.
ignorance, inscientia.
ignorant of, inscius, imperitus.

ill, aeger.
   to be, aegrotare.
   take, aegre ferre.
imagine, reri.
immediately, statim.
immense, ingens.
importance, to be of, interesse, referre. *Voc. 109.*
impose tribute, impongre tributum.
impossible, it is, fieri non potest (quin).
impregnable, inexpugnabilis. **impression on, to make**, commovere.
incite, adducfire.
increase (*trans.*), augere; (*intrans.*), crescere.
incur, subire.
incursion, to make an, incursionem-facere.
indeed, quidem.
   (**really**), revera.
   (**at least**), certe, saltem.
independence, libertas.
indignant, to be, irasci.
indignation, ira, dolor.
induce, to, adducere.
inexperienced. See *ignorant*.'
infantry, peditatus (*sing.*), pedites (*plu.*).
inferior, inferior.
infirm, infirmus.
inflict on, afficere (*acc.* of person, *abl.* of thing), inferre (*dat.* of person, *acc.* of thing).
influence, auctoritas.
   to have very great, plurimum valere.
inform, certiorem (aliquem) facere.
infringe upon, deminuere.
inhabit, incolere.
inhabitants, incolae.
   (**of a town**), oppidani.
   (**of city**), cives.
injure, laedere, nocere. *Voc. 61.*
injury, injuria, damnum.
innocent, insons, innocens.
insolence, arrogantia, superbia.
Inspire, to, injicere (*acc.* of thing, *dat.* of person).
instead of, loco.
insult, contumelia, injuria.
intend, to, in ammo habere.
intend, I, mihi in animo est.
intention (**with the intention of**), eo consilio ut.
interior, pars interior.
invade, incursionem facere in, invadere.
invasion, incursio.
invite, to, invitare.
involved in, to be, occurrere.
Ireland, Hibernia.
Irish, Hibermcus.
Irishman, Hibernus.
iron, ferrum (*adj.* ferreus).
island, insula.
issue, eventus, exitus.

J

jealousy, invidia.
jest, jocus,

join, to, *trans.*, conjungere; *intrans.*, se conjungere cum.
journey, iter.
joy, gaudium, laetitia.
joyful, laetus.
judge, judex.
Jupiter, Juppiter.
just as, just as much as, aeque ac, haud aliter ac. *Rule 30.*
justify, excusare.

K

keep, conservare.
   (**observe**), colere.
   (**one's word**), fidem praestare.
key, clavis.
kill, interficere.
   (**cut down**) occidere.
   (**murder**), necare.
   (**massacre**), trucidare.
kind, sort, genus.
kind, benignus.
kindly, *adv.* benigne.
kindness, benignitas, humanitas, benevolentia.
act of kindness, beneficium
king, rex.
kingdom, regnum.
kingly, regius.
kingly power, regnum.
knight, eques.
know, scire. *See Syn.*
   (**ascertain**), cognoscere.
   not to, nescire.
   it is well known, constat.
knowledge (**of things**), cognitio.
   (**of persons**), consuetudo.

L

labour, labor.
lack, to, carere. *See Syn.,* '**want.**'
ladder, scala.
laden, oneratus.
land, *trans.*, exponere; *intrans.*, e nave egredi.
land, ager, patria. *See Syn.*
landing, egressus.
last, proximus.
   at, tandem.
last, to the, ad extremum.
late at night, multa nocte.
   till late in the night, ad multam noctem.
   too, sero.
lately, nuper. **latter**, hic (*opp. to* ille).
launch, deducere.
law, lex.
   pass a, legem jubere.
   propose a, legem ferre.
law of nations, jus gentium.
   contrary to, contra jus gentium.
lawful, fas, *indecl. or use* licet.
lay down, deponere.
lead, ducere.
leader, dux.

lead back, reducere.
    out, educere.
    round, circumducere.
    aside, deducere.
learn, discere.
    (**ascertain**), cognoscere, comperire.
least, at, certe, saltern.
leave, relinquere.
leave one's post, loco cedere.
leave behind, relinquere.
leave, by your, pace tua.
legion, legio.
legionary, legionarius miles.
leisure, otium.
lend, mandare.
length, at, tandem.
lessen, deminuere.
let, allow, smere.
let down, demittere.
let go, dimittere, omittere.
letter, epistola, litterae.
levy, hold a, dglectum habere.
liable to, obnoxius.
liberate, liberare.
liberty, libertas.
lie, jacere.
    (**speak falsely**), mentiri.
lieutenant (**general**), legatus.
life, vita.
light, lux.
like, similis.
line of battle, acies.
lines (**of army**), munitiones.
listen, audire (parere).
litter, lectica.
little, parvus, extguus.
little, a, paulum.
    (**with comp.**), paulo.
    too, parum, *adv.* (*used as noun with partitive gen.*).
    for a little time, paulisper.
little by little, paulatim.
live (**exist**), vivere.
live in, habitare in, incolere.
long, longus.
    (**of time only**), diuturnus.
    (**for a long time**), diu, *adv.*
    (**now for a long time**), jamdudum, jamdudum.
    (**as long as**), donee, quoad. Rule 25.
    (**= provided that**), dum, dummodo. *Rule 27.*
look after, curare.
looks (**expression**), vultus.
lose (**let slip**), amittere.
    (**wilfully**), perdere. *See Syn.*
lose heart, animum demittere.
loss, incommodum, damnum.
    with great (**of a battle**), maxima strage, *or* multis amissis.
lost, to be, "actum est de" = **it is all over with**, lot, sors.
loud, *use* magnus.
love, amare, diligere.
loyal, fidelis.
loyalty, fides, fidelitas.
luxury, luxus.

M

mad, insanus., **to be**, furere.
magistrate, magistratus.
maidens (**servants**), ministrae, famulae.
maimed, saucius.
main road, via.
mainly, imprimis.
majority, major pars, *with part. gen.*, plerique, *adj. pl.*
make (**cause that**), efficere ut (**final**).
    trial of, experiri, temptare.
man (**human being**), homo.
    (**individual of male sex**), vir.
    to a, ad unitin.
    to man, *vb.*, complere.
manner, modus.
    (**custom**), mos.
many, raulti.
times (**larger**), multis partibus.
how, quot, *indecl. adj.*
march, iter.
    to, iter facere, contendere.
    a forced, magnum iter.
    on the, in *or* ex itinere.
    to continue, iter continuare.
marry (**woman as subject**), nubere.
    (**man as subject**), ducere. Voc. 6l.
marsh, palus.
marvellous, mirus.
massacre, caedes.
master (**of pupils**), magister.
    (**of slaves**), dSminus.
    of the horse, magister equitum.
match for, par.
matters a great deal, it, multum, *or* magni interest. Voc. 109.
mean, velle dlcere.
    (**indicate**), significare.
means (**manner, way**), modus.
    by this, ita.
    by no, haudquaquam.
meanwhile, interim, interea.
meet, obviam ire, *dat.*
    (**obtain**), nancisci.
meeting, concilium, conventus.
mention above, to, supra commemorare.
mercenaries, mercenarii milites.
merchandise (merx), *pl.*, merces.
message, nuntius.
messenger, nuntius.
middle, medius. See note, p. 23.
might, with all one's, summa vi.
mile, mille passus.
miles, two, duo millia passuum.
mind, animus.
    (**intellect**), mens. *See Syn.*
with minds made up, obstinatis animis.
mindful, memor.
misfortune, calamitas, malum.
moat, fossa.
mob, turba, multitudo.
mock, irridere.
modern times, in, his temporibus.
money, pecunia.
month, mensis.
moon, luna.

moreover, praeterea. (= **now**, continuing a narrative), autem.
morning, in the, mane, *indecl. abl.*, only.
mortal (**subject to death**), mortalis.
    (**causing death**), mortifer.
most, plerique, *adj.*
mother, mater.
mound, tumulus, agger.
mountain, mons.
mouth, os.
    (**entrance**), ostium, aditus.
move, movere.
    (**affect**), commovere.
much, just as much as, aeque ac.
    too much, nimius, *adj.*, nimium (*used as noun*), nimis, *adv.*
mule, mulus.
multitude (**great number**), multitudo.
    (**common people**), plebs.

N

name, nomen (**by name, named**, nomine).
narrow, angustus, artus.
nation, gens. *See Syn.*, 'people.'
naval, navalis.
near, prope.
near, to be, adesse.
nearly, paene, fere.
nearest, proximus, *followed by acc., dat., or* ab *with abl.*
necessary, necessarius.
necessity, necessltas.
neck, collum, cervices.
need, egere, indigere. *Voc. 134.*
    (*be without*), carere.
needs money, he, opus est ei pecunia.
neglect, negligere.
negligence, negligentia.
neighbour, neighbouring, vicinus, finitimus.
never, nunquam.
nevertheless, tamen, nililominus.
new, novus. *See Syn.*
    (= **fresh**), recens.
news, nuntius.
    what? quid novi ?
to bring, afferre, referre.
next, proximus.
night, nox.
    by, noctu.
    until late in the, ad multamnoctem.
noble, nobilis.
nobody, no one, nemo (*adj.* nullus).
none the less, nihilominus.
noon, meridies.
north, septentriones, *pl.*
not only . . . but also, non solum . . . sed etiam.
not yet, nondum.
nothing, nihil.
notice, animadvertere.
now, jam.
    (**at present time**), nunc.
    (**continuing narrative**), autem.
nowadays, his temporibus.
now for a long time, jampridem, jamdudum.

number, numerus, *only singular. a great number*, multitudo.
nymph, nympha.

O

oath, jusjurandum.
obey, to, parere.
object was, his, id egit ut.
observe (keep), colere.
 (notice), animadvertere.
obstacle, difficultas.
obstinacy, pertinacia.
obstinate, pertinax.
obstinately, obstinate.
occupy, occupare.
off (promontory, *etc*.), contra.
offence, noxa. delictum.
offend, offendere, *acc*., displicere, *dat*.
offer, offerre.
office (of state), honor.
officer, praefectus, legatus. *See note on p. 80*.
often, saepe.
 at often as, quoties. *See Rule 25*.
old (*that has lasted a long time*), vetus. *See Syn*.
 (Belonging to former times), antiquus.
 old man, senex.
 10 years old, etc. See p. 53.
older, natu major.
once (upon a time), aliquando, olim.
at once, statim.
one . . . another (*of several*), alius . . . alius.
 the one . . . the other (*two contrasted*), alter . . . alter.
 on one side . . . on the other, ab altera parte . . . ab altera.
 with one another, inter se.
one in ten, decimus quisque, *lit*., **each tenth man**.
only, solum, tantum, modo.
onset, impetus.
open, apertus.
to, aperire.
to be, patere.
throw open, patefacere.
openly, aperte.
opinion, sententia.
 to give an, sententiam ferre.
opportunity, facultas, locus, occasio.
 to give an, dare occasionem, facere potestatem, *gen. Voc. 100*. **should an opportunity offer**, data occasione.
oppose, obstare, obsistere, resistere.
opposite to, contra, e regione.
opposite (bank, *etc*.), alter.
oppress, to, vexare, opprimere.
oracle, oraculum.
orator, orator.
ordain to, edicere.
order, disciplina.
 to lose, omittere disciplinam
 (in close), confertus, conferto agmine.

order (command), jussum.
 by order of, jussu.
 without the order of, injussu.
 (*vb*.) **command**, jubere, imperare.
origin, origo.
others (all others), ceteri, reliqui.
other people, belonging to, alienus.
otherwise than, aliter ac. *Rule 30*.
ought, debere.
outpost, statio.
outside, extra.
overcome, superare.
 (with fear, *etc*.), perculsus.
overtake, assequi, consequi.
overthrow, sternere, prosternere.
owe, debere.
it is owing to you, per te stat
ox, bos.

P

pace, passus.
pacify, pacare.
pain, dolor.
palace, regia.
panic, pavor.
pardon, venia.
 to, ignoscere.
parent, parens.
part, pars.
part in, to take, interesse.
particularly, praeter omnes.
partly . . . partly, partim . . . partim.
pass, saltus, angustiae.
 spend, agere.
 by, practerire.
past, praeteritus.
 the, praeterita, *n. f*.
path (byway), trames.
patiently, aequo ammo.
pay, stipendium.
 to, solvere.
peace, pax.
peasant, agricola, rusticus.
penalty, poena.
 undergo, poenam siibire.
people (population, nation), populus. *See Syn*.
 (persons), homines.
 (common), plebs, vulgus.
perceive, sentire.
perform, fungi.
perhaps, forte, fortasse, forsitan. (Forsitan *always takes subj*.)
peril, to bring into, in perlculum adducere.
perish, perire.
 (of ship), frangi.
perjury, perjurium.
permit, smere.
Persian, Persa.
persuade, persuadere. *Rules 11, 12*.
pestilence, pestis, pestilentia.
philosopher, sapiens, philosophus.
philosophy, philosophia.
pierce, transfigere.
piece (of money), nummus.
piety (duty, natural affection), pietas.

pile up, congerere.
pitch a camp, to, castra ponere, munire.
pity, miseret, *impers. See Voc. 128*.
place, locus.
 first, principatus. (*vb*.) ponere. **before (prefer)**, anteponere.
 to take the place of, succedere.
plague, pestilentia, pestis.
plain, campus, planities.
plainly, aperte, plane.
plan, consilium.
 to form a, consilium capere, inire.
play (of artillery), immittere tela.
play, ludere.
pleasant, jucundus.
pleases, it, juvat, libet, placet. *Voc. 128*.
please, placere, juvare. *Voc. 61*.
plunder, vastare, diripere, spoliare
Po, Padus.
poet, poeta.
point out, ostendere, monstrare.
poison, venenum.
poor, pauper.
population, populus.
position, locus.
 to take up a, considcre.
possession, get, potiri.
possible, *use* facere, *or* fieri posse.
 as soon as, quam primum.
post, to leave one's, loco cedere.
power, potentia, potestas. *See Synonyms*.
 (energy), vis.
 kingly, regnum.
 with all one's, summa vi.
powerful, potens.
practise, studere, exercere.
praise, laus, *vb*. laudare.
pray, orare, precari.
prayers, preces.
prefer, malle.
prepare, parare.
 for, se parare ad.
 for battle, arma expedire.
presence of mind, to show, impavidus esse, se intrepide gerere.
presence of, in, coram.
present, donum.
 to be, adesse.
preserve, conservare.
press hard, urgere, premere.
 on, instare, *dat*.
pressed hard, to be, laborare.
pretend, simulare. **prevail**, superare.
prevent, prohibere.
prey, praeda.
price, pretium. *See p. 72*.
 at a low, vili.
pride (spirit), animus, superbia.
priest, priestess, sacerdos.
prison, carcer, vincula, *pl*. "bonds."
 put in, in carcerem (vincula) conjicere.
prisoners, captivi.
prisoner, take, capere, captivum facere.
private (not in office), privatus. **produce**, edere.
prolong a war, bellum ducere. **promise, to**, promittere, polliceri. **promontory**, promontorium.

proof, indicium.
property, bona, *n. pl.*, res.
private, res familiaris.
prophet, **prophetess**, vates.
propose (intend), in ammo habere.
    (a law), ferre.
proscribe, proscribere.
prospect (hope), spes.
prosperity, res prosperae.
prosperous, felix.
protection, to be, praesidio esse. *Voc. 85.*
    to be under, fidem sequi (ali cujus).
proud, superbus.
prove, demonstrare.
prove oneself false, se praebere infidelem.
provide, praebere.
provided that, dum, dummodo
province, provincia.
provision, rem frumentariam expedire.
provisions, commeatus, cibus.
provoke, lacessere, incitare.
prudent, prudens.
punish, punire, poena *or* supplicio afficere.
punishment, poena, supplicium.
purpose, for this, ad hoc.
    for the purpose of, causa (*after its case*).
    on, consulto, de industrial.
    on purpose to, eo consilio ut.
    to no purpose, frustra, nequic- quam.
pursue, sequi, persequi. *See Syn.*,
put back, reponere.
    on trial, reum facere, nomen deferre; *adj.*, reus.
    out to sea, evehi.
    to death, interficere.

Q

quantity, copia.
quarters, at close, comminus.
quickly, celeriter.
quiet, tranquillus.
    (*nn.*) quies.
quite, admodum.

R

rabble, turba.
race (birth), genus.
    (tribe, family), gens.
raiment, vestis.
raise a siege, relinquere obsidionem, obsidione desistere.
    (of relieving army), obsidione liberare.
rampart, vallum.
range, within, intra conjectum teli.
rank, ordo.
    First, prima acies.
rash, temerarius, inconsultus.
rashly, temere, inconsulte.
rashness, temeritas.
ravage, populari, vastare.
reach, pervenire ad.
read, legere.
    through, perlegere.
reading, lectio.

readily, libenter.
ready, get, parare, comparare.
    to, paratus, *with inf.*
really, revera.
rear, in the, a tergo.
rearguard, novissimum, agmen.
reason that, for the, propterea quod.
rebel, rebellis.
recall, revocare.
call to mind, repetere, ace.;
reminisci, gen.
receive, accipere.
recent, recens.
recently, nuper.
recognise, agnoscere.
recollect, remmisci.
    I recollect, venit mihi in mentem.
recollection, memoria.
recommend, suadere.
recover (*trans.*), recipere. (*intr.*), se reficere.
recruit, tiro.
red, ruber.
reduce, redigere.
refer, (to senate), referre.
refrain, temperare, prohiberi.
refuge, to seek, to fly for, confugere ad.
refuse, nolle, recusare. *Voc. 170.*
regard as, ducere ; habere pro.
regiment, cohors.
regret, deplorare.
    (be sorry for), paenitet.
reinforcements, supplementum, novae copiae.
reject, rejicere, respuere.
rejoice, gaudere. *Rule 22.*
relate, narrare.
relief, auxilium.
relieve, to, succedere, *dat.*, suble vare, *acc.*
    from a siege, liberare obsidione.
relying on, fretus.
remain, manere.
    faithful to Caesar, fidem Caesaris sequi.
remarkable, insignis, praeclarus.
remedy, remedium.
remember, meminisse, memor esse.
remembrance, memoria.
remind, admonere. **remove**, transferre.
renew, redintegrare.
    battle, redintegrare, restituere proelium. **repair**, reficere.
repay, reddere. **repeatedly**, identidem.
repel, repulse, repellere.
repent of, poenitet. *Voc. 128.*
replace, reponere.
reply, respondere.
report, nuntiare referre.
resentment, dolor, invidia.
reserves, subsidia.
resign, se abdicare.
resist, resistere.
resolutely, constanter, obstinate.
resolution, constantia.
resolve, constituere.
resolved minds, with, obstinatis animis.

responsible for, auctor, gen.
    to be responsible for, rationem reddere (to render an account).
rest, the, ceteti, reliqui; reliqua pars.
rest (*vb.*), quiescere, se teficere.
restrain, temperare. *Voc. 6l.*
result, eventus, exitus.
    to, evenire, evadere.
results, it, evenit. **retreat**, se recipere, pedem referre.
    sound a retreat, receptui canere. *Voc. 85.*
return, *intr.*, redire, regredi. *trans.* (= **give back**), reddere.
revenge, poena, ulciscendi libido, vindicare.
    (take verigcance on), ulcisci, poenam sumere de.
review (an army), recensere.
revolt, defectio.
    from, deficere ab.
revolution, res novae.
reward (*vb.*), praemio afficere, (*nn.*) praemium.
Rhine, Rhenus.
Rhone, Rhodanus.
rich, dives.
riches, divitiae.
ride, equo vehi.
ride at anchor, stare in ancoris.
right, it is, oportet. *Voc. 128.*
rightly, jure.
riot, tumultus.
ripe (ready, early), maturus.
ripen. maturescere.
rise, surgere, oriri, cooriri.
rising ground, locus editus.
risk, periclitari.
run risk, perlciilum subire.
risk all, rem in summum discrimen adducere.
risk one's life, periculum capitis subire.
river, fluvius, flumen.
    up, adverso flumine, in adversum flumen.
    down, secundo flumine.
road, via.
    (route), iter.
    make a, viam (iter) munire.
rob, spoliare.
robber, latro.
robes of state (of senators), tunica laticlavia.
rock, saxum, rupes.
rod, virga.
Rome, Roma.
Roman, Romanus.
rout, fundere, fugare.
    utterly, profligare.
rule, regere, regnare.
run, currere.
run out, procurrere.
    short, deficere.
    the risk, in periculum adduci. **away**, aufugere.
rush into, irruere.
    out, eruere, effundi.
    forward, proruere.

S

sacred, sacer.
sacrilegious, sacrilegus.
sad (feeling sad), gloomy, tristis.
    (showing sadness), maestus.
safe, in safety, tutus, incolumis.
safety, salus.
said he, inquit.
sail, navigare.
    past, *or* **along**, praetervehi.
    along coast, oram legere.
    to set sail, solvere navem.
sailor, nauta.
sake of, for the, causa (*following its case*), pro.
sally, sortie, eruptio. salvation of, to be, saluti esse. *Voc. 85.*
same as, the, Idem ac.
same time, at the, simul.
satisfy, satisfacere.
    (indulge), indulgere.
savage, saevus.
save, servare.
say, dicere.
    men say, it is said, ferunt.
scale, ascendere.
scarcely, vix, aegre.
scatter, *trans.*, dispergere, *intr.*, *use passive.*
schoolmaster, magister.
scorn, contemptus, contemptio. *vb. See 'despise?'*
scout, explorator, speculator.
scruples (religious), religio.
sea, mare.
sea, to put out to, evehi.
search for, quaerere, petere.
seat of war, sedes belli.
secretly, clam.
see to, curare. *See Voc. 149.*
see to it that, take care that, cura ut.
seek, quaerere, petere.
seek refuge, confugere ad.
seem, videri.
seize, capere. *See Syn, 'take.'*
    (snatch), rapere.
    (arrest), comprehendere.
seldom, rarely, raro.
sell, vendere.
senate, senatus, patres.
house, curia.
senator, senator.
send, mittere.
    away, dimittere.
    back, reddere, remittere.
    for, arcessere.
    forwards, praemittere.
    to the aid, subsidio mittere, submittere.
sentence, to undergo, poenam subire.
sentinels, vigiliae, custodes.
separate, sejungere.
serious, gravis.
serve, to, prodesse, servire.
    (as soldier), stipendia merere (*sometimes* merere *alone*).
sesterce, sestertius.

set free, to, liberare.
    out, proficisci.
    sail, solvere navem, ancoram tollere.
settlement, colonia.
several, complures.
severe, gravis.
severely, graviter.
share (divide), partiri.
    (take part in), particeps esse.
shed, effundere.
shield, scutum.
ship, navis.
    (of war), navis longa.
    (merchant, *or* **transport)**, navis oneraria.
shipwreck, naufragium.
shipwrecked, ejectus in litore *or* litus.
    to be, naufragium facere.
shirk, vitare, detrectare.
shoot, to (missiles), mittere.
shore, litus, ora.
short, brevis.
    to run short, deficere.
shout, clamor.
    to, clamare.
show, ostendere, demonstrare. *See Syn.*
    courage, virtutem praestare.
show oneself brave, se fortem praebere.
shower, imber.
    (of missiles), vis, multitudo, crebra tela, *pl.*
shut up, elaudere.
Sicily, Sicilia.
sick, aeger.
    to be, aegrotare.
side, latus.
    (of a river), ripa.
    to be on our, stare a nobis.
    on the one . . . on the other, ab altera parte . . . ab altera.
    on this side of, citra.
sides, on all, undique, passim.
    on both, utrimque.
siege, obsidio.
    to raise a, relinquere obsidionem, obsidione desistere.
    to relieve from, liberare obsidione.
sight, conspectus.
    of, to catch, conspicere, conspicari.
sign, signum.
signal for, signum, gen.
    to serve as, signo esse. **Voc. 85.**
signally, so, tanta strage.
signs of office, insignia.
silence, silentium.
silent, silens, tacitus.
    to be (*make no noise at all*), silere.
    to be (*not to speak*), tacere.
silently, silentio.
silver, argentuia
since, quoniam, quum. Rule 22.
    (from the time when), ex quo tempore.
sink (*trans.*), submergere.
sister, soror.
sit, sedere.
she, magnitudo.

skill, sollertia.
    (gained by experience), peritia, usus.
skin (of men), cutis.
    (of beasts), pellis.
slaughter, trucidare.
    (*nn.*), caedes.
slave, servus.
slavery, servitus.
slay, to, occidere, trucidare. *See Syn., 'kill.'*
sleep, dormire.
slight, aspernari.
slip, labi.
    let, dimittere, omittere.
slope, clivus.
slow, lentus.
small, parvus, exiguus.
    so, tantulus.
smile, risus.
    to, subrIdere. snow, nix.
so (with *adv.* and *adj.*), tam. **Voc. 6.**
    (in such a way), ita.
    (to such an extent), adeo.
    great, tantus.
    many, tot.
    much (*adv.*), tantopera, tantum.
    often, toties.
soil (ground), solum.
soldier, miles.
    of line, legionarius.
some, nonnulli.
some days after, aliquot post diebus.
some . . . others, alii. . . alii.
sometimes, nonnunquam, interdum.
son, filius.
    of, nalus. *Ex. 87.*
song, cantus.
soon, mox, brevi (tempore).
as soon as, simulac. Rule 25.
as soon as possible, quam primum.
sorrow, dolor.
sorry, use paenitet. Voc. 128.
sound, sonus, sonitus.
sound a retreat, to, receptui canere.
south, meridies.
sow, to, serere.
Spain, Hispania.
Spaniard, Hispanus.
Spanish, Hispanicus.
spare, parcere.
Spartan, Lacedaemonius.
speak, loqui.
speaker, orator.
spear, hasta.
speech, oratio.
to make a, orationem habere.
speed, celeritas.
spend, agere.
splendid, insignis.
spoil, spolia, *n. pl.*
sports, ludi. spring, ver.
spy, speculator.
squadron, ala, turma.
staff (officers), legati.
stand, stare.
    firm, resistere, in loco perstare.
    by, adstare.
    for the consulship, consulatum petere.
standards, to advance, signa ferre.

Appendix

start, proficisci.
starvation, fames.
starve, fame perire.
state, civitas. *adj.*, publicus.
state of affairs, in this, quae quum ita sint, essent.
statue, statua.
stay, manere, morari.
steal, abripere.
stealthily, furtim.
steep, praeruptus.
still (till now), adhuc.
    (even), etiam.
sting (provoke), incitare, lacessere.
stone, lapis.
storm, tempestas.
    to, expugnare.
story, fabula.
    to tell a, narrare.
straight (*adv.*), directo.
    (make straight for), recto itmere petere.
strange, minis, mirabilis.
stranger, hospes, advena.
straw, not care a, flocci non facere.
stream, rivus.
street, via.
strength, robur, vires.
stretch out, to, extendere, porrigere.
strict, severus.
    (careful), diligens.
strike, to, percutere, ferire.
    a camp, castra movere.
    terror, injicere terrorem, *dat.*
stroke, mulcere.
strong, firmus, validus.
strongly, valide.
stubbornly, acriter.
stumble, prolabi.
stupefied, obstupefactus.
subdue, subigere, in potestatem redigere.
subject, imperio subjectus.
    to (liable to), obnoxius.
succeed, get on well, proficere.
    turn out well, prospere evenire.
success, successus.
    without, frustra, nequicquam.
    win a, rem prospere gerere.
such, tails.
such . . . as, talis . . . qualis.
suddenly, subito.
suffer, pati.
suffering, dolor.
sufferings, mala.
sufficient, satis.
to be (of supplies), suppetere.
suitable, idoneus.
suits, it, convenit.
sum, summa.
summer, aestas.
summon, arcessere.
    back, revocare.
sumptuous, lautus.
sun, sol.
sunset, soils occasus.
superior, to be, praestare.
superstition, superstitio, nimia *or* prava religio, inanis timor deorum.
supper, cena.
supply, praebere.
support (military), subsidia, *n. pl.* to, sustmere, tolerare. *See Syn.,* '*bear.*'
    (aid), adjuvare.
supreme power, summa imperil.
sure, to be, pro certo habere.
surmount, superare.
surpass, superare, praestare.
surprise, opprimere.
surrender (*trans.*), tradere, dedere. (*intr.*), se dedere.
surround, circumvenire, cingere.
survive, superesse.
surviving, superstes.
sustain (encourage), confirmare.
swear, juro.
swim, natare.
sword, gladius.
Syracusan, Syracusanus.
Syracuse, Syracusae.

T

take, capture, capere.
    away, auferre.
    from, privare.
    by storm, expugnare.
    captive, capere.
    ill, aegre ferre.
    part in, interesse.
    to flight, terga vertere.
    the place of, succedere.
    up arms, arma sumere.
    up one's position, considere.
take on board, in navem excipere. taking place, to be, pass, of agere. talent (money), talentum.
talents, ingenium.
talk, loqui. tax, vectigal.
teach, docere.
tear, lacrima.
temper, mens, animus.
temple, templum, aedes.
tempt, temptare.
ten, one in (each tenth man), decimus quisque.
tent, tabernaculum.
tenth, one, decima pars.
tenths, three, tres decimae partes.
terms, conditiones.
    on equal, aequo Marte, aequa contentione.
terrible, terribflis.
terrify, terrere.
territories, fines (*in sing*, finis = **boundary**).
terror, to inspire with, injicere terrorem, *dat.*
thank, gratias agere, *dat.*
theft, furtum.
then, tum, tune.(= **next**), deinde.
therefore, itaque.
thereupon, deinde, quo facto.
thick, densus.
thicket, virgultum.
thief, fur.
think, putare, existimare, arbitrari.
    I almost; haud scio an.
thirds, two, duae partes.
thirst, sitis.
threats, mmae.
threaten, minari. *Voc. 61.*
    (by proximity), imminere, instare.
threatening, minax.
throw, jacere.
    away, abjicere.
throw a bridge, over a river, pontem in flumine faccre.
thus, ita, sic, hoc modo.
Tiber, Tiberis.
time, tempus.
    at the same, simul.
    for a little, paulisper.
    for a long, diu.
    in, ad tempus, temperi.
    in a short, brevi (tempore).
    till that, ad id temporis.
    to waste, tempus terere.
    for some, aliquamdiu.
    now for a long, jampridem, jadudum. (*p. 201.*)
    in our, nostra aetate, his temporibus.
tinge, tinguere.
tired, defessus.
tired of, to be, piget, taedet. *Voc. 128.*
to-day, hodie.
toga, toga.
together, una.
to-morrow, cras.
too late, sero.
    little, parum, *adv.* used as noun.
    much, nimius, *adj.*, nimium; *adv.*, used as. *noun*, top.
torment, torture, cruciate.
torture, cruciatus.
touch, tangere.
towards, erga.
    evening, sub vesperum.
town, oppidum.
town, people of, oppidani.
traitor, proditor, perfidus.
transfer, transferre.
traveller, viator.
treachery, proditio.
treason (accuse of), majestatis accusare.
treasure, thesaurus.
treat, afficere.
    well, beneficio afficere.
    for, agere de.
treaty, foedus.
tree, arbor.
trench, fossa.
trial of, to make, experiri, temptare.
    to be on, reus esse.
    to put on, reum aliquem facere, nomen alicujus deferre.
tribe, trtbus.
tribune (of people), tribunus plebis.
    (of soldiers), tribunus militum.
tribute, tributum, stipendium, vectigal.
trick, dolus, ars.
triumph (precession), triumphus,
    in triumph, victor.
troop (of horse), turma.
troops, copiae.
Troy, Troja.

true, verus.
trust, credo, committo. *Voc. 6i.*
truth, to tell the, vera dicere.
try, conari.
turn, in turn, invicem, singuli.
    back, reverti.
    round (*intr.*), converti, se convertere.
two divisions, in, bipartito.
tyrant, tyrannus.

U

unaccustomed, insuetus.
unanimously, consensu (omnium).
    approved, to be, omnium consensu comprobari.
uncertain, dubius.
unconquerable, indomitus, invictus.
under arms, in armis.
undergo sentence, poenam subire.
understand, intellegere.
undertake, suscipere.
unexpected, subitus, inopinatus.
unfortunate, infelix, funestus.
union, consensus.
universe, mundus.
unjust, injustus.
unlike, dissimilis.
unmolested, incolumis.
unmoved, immotus.
unshaken, immotus.
until, dum, donec, quoad. *Rule 25.*
    (*prep.*), usque ad.
untouched, integer.
unwilling, invitus.
    to be, nolle.
unworthy, indignus.
upright, probus.
upset, evertere.
urge, hortari, admonere.
    on, urgere.
use, uti.
useful, utilis.
useless, mutilis.
utmost (**extreme**), summus.
    to do one's, id agere ut (*final*).

V

vain, in, frustra, nequicquam.
value, aestimare.
vanguard, primum agmen.
various, varius, diversus.
vengeance on, to take, ulcisci, poenas sumere de.
veteran, veteranus.
vexed, to be, aegre ferre.
victorious, to come off, evadere victor.
victory, to win a, victoriam reportare.
    vigorous, alacer.
vigour, alacritas.
village, vicus, pagus.
vine, vitus.
vineyard, vinetum.
violate, violare.
violence, vis.

virtue, virtus.
visit, to, vIsere.
voice, vox.
    with a loud, magna voce.
vow, to, jurare, se jurejurando obstringere.

W

waggon, plaustrum.
wage war, bellum gerere, bellum inferre.
wait, manere.
    for, exspectare.
wake, excitare.
wall, munis, moenia, *n. pl.*
wander, vagari, errare.
war, bellum.
    prepare for, bellum parare.
    declare, indicere.
want, inopia. *vb.*, carere, egere. *See Syn.*
warn, admonere.
warning, exemplum.
warrior, juvenis.
waste time, to, tempus terete.
watch, spectare, intueri.
    about the third, de tertia vigilia,
way (**manner**), modus.
    (**route**), via.
weak, infirmus, invalidus.
weakness (**want of energy**), infirmitas, imbecillitas (animi, consilii).
    (**of forces**, *etc.*), *use* exiguus (small).
wealth, divitiae.
weapon, telum.
wear, *passive of* induere, vestire.
weary, essus, *or use* taedet. *Voc. 182.*
weave, to, texere.
weep, lacrimare.
weigh anchor, ancoram tollere.
well, bene.
west, solis occasus, occidens.
western (**terra**) quae ad occasum solis special.
what news? quid novi?
    sort of? qualis?
when? quando.
whence? (**where from?**) unde.
whenever, quandocunque.
where? ubi, qua.
whereupon, quo facto.
whether. .. or (*double cond.*), seu ... seu, sive ... sive.
    (**double question**), utrum . . . an.
which of two? uter.
whilst, donec, quoad. *Rule 25.*
white, albus, candidus.
whither, where to? quo.
who? quis, quisnam. *adj.*, qui.
whoever, whatever, quisquis, quicumque.
whole, tutus, omnis, universus. *See Syn.*
wholly, ornnino.
why? cur, quare, quamobrem.
wide, latus.
wife, uxor.
willingly, libenter.

win (**obtain**), nancisci, adipisci.
win a victory, victoriam reportare.
wind, ventus.
wing, ala.
winter, hIems.
    quarters, hiberna (*n. pl.*).
wisdom, sapientia.
wise, sapiens, prudens.
    in no, haudquaquam.
wiser than to, sapientior quam qui.*Rule 18.*
wish to (**be willing**), velle.
wish not to (**be unwilling**), nolle.
withdraw, pedem referre, se recipere.
within (*prep.*), intra.
without accomplishing anything, re infecta.
withstand, resistere.
wolf, lupus.
woman, mulier.
wonder (**at**), mirari, admirari.
wonderful, mirus, mirabilis.
wood, silva.
wool, lana.
woollen, laneus.
word, verbum.
    to keep, fidem praestare.
work, labor, opus. *See Syn.*
    to, laborare.
world, orbis terrarum.
    (**universe**), mundus.
worn out, confectus.
worship (*vb.*) colere, (*nn.*) cultus.
worth, to think, aestimare. *Voc. 57.*
worthy, dignus.
would that, utinam. *See Voc. 254.*
wound, vulnus.
    deadly, mortale vulnus.
    to, vulnerare.
wounded, vulneratus, *adj.*, saucius.
wreck (**of ship**), frangere.
write, scribere.
wrong, to do, peccare.
    to, injuriam inferre, *dat.*
wrongfully, injuria.

Y

year, annus.
yearly (*adv.*), quotannis.
yesterday, heri.
yet (**still**), adhuc.
not yet, nondum.
yield (**produce**), ferre.
    (**give up**), dedere, *intr.*, cedere.
yoke, send under, sub jugum mittere.
young, juvenis.
younger, natu minor.
youth, juvenis, adolescens.
    (**collective**), juventus.

Z

zeal, studium.

Appendix

Answer Key

Exercise 1
1. Present
2. Imperfect
3. Imperfect
4. Present
5. Imperfect
6. Present
7. Perfect
8. Imperfect
9. Present
10. Pluperfect
11. Present
12. Pluperfect
13. Perfect
14. Imperfect
15. Present
16. Present

Exercise 2
1. Ad urbem eo ut panem emam.
2. Ad urbem ivit ne patrem videret.
3. Domum ivimus ut amicos videamus.
4. Ad Caesarem ibimus ut pacem rofemus.
5. Ne me miseris ut pacem rogem.
6. Celeriter currebamus ne caperemur.
7. Equum emi ne fessus sim.
8. Date ei gladium ne interficiatur.
9. Ad Italiam ieratis ut regis filium videretis.
10. Missi sumus ut pacem rogaremus.

Exercise 3
1. Hostes se receperunt ut pugnam vitarent.
2. Ducentos mitimus ut hostium iter impediamus.
3. Celeriter iter fecerunt ne hostes conslia (sua) cognoscerent.
4. Ad summum collem processimus ut hostium castra videremus.
5. Cum Caesare iter facit ne a nobis accusetur.
6. Laboramus ut divites fiamus.
7. Venerunt ut arma nos rogent.
8. Ne ignavum te putemus, fortiter pugna.
9. Hoc fecit ne pauer consul esset.
10. Non debemus hoc facere ut laudemur.

Exercise 4
1. Missus sum ut pacem rogarem.
2. Hoc faciam ut amicos juvem.
3. Abierunt ne videantur.
4. Abierant ne viderentur.
5. Aegros relinquemus ne impediamur.
6. Ut amicos juvemus dolorem pati volumus.
7. Ut nor juvarent (*or* nobis subvenirent) celerrime contenderant.
8. Hoc fecit ut consul fieret.
9. Se receperunt ne occiderentur.
10. Ad summum collem camus ut campum videamus.

Exercise 5
1. Ne ipse accusarer, amicum meum accusavi.
2. Bonos laudare debemus ut alios bonos faciamus.
3. Ut hostes vitetis celerrime, contendite.
4. Aegros reliquimus ne impediremur.
5. Non veni ut inimicos vitem.
6. Ut tutus sis mane in urbe.
7. Nos omnes tecum veniemus, ut tutus sis.
8. Ne veneris ut me serves.
9. Ne hostes urbem caperent totus exercitus profectus est.
10. Ne ab hostibus capiantur noli multos mittere.

Exercise 6
1. Tam fortes sunt milites ut semper hostem vincant.
2. Ita hoc fecit ut non eum laudemus.
3. Tot erant hostes ut nostri omnes timerent.
4. Tam celeriter effugit ut nemo eum capere posset.
5. Tam ferociter pugnatum est ut omnes milites occisi sint.
6. Tantum est periculum ut nullae naves servari possint.
7. Tam altum est flumen ut nemo id possit transire.
8. Toties hostes vicerunt ut nunc eos despiciant.
9. Tantus erat eorum timor ut non auderent flumen transire.
10. Tanta tempestas coorta erat ut omnes nautae timerent.

Exercise 7
1. Adeo eramus defessi ut campo maneremus.
2. Satisne estis fortes ut hostem vincatis?
3. Tam alta nix erat ut non proficiscceremur sed in castris maneremus.
4. Toties hoc dixit ut jam deffesus sim.
5. Tot erant hostes ut facile urbem ceperint.
6. Tam alta erat arbor ut ceciderit et humi jaceret.
7. Non satis fortes eramus ut in pugnam rediremus.
8. Tanta erat ejus fortitudo ut omnes eum laudarent vellentque eum sequi.
9. Tam facile hoc fecit ut non defessus sit.
10. Tales erant hae arbores ut non eas ascendere possemus.

Exercise 8
1. Ita laboremus ut omnes nos laudent.
2. Tot milites advennerant ut castra plena essent.
3. Toties mare transvimus ut tempestates non timeamus.
4. Toties me rogavit ut librum ei dederim.
5. Copiae hostium tantae sunt ut eas despicere non possimus.
6. Adeo territi sumus ut omnes fugeremus.
7. Tot homines occisi sunt ut non rursus pugnaremus.
8. Tam ignavi sunt ut in proelium redire non audeant.
9. Satis validi sumus ut te servemus.
10. Non satis validi eramus ut contra eos pugnaremus.

Exercise 9
1. Arbor tam alta erat ut caderet (*or* ceciderit).
2. Mare tantum est ut id transire non possimus.
3. Tam alta erit nix ut proficisci non possimus?
4. Nautae adeo territi sunt ut navem relinquerent (*or* reliliquerint.)
5. Tam fortis erat ut mare transiret et domum rediret (*or perf. subj.*)
6. Collis tam altus est ut eum ascendere non possimus.
7. Pueri tam ignavi erant ut eos non laudarem.
8. Tam fortis est ut laudari debeat.
9. Tanta erat virtus ejus ut omnes eum laudarent.
10. Insula talis est ut nolim eam videre.
11. Tam bene laborabant ut divites fierent et ab omnibus laudarentur.

Exercise 10
1. Venimus ut muros defendamus.
2. Tam fortis adest nemo ut solus muros ascendat.
3. Murus tam altus factus est ne quis unquam eum ascenderet.
4. Murus tam altus factus est ut nemo unquam eum posset ascendere.
5. Tam defessus sum ut non possim laborare.
6. Nuntii qui missi sunt ut pacem rogarent redierunt.
7. Leges quas Romani fecerunt tam bonae erant ut nemo eas violare vellet.
8. Loquere de me ne unquam rursus me accuset.
9. Divites pauperes juverant ne fame morerentur.
10. Adeo laesus est ut mortuus sit.

Exercise 11
1. Ut pacem rogaret missus est ne cives fame morerentur.
2. Tam celeriter nuntii advenerunt ut nemo mortuus sit.
3. Abito celeriter ne quis te videat.
4. Tam bene muros defendebamus ut hostis se reciperet neque urbem caperet.
5. Tam alta nix erat ut multi frigore morentur.
6. Celeriter proficiscere ne quis te videat.
7. Satisne fortis et ut solus proficiscaris?
8. Ne hoc feceris ne ignavus esse videaris.
9. Altam fossam fecimus ne quis eam transeat.
10. Tam alta fossa facta est ut nulli milites eam transire possent.

Exercise 12
1. Tot tela missa sunt ut nullus locus tutus esset.
2. Scutum satis magnum erat ut eum defenderet.
3. Ne quis ignavus sit hoc opus omnibus datum est.
4. Tam ignavi erant ut se reciperent neque urbem defenderent.
5. Copiae nostrae satis magnae sunt ut hostes repellant.
6. Eum interficimus ne nos laederet.
7. Tam fortis est ut hostes non timeat sed pugnas amet.
8. Hoc opus ita fecit ut omnes id laudarent.
9. Fortis esto ut te laudemus et amicum appellemus.
10. Tam celriter abiit ut nunquam rursus eum videremus.

Exercise 13
1. Tam paucos misit ut muros defendere non possemus.
2. Tam celeriter redibimus ut non debeas mortem timere.
3. Is qui audet hostes despicere satis fortis est ut eos vincat.
4. Nemo tam fortis est ut nunquam timeat.
5. Subvenimus vobis ne quid opus impediat.
6. Scutum ferebat ne ullum telum se laederet.
7. Scutum tantum ferebat ut nullum telum eum laedere posset.
8. Omnes interfecti sunt, ne ullus nuntius domum unquam rediret.
9. A tot viris accusor ut me ipsum defendere non possim.
10. Ne unquam vincaris ne timueris unquam.

Exercise 14
Miles pauper aliquando mulum ducebat auro oneratum quod ad Alexandrum Magnaum missum erat. Tam fessus erat mulus ut non diutius onus ferre posset et miles aurum ipse portare cogeretur. Sed casu ipse Alexander illium sequebatur adeoque humanitatem ejus mirabatur ut diceret "Conare, mi amice, domum aurum portare, nam do tibi omne."

Exercise 15
Celeriter hostes progressi sunt ut urbem caperent. Tam pauci milites in urbe erant ut vix muros defendere possent. Sed novae copiae progrediebantur et illi constituerunt fortiter resistere, ut hae advenirent hosteque vincerant. Tam ferox erat impetus ut muri paene caperentur; sed tandem novae copiae advenerunt et hostes se recepere. Tanata erat civium laetitia ut in templa se conferrent et dis multa dona darent.

Exercise 16
Milites, qui totum illum diem iter fecerant, tam defessi erant ut vix collem ascendere possent. Alii ut celeriter contenderent arma abjiciebant; alii adeo labore confecti erant ut amici eos portarent. Sed tanta erat eorum fortitudo ut tandem ad summum collem advenirent hostiumque castra conspicerent. hic se celabant ne ab hostibus viderentur.

Exercise 17
Toties a Caesare victi erant un nuntios ad eum mitterant et pacem peterent. Ne rursus pugnare vellent, Caesar eos obsides rogavit, quos ei dederunt. Execitus antem Gallorum tantus erat ut Caesar prope eos manere, nollet, et discederet. Ne hostes sequerentur suos celerrime duxit, et ante noctem (in) castra inierunt.

Exercise 18
Persa quidam e Persia expulsus ad urbem Athenas venit ut Cimonem videret. Multum aurum et argentum attulit ut donis Cimonem amicum faceret. Roganti Cimoni "Affersne hanc pecuniam ut amicitiam meam emas?" respondit Persa: "Volo te amicum facere." "Aufer," inquit Cimon, "pecuniam ne te inimicum existimem, amicitia enim neque vendi neque emi potest."

Exercise 19
Pyrrhus, rex Graecus, pecuniam dedit Fabricio, duci Romano, ut exercitum Romanum proderet. Nullum autem donum tentum erat ut Fabricium temptaret. Graecus quidam ad castra Romana venit ut donum acciperet et tune (or dono accepto) regem interficeret. Sed tam probus erat Fabricius ut hominem regi redderet ut ab eo puniretur.

Exercise 20
1. Speare facilius est quam credere.
2. Qui imperare volunt ei discere debent parere.
3. Bonus imperator esse putabatur.
4. Omnium militum est vello pro patria mori.
5. Desine ignavus esse et disce laborare.
6. Constituimus amicis subvenire.
7. Hi non solent pugnare.
8. Verine esse amici tibi videbantur?
9. Dux constituit in colle castra ponere.
10. mentiri non audebant.
11. Nonne coacti estis domum relinquere?
12. Non sinunt nos in urbe manere.

Exercise 21
1. Bonorum civium est conari pauperibus succurrere.
2. Discere facilius est quam docere.
3. Si milites iter facere nolunt, punientur.
4. Sibi soli vult prodesse.
5. Barbari dicuntur fortissimi esse.
6. Constituerunt hostem in urbem sequi.
7. Jucundum est eos juvare qui se juvare possunt.
8. Omnes mentiri turpe debent putare.
9. Alii imperare solent, alii parere.
10. Ii qui aliis imperare solent discere debent parero.
11. Stultum putant pro patria mori.
12. Omnes debent eos qui sapientes esse videntur laudare.

Exercise 22
1. Celerius quam nunc possum discere solebam.
2. Queri inutile est.
3. Nunquam desinit de amicis queri.
4. In campo manere constituimus.
5. Fortissimus esse mihi visus est.
6. Regere difficilius est quam regi.
7. Si alios juvare conamur, illi nos juvare volunt.
8. Ego manere malo, tu discedere.
9. Constituerunt laborare ne punirentur.
10. Domum cum amicis ire solebant.
11. Coacti sunt se recipere.

Exercise 23
1. Non debes vir esse cupere.
2. Dux contra hostes proficisci constituit.
3. Dicere facilius est quam persuadere.
4. Nunquam desinere debes discere.
5. Si discere cupimus magistros semper habere possumus.
6. Amicos non juvare idem est atque eos laedere.
7. Puni eum se discere nonvult.
8. Urbem defendere constituimus.
9. Multa emere coacti sumus quae utilia esse non videntur.
10. Me invitum loqui cogis.

Exercise 24
1. Victo exercitu dux fugit.
2. Regulus hosti traditus interfectus est.
3. Victis hostibus dux domum rediit.
4. Civibus arcessitis haec dixit.
5. Capti milites arma tradidere.
6. Copias collectas in hostes duxit.
7. Galli armis abjectis ab Romanis capti sunt.
8. Captum nuntium interfecerunt.
9. Fratre occiso in silvas fugit.
10. Hostes nuntios captos interfecerunt.

Exercise 25
1. Rex factus civitati prodesse conabatur.
2. Regibus exactis consules creati sunt.
3. Milites, armis abjectis, e proelio effugerunt.
4. Caesar Gallis victis obsides imperavit.
5. Nostri duces captos as Caesarem adduxerunt.
6. Gladio rapto hostem occidere conatus est.
7. Castra capta incendimus.
8. Hostibus victis milites domum redire volebant.
9. Captivos liberatos domum misit.
10. Galli victi pacem petierunt.

Exercise 26
1. Lapso equo captus sum.
2. Nuntius haec locutus abiit.
3. Quum ad urbis portam advenissent constiterunt.
4. Nostri decem milia passum progressi ad flumen pervenerunt.
5. Visis hostium copiis nostri se receperunt.
6. Timentibus nostris dux se recepit.
7. Quum constitissemus castra posuimus.
8. Moriturus filios convocavit.
9. Profectis hostibus nos pedem rettulimus.
10. Gallis muros adortis urbs expugnata est.

Exercise 27
1. Nostri, cum ad portas advenissent, eas aperire conati sunt.
2. Nostri portis apertis ingressi sunt.
3. Galli moenibus oppugnatis urbem expugnarunt (or viceperunt)
4. Domo mea collapsa domum ad Caium me contuli.
5. Domum ingressus Caium appelavi.
6. Nocte appropinquante castra appellavi.
7. Hieme ineunte trans (ultra) flumen nos posuimus.
8. Patre morituro domum rediit.
9. Ille, cum domi dormiisset, mane discessit.
10. Nuntius regressus hoc responsum rettulit (*or* rētulit).

Exercise 28
1. E silva egressi castra hostium vidimus.
2. Haec locuti discessimus.
3. Haec locutus e castris egressus est.
4. Capta Troja Graeci dpmum redierunt.
5. Regnate Romulo Roma urbs erat parva.
6. Juvenis interfectus est pro patria pugnans.
7. Captum nuntium hostes contenderunt.
8. Castra posita vallo munierunt.
9. Exercitu collecto in hostes contenderunt.
10. Galli, quum nobis resistere non possent, arma abjecerunt.

Exercise 29
1. Silentio facto haec dixit.
2. Mortus est dormiens.
3. Mortuo Remo Romulus solus rex factus est.
4. Magnis moenibus visis non urbem oppugnavimus.
5. Accepto supplemento hostibus resistere poteramus.
6. Consule Crasso pax erat.
7. Horatus milites eduxit.
8. Incenso oppido discessimus.
9. Fratre occiso in silvas fugit.
10. Hostibus secutis (*or* sequentibus) non constitimus.

Exercise 30
1. Illi domum regressi libenter ab amicis accepti sunt.
2. Milites ex urbe egressi ad castra redierunt.
3. Occisus est amicum servare conans.
4. Nocte appropinquante castris relictis in hostes progressi sumus.
5. Hoc (*or* quo) audito dux pedem referre constuit.
6. His dictis se ad pedes regis projecit.
7. Hic decimus annus est ab urbe condita.
8. Gallum interfectum in silva sepelivit.
9. Veris initio (*or* vere appetente) profecti in hostes contenderunt.
10. Haec dona accepta filio auo dedit.

Exercise 31
1. Illi castra munientes ab hostibus oppugnati sunt (*or* Hostes eos castra munientes adorti sunt).
2. Castra, nonnullis jam egressis, ab hostibus oppugnata sunt.
3. Hostes nonnullo e castris egressos aggressi sunt.
4. Caesare in castra ingresso milites hostium impetus fortius sustinebant.
5. Suos ita (in hunc modum) hortatus discessit.
6. Urbe prodita abierunt.
7. Exercitu in urbem reducto obsides imperavit (or poposcit).
8. Regibus expulsis Romani consules habebant.
9. Aegris in castris relictis hostem secuti sunt.
10. Hostem sequens occisus est.

Exercise 32
Victis jam hostibus dux suos in castra reduxit, quae vallo munita erant. Legatus in castris relictus de proelio non certior factus est; qui, ut exercitum procul visum exspectaret in summum vallum ascendit. Egressus (autem) appropinquantes de proelio interrogavit. Adeo tamen erant defessi ut nihil ei dicere vellent sed armis abjectis ad tabernacula se conferrent.

Exercise 33
Pane jam eso omni nos fame peribamus. Dux autem convocatis nobis panem dedit quem in sua domo celatum servaverat; tum apertis portis et ipse et milites per hostium castra effugerunt. Sauciis solis in urbe relictis nos ipsos hostibus dedidimus; qui multo auro argentoque ex urbe ablato brevi nos reliquerunt.

Exercise 34
Hostibus conspectis Galli flumen transierunt et ponte rescisso Caesaris adventum exspectabant. Hic statim pugnare noluit cum sui defessi essent (or suis) defessis). Itaque, cum in colles contendisset, castris positis, contra hostes egressos castris et frumentum petentes descendit. Quibus victis captos vendidit, et ponte refecto ad urbem rediit.

Exercise 35
Explorator ad summum collem regressus hostes gradatim trans campum progedientes conspexit. Quod, cum ad castra venisset, imperatori nuntiavit. Castris igitiur statim motis ultra flumen profecti sumus. Ponte rescisso, ne hostes nos sequerentur, totum diem iter per silvas fecimus, et nocte appropinquante (*or* sub noctem) ad urbem Spoletium appropinquavimus. Hic commeatu collecto nos defendere constituimus; moenia enim et portae urbis a Romanis facta validissima erant.

Exercise 36
1. Ruri (*or* -e) Domi. Ex Asia. Athenis, Aestate. Nocte *or* noctu. Totam noctem.
2. Omnes copias ad Labienum in castra misit.
3. Augustus Nolae mortuus est septuaginta annos natus.
4. Cicero consul fuerat paucis ante annis.
5. Proxima aestate rus ibo.
6. Decem annos domi tuae (apud te) manebam.
7. Tribus diebus Athenas advenies.
8. Hieme Syracusae me contuli. Nix duos pedes alta erat.
9. Tribus abhinc mensibus Carthagini meum amicum vidi.
10. Nix ruri altior erat quam in urbe.

Exercise 37
1. Nova navis quinquaginta longa est.
2. Messanae. Carthagini (*or* -e). Sagunti. In Sicilia. Florentia, Pisas.
3. Aut Athenis aut Corinthi tres annos manebimus.
4. Eo die quo pugnatum est.
5. Novem post annis nocte domum regressus sum.
6. Novem diebus Carthaginem redibo.
7. Nonne vis in Italiam abire ut amicos tuos visas?
8. E Sicilia profectus Brundusium se contulit, deinde in Graeciam.
9. Domi eritis?
10. Decem abhinc diebus rure in urbem regressus sum.

Exercise 38
1. Romani Cannis gravem cladem acceperunt.
2. Quinque dies exercitus progressus est.
3. Quattordecim diebus auxilium ad urbem veniet.
4. Quum iter Athenas faceret Corinthi cunctatus est.
5. Cum ex Asia Brundisium navigaret tempestate perit.
6. Rus ibo ut meum fundum videam.
7. Hannibal bellum in Italia quattordecim annos gessit.
8. Tribus post diebus a fratre interfectus est.
9. Quinto die tempestas coorta nos coegit ad portum Tarentum ire.
10. Visne Florentiam venire ut domum meam videas?
11. Ego jam undeviginti annos natus Athenas nunquam visi.
12. Hostibus nos prima luce adortis totum diem pugnabamus.

Exercise 39
1. Ex Hispania. Romam. Florentiae. Alba. In Galliam. Zamam.
2. Urbs tam pulchra erat ut in ea multos annos manerem.
3. Multis jam annis amicos non vidi.
4. Totam aestem ruri manserunt, et hieme appropinquante ad urbem redierunt.
5. Amici mei Athenis Corinthum venerunt ut me viderent.
6. Castris solis occasu relictis ad proximum oppidum uno cum comite se contulit.
7. Postridie castra septem circiter millia passum ab hostibus posuit.
8. Vespere ad flumen Alliam pervenerunt, quod undecim circiter millia passum abest Roma.
9. Hic fluvius triginta pedes latus est et decem pedes altus.
10. Illo die ad patriam rediit, ex qua quindecim annos natus profectus erat.

Exercise 40
Tribus post diebus flumen quinque et quadraginta pedes latum transiimus. Inde bona via quattor dies progressi Carthaginem advenimus. Paulisper in urbe morati, mox metu civium ea relicta in litore castra posuimus. Cibus quotidie in castra ruro apportabatur. Initio veris Uticam contendimus, quae urbs ab Romanis quinque ante annis capta erat.

Exercise 41
Multos dies in castris mansimus impetum hostium exspectantes. Noctem quidem omnem clamores cantasque audiebamus, sed interdiu neque eos vidimus neque ausi sumus exire ut exploraremus (better, ad explorandum). Castra eorum visa sunt circiter sescentos passus a nobis esse posita, et flumen (usi) effugere constituimus, Nocte igitur obscura castra relinquimus, et magna lintre parata insciis hostibus adverso flumine (or i .. adversum flumen procedere incepimus.

Exercise 42
1. Castris hostium potitus praedam militibus dedit.
2. Civis fame peribant plures quam morbo.
3. Frater meus vir infirmo corpore erat.
4. Sapiens sua sorte contentus est et officiis suis bene fungitur.
5. Nunquam aedes quam has pulchriores vidi.
6. (Qui) quum vir magna fortitudine esset mansit.
7. Hercules duodecim magna difficultate labores suscepit.
8. Ecercitus quem ille paravite multo quam noster major est.
9. Mercurio alis freto nullum nave opus erat.
10. Sagitta (quae) ab milite quam missa (erat) interfectus est.
11. Multo saepius mari quam terra bellum gerebatur.
12. Frater meus me est duobus pedibus altior.

Exercise 43
1. Eodum cibo vescamur quo milites.
2. Ille multo similior est tibi quam Caesar.
3. Solon, vir magna sapienta, leges Athenis dedit.
4. Muri, a Balbo aedificati, magna sunt altitudine.
5. Virtute magis quam muris servabimur.
6. Ex itinere plures amicos quam hostes vidimus.
7. Nulli muri altiores sunt quam Babylonia.
8. Hanc domum multo plus admiramur quam illiam.
9. Hostium copiae paullo minores sunt nostris.
10. Hostes nos crebris telis aggressi sunt.
11. Caesus est arcubus quibus milites utebantur.
12. Flumen transiimus multis pedibus Rhodano altius.
13. Urbs nostra multis partibus vestra (or quam vestra) major est.

Exercise 44
1. Scimus copias adventuras esse.
2. Dicunt regem mortuum esse.
3. Audiimus pacem factam esse.
4. Nuntiatum est hostem castra movisse.
5. Nuntii dicunt urbem captam esse.
6. Sensimus regem interfectum iri.
7. Constat cives ignavos esse.
8. Dic amico tuo me paratum esse.
9. Promisimus nos Caesari arma daturos esse.
10. Nonne seitis arma captum iri?

Exercise 45
1. Promisimus nos obsides daturos esse.
2. Nuntiatum est urbem captam esse.
3. Dicunt novas copias adesse.
4. Speramus nostros non cessuros esse.
5. Constat Gallos bonos esse milites.
6. Nuntiatur magnam cladem a nostris acceptam esse.
7. Nuntiatum est Caesarem Gallos vicisse.
8. Speramus Caesarem ab Arivisto capta iri.
9. Senserunt castra ab Ariovisto capta esse.
10. Nonne putasti tuos amicos venturos esse?

Exercise 46
1. Se — sua
2. Ipse.
3. Ipse.
4. Ipsi.
5. Eos ipsos.
6. Sibi.
7. Se — eos
8. Ipse — eos
9. Se — eos
10. Se — Ipsas
11. Suos (fecit certiores) - eos.
12. Se.

Exercise 47
1. Pauci sciebant muros captos esse.
2. Audiistine regis exercitum progredi?
3. Non credit nos unquam iter confecturos esse.
4. Negat nos iter confecturos esse.
5. Promitte te non me secuturum esse.
6. Spero me paucis diebus id tibi daturum esse.
7. Milites exclamabant nunquam se victos esse neque jam cessuros.
8. Simulo me ejus amicum esse.
9. Nesciebam eum te decepisse.
10. Negaverunt se de regis adventu certiores factos esse (or audiisse).
11. Minabamur nos eos aggressuros esse domum redeuntes.
12. Ferunt cives ditissimos esse.

Exercise 48
1. Ducem certiorem fecerunt obsides ab omnibus civitatibus datum iri.
2. Nostri certiores facti sunt hostem castra muniisse et impetum exspectare.
3. Nuntiatum est Gallos adesse.
4. Omnes milites affirmabant se nunquam ducem {desertos relicturos} esse.
5. Promisisti te ad me in castra venturum esse.
6. Affirmaverunt novas copias visas esse atque brevi adventuras.
7. Scio eos promisisse se ante solis occasum venturos esse.
8. Adeo erant territi ut non viderent hostes impetum facere.
9. Legati regem certiorem fecerant bellum confectum esse.
10. Simulabant se regem de clade certiorem fecisse.
11. Ne simulaveris te patre sapientiorem esse.

Exercise 49
1. Hostes dicuntur adesse.
2. Nuntiatum est hostes adesse.
3. Certior factus est legiones quam primum secuturas esse.
4. Spero me Romae te proximo anno visurum.
5. Illi cum cognossent hostem se mox aggressurum esse, se recipiebant.
6. Certiores facti de hac clade affirmarunt se pedem relaturos esse.
7. Ipsi animadvertimus nostros cedere velle.
8. Nonne sentis nos ab hostibus cinctos esse?
9. Nuntii nos certiores faciunt hostes castra biduo abhinc reliquisse.
10. Legati regem certiorem fecerunt se auxilia ei daturos esse.

Exercise 50
1. Dux sensit hostes aggressuros esse.
2. Nuntiatum est per exploratores supplementa advenire.
3. Negaverunt eum sibi praemium promissum dedisse.
4. Spero me Romae te proximo anno visurum.
5. Illi cum cognossent hostem se mox aggressurum esse, se recipiebant.
6. Certiores facti de hac clade affirmarunt se pedem relaturos esse.
7. Ipsi animadvertimus nostros cedere velle.
8. Nonne sentis nos ab hostibus cinctos esse?
9. Nuntii nos certiores faciunt hostes castra biduo abhinc reliquisse.
10. Legati regem certiorem fecerunt se auxilia ei daturos esse.

Exercise 51
Senex uxori suae his verbis querebatur: (dicebat) se in agros quotidie exire domumque vesperi regredi labore confectum: illam autem domi sedere ignavam. (Ad haec) uxor respondit se ignavam esse nolle promisitque se ipsam postero die in agros exituram esse. Vir igitur domi manebat ut cenam pararet; sed haud talium rerum peritus nihil paravit quod vesperi possent edere; et postridie dixit se laborare atque edere malle quam dormire atque esurire. Itaque ipse in agros exiit.

Exercise 52
Philippo nuntiatum est Romanos adesse. In forum igitur procurrit se proditum esse exclamans misitque alios qui thesauros in mare abjicerent, alios qui naves incenderent. Ii qui eum videbant dicunt (eum) similem fuisse furenti. De industria saltus ab suis ducibus desertos fuisse affirmabat atque se nocentes poena esse affecturum. Simul pollicebatur se multam pecuniam daturum esse pro unoquoque Romano intra regni sui fines interfecto.

Exercise 53
Certiores facti ducem Romanum tria milia militum misisse qui oppidum obsiderent, cives, quibus cibus jam deficiebat, magnopere territi sunt. Constituerunt igitur legatos in castra mittere qui pacem rogarent. (Quibus) Romani responserunt hanc datum iri traditis obsidibus; quos ante noctem dux Romanus postulavit. Sed cives se jusso parituros esse negabant: (dicebant) se mori quam talem pacem accipere negabant: (dicebant) se mori quam talem pacem accipere malle. Urbs igitur quattor menses obsidebatur; deinde Romani ut suos fines contra Suevos defenderent se receperunt.

Exercise 54
Prima luce Leonidas sensi se ab hostibus circumventum esse. Magna tamen virtute praeditus constituit proelio commisso pro patria mori. Socios igitur laudatos domum dimisit, multosque etiam Lacedaemoniorum dimittere voluit, sed omnes negabant se regem deserturos. Tandem Leonidas hostes appropinquare conspicatus, suos acie instruxit ut impetum (eorum) sustinerent. Constabat quidem inter omnes copias hostium tantas esse ut spes nulla fugae esset, sed cum multas horas fortiter pugnassent omnes ad unum occisi sunt.

Exercise 55
Romulus ad Campum Martium regressus ut exercitum recenseret, magna subito coorta tempestate, tam densa nube celatus est ut cives eum videre non possent. Nec postea ab ullo mortali visus est. Postridie autem juvenis quidam, nomine Proculus Julius, Romam ingressus rettulit Romulum sibi visum dixisse deos velle Romam caput esse orbis terrarum. Itaque Romani senserunt se debere arti militari studere bonosque milites fieri, ut omnes scirent Romulum vera locutum esse.

Exercise 56
Multi quidem amici mihi sunt, sed ex omnibus Caius mihi callidissimus esse videtur. Olim fratre Caii ob delictum accusato Caius ipse testimonium dicere coactus est. Accusatores quidem voluerunt eum lacessere ut negaret quae jam (antea) dixerat. Ille autem quum eos haec cupere sciret testimonium sine ira dixit. Tandem accusatorum quidam, "Abi," inquit, "amico, callidissimus es." Respondit Caius se velle eadem de eis dicere sed jurasse se vera locuturum.

Exercise 57
1. Quanti hunc equum aestimas?
2. Quattor denariis hunc librum emi.
3. Magnine libertatem aestimas?
4. Vili hanc domum emi quod Caius nihili aestimabat.
5. Haec domus quinque millibus sestertium mihi stetit.
6. Equum mille quingentis sestertiis vendet.
7. Fundum meum magna pecunia vendo.
8. Non flocci facio sapientiam.
9. Servus libertatem talento potest emere.
10. Hoc minoris aestimo quam illud.

Exercise 58
1. Equum eme mille ducentis quinquaginta sestertiis.
2. Hoc tanti aestimo ut (id) vendere nolim.
3. Haec domus eis maxima pecunia stetit.
4. Virtutem maximi aestimant.
5. Victoria Hannibali multis militibus stetit.
6. Quot talentis vis hunc servum vendere?
7. Quanti servum aestimas?
8. Argentum fac minoris, pluris virtutem.
9. Fundum novem millibus sestertium emit, quem jam nihili aestimat.
10. Quanto argento liberatus est?

Exercise 59
1. Scio eos nimis temporis terere.
2. Parum erat ei fiduciae.
3. Utrique vestrum est satis audaciae.
4. Hoc faciunt ne quid detrimenti respublica capiat.
5. Tria milia optimorum nostrorum perierunt.
6. Alii civium se dedere volebant, alii resistere.
7. Civitas nostra, quae aliquando orbis terrerum mixima erat, aliquid antiqui roboris etiamnunc servat.
8. Vos plerique plus virtutis quam sapientiae praestitistis.
9. Aliquid puto inesse omnibus boni.
10. Ubi gentium habitas?

Exercise 60
1. Plurimi antiquorum amicorum mortui sunt et nonnulli destiterunt esse amici.
2. Caesar maximus Romanorum semper habitus est.
3. Gallis nimis eloquentiae parum autem sapientiae est.
4. Dixerunt Helvetios gentem totius Galliae maximam esse.
5. Tanta tempestas coorta est ut major pars navium amissa sit.
6. Aliquot nostrum spem omnem amisimus.
7. Vos qui aliquid amoris habetis patriae vestrae hoc facere non debetis.
8. Ille primus in hanc partem terrae iter fecit.
9. Non existimo Crassum virum nostrae terrae (civitatis) maximum.
10. Optimas navium tuarum nobis submitte.

Exercise 61
1. Divitias mihi promisit neque ulla est ipsi pecunia.
2. Mihi satisfecit et puto me ei rursus credere posse.
3. Eis qui pugnae supererant hostis pepercit.
4. Labienus a Caesare exercitui praefectus est.
5. Is qui amicis nulla causa irascitur sibi ipsi magis quam illis nocet.
6. Hic locus non mihi videtur ad castra idoneus esse.
7. Difficile est tali morbo mederi.
8. Atticus amicus meus ex urbe mihi obviam ivit.
9. Legioni praefectus multis proeliis in Gallia intererat.
10. Equites fugientibus Gallis instabant.
11. Mille Galli se nobis objecerunt quibus vix resistebamus.
12. Caesar in Gallos bellum gerebat: sed ejus victoriae inimicis Romanis non placebant.
13. Mihi mortem minabantur; sed non illis nocueram.

Exercise 62
1. Bellum statim Gallis indicamus.
2. Tu qui legioni praefectus es, nos in hostes ducere debes.
3. Claudiamne duxit amicus tuus?

4. Regi placet tibi imperium committere.
5. Civibus bellum intulerunt.
6. Judices captivis cruciatus minati sunt.
7. Caesar multos obsides Aeduis imperavit.
8. Imperator has copias nobis submisit.
9. Quis non libertatem servituti anteponit?
10. Nolo hanc pecuniam Caio committere.
11. Labienus, qui sextae legioni praeerat, Gallorum impetum sustinuit.
12. Agriculturae multo magis quam bello student.

Exercise 63
Tanti libertatem Graeci aestimabant ut Persia resistere neque unquam cedere constituerent. Themistocles copiis Graecorum praefectus est; cujus consililio illi navibus confisi mari in Persas rem gerebant. Classis Graeca ad Salamina insulam aderat, unde plerique ducum se recipere volebant et Athenas in hostium potestate relinquere; suam enim salutem pluris quam urbem Athenas aestimabant. Tum Themistocles se Atheniensesque cum classe ducentarum navium Athenas navigaturos esse affirmavit; neque tamen ceteris potuit persuadere.

Exercise 64
Quo facto Themistocles ut et Athenas et ceteras civites Graecas servaret hoc iniit consilium. Nuntium ad regem Persarum clam misit qui Graecos jam se recepturos esse nuntiaret: (ostendit) persas magna sua classe paucas Graecorum copias facile posse circumvenire. Sunt qui dicant hoc consilio eum voluisse regi placere suamque salutem libertati patriae anteposuisse; quod tamen consilium Graecis multum profuit: Persicae enim naves se ipsas impediebant Graecique hostem fuderunt.

Exercise 65
Proelio in hoc loco cum Gallis commiso Caesar multos suorum amisit. Cum enim ad summum collem advenisset castraque coepisset munire, subito hostis adortus est. Romani qui non in acie instructi erant primum non poterant resistere et pedem referebant; deinda Caesar decima legione, quam secum habebat, auxilio illis missa tandem Gallos ad flumen depulit. Ilic tamen iterum resistebant et ut ipse Caesar affirmat fortissimo pugnabant.

Exercise 66
Rex de hac re certior factus centurionem cum centum quinquaginta militibus misit qui latrones captos ad se ducerent. Hi (autem) cum ad locum ubi latrones erant advenissent cognoverunt firma castra in silva munita aditusque omnes succis arboribus obsessos esse. Tandem vero loco expugnato capti latrones occisi sunt; sed ducis filio puero duodecim annos nato rex pepercit.

Exercise 67
Quum segetes jam maturescerent imperator per silvam contendit duce usus quem equites ceperant. Ex itinere exploratores dimsit qui castra hostium reperirent. Hi regressi eum certiorem fecerunt hostes cum feminis liberisque et magno pecorum numero castris in media palude munitis adventum ejus exspectare. Quo cognito tam celeriter progressus est ut ad castra media nocte perveniret; el tanta fuit Romanorum virtus ut pauci Germanorum incolumes effugerent.

Exercise 68
Calenus literas a Caesare accepit, qui eum certiorem fecit portus omnes et litus ab hostibus occupata esse. Quo audito naves omnes revocavit; una autem, quae jussis ejus non paruit, a Bibulo capta est. Nautae omnes a saevo imperatore interfecti sunt, qui neque viris neque pueris pepercit et speravit se saevitia bellum celerius confecturum. Calenus autem classem quadraginta navibus secutus eum Orici triduo post caedem vicit.

Exercise 69
Reges Britanniae et Germaniae bellum Philippo regi Galliae indixerunt. Pro certo enim habebant se eum victuros esse et propter navium multitudinem et quod copias Gallorum parvi aestimabant. Ille tamen eos magno proelio Bovinii vicit. Atrociter proelio commisso omnes summam virtutem praestiterunt. Animadservum est sacerdotem quendam magnum hostium numerum occidisse, clava ferrea pro telo usum. Tale delegerat telum quod negavit sacerdotem debere sanguinem hominum effendere, et hoo modo hostos vi ictus peirre.

Exercise 70
Rex Gallorum fuit ipse eques exercitus sui fortissimus, qui, equo suffosso, ipse quidem volneratus statim surrexit et iterum suos in hostes duxit. Impetum in turmam Germanorum fecerunt; inter quos fuit ipse imperator. Germani igitur, rati imperatorem captum iri, auxilio ei progressi viam fugae patefecerunt. Quo facto Philippus suis dixit se tergum modo imperatoris illo die visuros esse. Fugato autem imperatore Galli exercitum persecuti maximum ei caedem intulerunt.

Exercise 71
1. Divitibus a pauperibus invideatur.
2. Ferociter Cannis pugnatum est.
3. Rursus non tibi credetur.
4. A multis nostrum (tibi suasum est or monitus es).
5. Tres fere horas hostibus resistebatur.
6. Romae multis nocentibus ignoscitur.
7. Tibi satisfiet.
8. Mihi a majore parte persuasem est.
9. Multi te aegriores sanati sunt.
10. Num talibus apud nos favebitur.

Exercise 72
1. Num hemini creditur qui semel mentitus est?
2. Operi a talibus solum obsistitur.
3. Ne tibi ab eo persuasum sit.
4. Laborantibus Romanis subventum est.
5. Nemini consilio nocetur.
6. Non illis placebitur.
7. Exercitui ab imperatore solo imperatur.
8. Cui diviti a sapientibus invidetur?
9. Tibi a nobis suadeatur.
10. Accusaberis neque tibi parcetur.

Exercise 73
1. In silvas confugiamus.
2. Me in urbem sequere.
3. Ne conatus sis (noli conari) effugere.
4. Romam eamus neve hic maneamus.
5. Ne in urbem regrediantur.
6. Ne manseris domi neve tempestatem metueris.
7. Fac hoc ut lauderis.
8. Ne ei gladium dederis sed dato arcum et sagittas.
9. Ne axilium amicos rogemus.
10. In loco persta neve pedem retuleris.

Exercise 74
1. Aufer hoc scutum.
2. Noli equites adducere (ne ... adduxeris) sed addue pedites et sagittarios.
3. Conemur auxilium amicis ferre.
4. Da mihi libros quos te rogavi.
5. Veni ad me neve timueris.
6. Ne inimicos juvemus neve amicis noceamus.
7. Maneant ubi sunt.
8. Pauperes ne speveris.
9. Pro patria moriamur.
10. Noli hanc occasionem dimittere.

Exercise 75
1. Eum rogavi ut in vias me sequeretur.
2. Te oro eum effugere sinas.
3. Minucio imperavit ne proelium temptaret. Minucium vetuit proelium temptare.
4. Eis persuadebo ne me hic solum relinquant.
5. Caesar suos horatus erat ut in loco perstarent.
6. Te vetui illum pecuniam rogare.
7. Te admoneo ne talis viri amicitiam spernas.
8. Caesar postulavit ne Germani Rhenum transirent neve ex suis finibus excederent.
9. Galli Caesarem oraverunt ut oppido suo parceret.
10. Tam longum erat iter ut suos impedimenta in oppido relinquere juberet.

11. Ei persuasi ut libris studeat.
12. Impera ut primum agmen consistat. Primum agmen jube consistere.

Exercise 76
1. Mihi persuaserunt ut domi maneam.
2. Jube tuos te sequi.
3. Rogati sumus ut civibus subveniremus (or auxilium ferremus).
4. Imperavi tibi ne nos hic solos relinqueres.
5. Moniti sunt ne agros suos relinquerent.
6. Amicos meos admonebo ut Romam ad me veniant.
7. Puero imperavi ne equum sibi emeret.
8. Impera fratri tuo ne flumen transeat neve in oppidum veniat.
9. Primum agmen consistere jussi et supplementum exspectare.
10. Tam grave vulnus acceperat ut servum rogaret ut se interficeret.

Exercise 77
1. Suis imperavit ut pontem qui in Rhodano factus erat rescinderent. [Suos jussit ... rescindere].
2. Suis persuasit ne pedem referrent, admonuitque eos totam regionem in hostium potestate esse.
3. Caesar suis dixit sibi persuasem esse Gallos Rhenum transiisse.
4. Cicero peditatu tribus post diebus se sequi jusso cum equitibus profectus est.
5. Nostri moniti sunt ut magna (cum) diligentia progrederentur ne in incautos hostis impetum facerent.
6. Captivi Caesarem oraverunt ut sibi parceret et ad amicos se remitteret.
7. Nunquam mihi persuadebis Romanos a barbaris victum iri.
8. Tanta captivis erat constantia ut nemo eos cegere posset loqui.
9. Certiorne factus es nostros arma deponere jussos esse? [nostris ut arma deponerent imperatum esse].
10. Quo facto dimissum concilium vetuit rursus convocari [dimisso consilio imperavit ne rursus convocaretur].
11. Sciebant Caesarem se vetuisse hostem aggredi, sed absente illo arma expedire coeperant.

Exercise 78
1. Rogatus sum ut consulatum petam.
2. Vetabo eos citra flumen transire.
3. Moneo vos punitum iri.
4. Caesar legionem multis precibus hortatus est ne se hostibus proderet neve spem ultimam salutis abjiceret.
5. Vetiti sumus domos spoliare (or Nobis imperatum est ne spoliemus).
6. Nobis imperatum est ut rursus oppidum expugnare conemur.
7. A Caesare monitus sum (or mihi suasum est) ne tibi confiderem neve te mecum ducerem.
8. Nostri praemio promisso adducti sunt ut thesaurum quaererent.
9. Creditur Catilina jussisse Romam incendi.
10. Persuade ei periculosum esse montem transire.
11. Divitiacus conatus est Gallis persuadere ut fidem Caesaris sequerentur neve ab eo deficerent.

Exercise 79
Cincinnatus ultra Tiberim habitabat in parvo fundo quem suis manibus colebat. Nuntii ab senatu missi in agro sedentem eum colebat. Nuntii ab senatu missi in agro sedentem eum invenerunt, et certiorem factum ipsum dictatorem creatum esse rogaverunt ut quam primum secum proficisceretur. Quo audito ille Paciliam uxorem jussit sibi togam afferre ne patram nuntiis displiceret; qua allata dixit se velle jussis parere et statim cum iis proficisci.

Exercise 80
Rex quidam unum ex servis suis invenit dormientem manuque litteras tenetem. Legit autem litteras in quibus pueri mater filio quod ad se pecuniam mississet gratias agebat eumque orabat ut domino fideliter pareret. Litteris igitur in pueri manum cum auro repositis alium servum jussit illum excitare. Primo puer auro viso territus est; rex autem locutus bonam fortunam saepe dormientibus contingere eum jussit matri aurum reddere et dicere regem talis filii matrem magnopere laudare.

Exercise 81
Vesperi speculator ab custodibus ad portam oppidi comprehensus est; qui praesidii praefectum ductus se prostravit et lacrimans ut sibi parceret orabat: se (affirmabat) posse multis obsidentium ut ad hostes transirent esse. Praefectus autem quum negasset se hoc modo bellum gerere custodes jussit illum ad hostium castra ducere. Simul epistola ad ducem missa monuit ne rursus proditoribus uteretur: semper enim eos ut se ipsos servarent dominos velle prodere.

Exercise 82
Hoc proelio facto dux Lacedaemonius nuntium Spartam misit qui cives certiores facerat se in calamitates incidisse (et) Mindarum mortum esse (et) milites fame mori. Mox tamen Darius filium suum natu minorem ad litus misit qui stipendium nautis Lacedaemoniis praeberet. Quo facto hi tam subito Athenienses adorti sunt ut facile illis victis omnem classem caperent (or perf. subj.) Tandem Athenienses fame adducti urbe tradita socii lacedaemoniorum facti sunt.

Exercise 83
Postero die Britanni magnis itineribus progressi sunt eo consilio ut Gallos improvidos aggrederentur. Hi tamen, cum jam per exploratores cognossent Britannos progredi, in summo tumulo consederant. Cum igitur Britanni intra teli conjectum venissent sagittariique in hostes sagittas mitterent dux Gallicus suis imperavit ne tela rejicerent sed Brittanos ad imum tumulum appropinquare sinerent. Inde cum paucos (modo) passus abessent, suis imperavit ne diutius manerent sed arma expedirent. Tum signo dato Galli tanta vi impetum fecerunt ut Britanni fusi se fugae mandarent.

Exercise 84
Dux suis frustra persuadere conatus est ut se per silvam sequentur. Ostendit hostes pedem rettulisse nec quemquam se in itinere aggressurum esse. Responderunt autem noctem appropinquare et multos hostes se pone arbores celare posse, et orabant eum ut sineret se noctem in castris agere. Quod cum duci non placeret, dixit se ipsum etiam cum paucis statim progressurum, et reliquis suasit ut ad urbem redirent et dicerent amicis se contra hostes progredi noluisse.

Exercise 85
1. Oneri solum tibi ero.
2. Recepti canere fugae signo erit.
3. Haec negligentia ei dedecori fuit.
4. Bono fuit Romanis reges expellere.
5. Poena causae mortis ei erat.
6. Patris constantia tibi sit esmper exemplo.
7. Aegio mihi pecuniam auxilio misit.
8. Laudi mihi erat quod domum tutus advenisti.
9. Magno tibi dedecori hoc erit.
10. Tibi odio esse non debet.
11. Ei persuaserunt tale consilium toti exercitui exitio fore.

Exercise 86
1. Avarita magno malo est hominibus.
2. Hoc magno exemplo est virtutis.
3. Tres legiones praesidio castris reliquit.
4. Jussit me receptui canere.
5. Puto hanc cladem magno Romanis dedecori fuisee.
6. Conemur exemplo esse aliis.
7. Credo hoc consilium exitio nostro exercitui fore.
8. Odio erat omnibus bonis.
9. Laudi tibi est captivis pepercisse.
10. Haec victoria saluti fuit civitati.
11. Locus ipse magno Gallis praesidio fuit.

Exercise 87[1]
1. Patria expulsus dixit se (ab) legibus esse liberum.
2. (Ab) regibus erat ortus: non tamen ipse regno fruebatur.
3. Exsules (ex) patria excedere (or ex patria discedere) coacti sunt.
4. Regi persuasum est ut captivos vinculis liberaret.

---

1. The prepositions are inserted in brackets, where they may be used or omitted at will.

5. Non modo (ab) culpa erat liber sed etiam laude dignus.
6. Tali patre nato omnes cives libenter parebant.
7. Tam procul (ab)[2] urbe habitabat ut ne amici quidem saepe eum viderent.
8. Ne cruciatu quidem ut loquerentur servis persuaderi potuit.
9. Regibus Roma expulsis cives pleni erant laetitia (or laetitiae).
10. Saepe hominibus ipsa laude nocetur.
11. Non modo et fructu et floribus insula abundat sed ab gente etiam incolitur (ab) dis orta.

Exercise 88
1. Haec victoria nos omni metu liberavit.
2. Castra in colle non procul (ab) oppido posita sunt.
3. Etiam boni non semper culpa sunt vacui.
4. Nobil henere ortus exemplo reliquis civibus esse conatus est.
5. Non solum viri sed etiam feminae liberique patria expulsi sunt.
6. Milites jussi sunt obsidione desistere.
7. Ne salutis quidem causa procul urbe habitabo.
8. Haec terra omnibus divitiis abundat.
9. Coacti sumus non solum (ex) urbe excedere sed etiam bona omnia tradere.
10. Nos omnes eos oravimus ut captivos vinculis liberarent.
11. Hi divites erant et pecore et pecunia.
12. (Ex) urbe iratus excessit.

Exercise 89
1. Pauci numero erant milites sed magna fortitudine pugnabant.
2. Magna voce respondit se nunquam cessarum esse.
3. Certiores facti sunt hostem magno tumulta progredi.
4. Armatis quam plurimus summo furore in hostem impetum fecerunt.
5. Injuria proditionis ab inimicis accusatus sum.
6. Dixerunt se more majorum vivere solitos esse.
7. Hi proditores jure quam celerrime interfecti sunt.
8. Natu minor est fratre sed sapienta ingenioque eum superat.
9. Tu, wui natu Britannus es, pro virili parte malis legibus debes resistere.
10. Ne audiveram quidem eos nobis esse numero inferiores.
11. Pace tua eum rogabo ut domum mecum quam seapissime veniat.
12. Ne tu quidem, inquit, mihi persuadebis jure Caesarem interfectum esse.

Exercise 90
1. Athenienses proelium summo furore commiserunt.
2. Quae cum cura didicit maximi aestimat.
3. Arte non virtute superiores sunt.
4. Haec cum dolore (or magno dolore) dixit.
5. Ceteris rebus utuntur Graecis litteris.
6. Credo nobis more majorum agendum esse.
7. Pace tua servos se recipere jubebo.
8. Videtur jure punitus esse.
9. More divitum vivere vobis, qui pauperes estis, jucundum videtur.
10. Magna ira respondit inimicum suum esse mentitum.
11. Consul cum risu (or subridens) "Domum abi," inquit "neve huc rursus veneris."
12. Numero quidem hostibus inferiores sumus, sed nostri ceteros virtute superant.

Exercise 91
Mortuo Numa Tullus Hostilius rex factus est. Eo regnante bellum inter Romanos Albanosque coortum est. Quod ut sine magno detrimento conficeretur reges imperaverunt ut tres Romani contra tres Albanos pro patria pugnantes rem decernerent. Diu pugnabatur: tandem tamen duo Romanorum interfecti, omnes tres Albani vulnerati sunt. Tertius Romanus, cui nomen erat Horatius. fuga simulata Albanis ut se sequerentur persuasit. Sequentes autem sejuncti sunt conversusque Horatius singulos interfecit.

Exercise 92
Tum Eurystheus Herculi undecim laborem laborem proposuit, qui iis quos supra commemoravimus difficilior erat. Nam imperavit ut mala aurea ex Hesperidium hortis abriperet. Hae nymphae erant insigni pulchritudine quibus in terra longinqua habitantibus ab Junone mala aurea commissa erant. Haec abripere multi antea conati erant. Hortotamen, in quo mala erant, alto muro undique cincto, difficile erat factu: portam praeterea draco eui certium erant capita interdiu noctuque custodiebat.

Exercise 93
Caesar certior factus Belgas contra Romanos conjurare constituite sine mora ipse in mediam Galliam cum duabus legionibus proficisci, jussi reliquis intra paucos dies se sequi. Cujus adventu Remi, qui Galliae fines incolunt, legatos miserunt qui dicerent se velle et obsides dedere et frumento Romanos juvare. Nuntiaverunt reliquos Belgas in armis esse Germanosque cum iis conjunctos. Quo audito Caesar promisit se quam celerrime auxilio Remis adventurum esse, ut conjunctis sopiis incursionem Germanorum repellerent.

Exercise 94
Romani de tertia vigilia profecti magna diligentia procedabant; nam certiores facti erant hostem adesse. Usque ad multam noctem progressi jussi sunt castra ponere. Media nocte clamoribus undique auditis magnas hostium copias impetum facere videbant, quem ut repellerant arma quam celerrime sumpserunt. Hostes tamen quum se non potuisse nostros improvidos adoriri sentirent, signo receptui dato pedem rettulerunt.

Exercise 95
Illo tempore Ludovicus Carthaginem obsidere non potuit, quod novas copias a fratre suo Carolo Siciliae rege non acceperat. Interea et exercitus morbo affectus est quo major pars militum paucis diebus periit, et ipse eodem morbo afflictus sensit se eo moriturum esse. Sed ut virtutem militum sustineret omnibus regis officiis functus omni modo saluti militum studebat. Tandem vero, in tabernaculo manere coactus, mox mortuus est cum suis imperasset ne unquam obsidione desisterent.

Exercise 96
Multos jam menses nullo nuntio de exercitu accepto cives credere coeperunt clade accepta suos omnes perisse. Mulieres quidem quotidie ad templa ibant deosque precabantur ut viros filiosque sibi incolumes redderent. Tandem, hieme appetente, cum omnes spem abjicere coepissent, nuntius procul visus est qui ad urbem summa celeritate appropinquabat. Cives omnes obviam effusi orabant ut se sine mora certiores de exercitu facerat. Nuntius tam fessus erat itinere ut primo loqui non posset; sed tandem dixit exercitum et multas victorias reportasse et multa hostium oppida cepisse, et milites sperare se brevi cum magna praedae copia multisque captivis domum regressuros esse.

Exercise 97
Veientibus incursiones praedae causa saepe facientibus, Romani suos fines vix defendere poterant. Milites dimum vere redibant ut sererent et auctumno ut messem colligerent, quo tempore Veientes agris magnopere nocebant. Tandem Fabii patribus promiserunt se totum annum in armis fore et ipsos totum bellum suscepturos. Gratiis a senatu actis Roma egressi ad (apud) Cremeram flumen castra posuerunt. Paulisper quidem Veientes cohibebant sed tandem circumventi omnes ad unum trucidati sunt.

Exercise 98
Tertia circiter vigilia Moscova profecti sumus, ne ullus tumultus ab amicis nostris exicitaretur. Nunquam me rursus fratres meos visurum esse speravi. Dies triginta tres secundum viam nive unum pedem alta apertam progrediebamur. Nonnunquam unus e nobis delapsus ultra se movere non poterat; quem custodes haud urgebant, bene enim sciebant lupos eum praedam ante proximum diem habituros esse. Nunc eis saepe invideo qui ita in via relicti sunt, et mortem antepono malis quae mihi quotidie instant. Laborare cogor, quod minimum est malorum; dolores videre cogor feminarum quae nobiscum omnia pro libertate audebant.

---

2. Most authors, except Livy, insert the **ab** after **procul**.

Exercise 99

Ars scribendi.
Ars scribendi litteras
Parendo legibus.
Mutandis legibus.
Amicis placendi causa.
Amicos servandi causa.
Ad nocendum Gallis.
Ad vincendos Gallos.
Signum procendi.
Signum castra movendi.
Cupido divitias habendi.
Moriendo.
{ Civitatis servandae causa.
{ Civitatis juvandae causa.
Subveniendi civitati causa.
Ad regem servandum.
Ad serviendum regi.

Exercise 100

1. Juvandi causa amicos hoc fecimus.
2. Alios docendo (aliis docendis) ipsi discimus.
3. Litteras discendo (litteris discendis) lectione possumus frui.
4. Romam festinaverunt defendendi causa urbem (ad urbem defendendam).
5. Nonne cupidus es amicos servandi?
6. Studio legibus parendi Romani magni facti sunt.
7. Ars alios regendi non facile discitur.
8. Adipiscendi causa honorem (honoris) multa patimur.
9. Occasio data est pugnandi.
10. Haec bona videtur esse occasio hostes vincendi (hostium vincendorum).

Exercise 101

1. Caesar equites misit ad auxilium sociis ferendum.
2. Praefecti suos in omnes partes pabulandi causa dimiserunt.
3. Legibus parendo nos cupidos praebemus reipublicae servandae.
4. Suis signum dedit progrediendi.
5. Signum datum est signa ferendi.
6. Athenienses quosdam Delphos miserunt ad deum consulendum.
7. Placendi causa amicis patres multa turpia fecerunt.
8. Nuntios as Aeduos misit postulandi causa obsides.
9. Nulla eis relicta est potestas se (sui) recipiendi,
10. Cupidi sunt litteris studendi.

Exercise 102

1. Spe urbis capiendae adducti sunt.
2. Adductus sum ut hoc facerem militibus placendi causa.
3. Missi sumus ad auxilium petendum.
4. Missi sunt ad auxilium sociis ferendum.
5. Tempus in libris scribendis saepe teritur.
6. Parendo legibus sapienter factis urbs Roma magna est facta.
7. Cives hujus urbis leges mutandi cupidi videntur.
8. Ne hanc faculatem victoriae reportandae dimittamus.
9. Cupidus sum tibi consulendi.
10. Caesar cupidus erat obsides Gallis imperandi.

Exercise 103

1. Ne de fugiendo loquamar, solum enim resistendo vincemus.
2. Ad patriam servandam homo semper mortem obire debet.
3. Quot nostrum apti dumus exercitui imperandum?
4. Signum dedit fluminis transeundi.
5. Studio equitatus persequendi langius progressi sumus.
6. Ad discendem opus est ingenio et magna discendi cupidine.
7. Arcessiti sumus ad regem a damno defendum.
8. Magna scelerum causa est divitias habendi cupido.
9. Jussi sunt legati arcem intrare ad arma accipienda quae hostes promiserunt se tradituros esse.
10. Navium complendarum causa et statim (navem) solvendi merces magno pretio emerunt.
11. Adsunt veniae petendae causa.

Exercise 104

1. Facile dictu est, factu difficile.
2. Negant urbem facile captum iri.
3. Exite lusum.
4. Quod esu est jucundum ne semper ederis.
5. Fabula narratu est mirabilis.
6. Mitte eum statim pecuniam solutum.
7. Dux praefectos jussit aliquos pabulatum mittere.
8. Ignis est tactu periculosus.
9. Roma exierunt novam coloniam conditum.
10. Inter omnes constat urbem nunquam traditum iri.

Exercise 105

1. Aeneas (e) castris excesserant rogatum auxilium.
2. Non credo pecuniam solutum iri.
3. Non fas est facu.
4. Et mater et uxor Corialani ad eum missae sunt veniam pro urbe petitum.
5. Mox cubitum ibo.
6. Saepe turpia dictu agunt.
7. Spero milites mox domum rursus dimissum iri.
8. Fabula facilis est narratu.
9. Viros mitte repsposum.
10. Voce difficili auditu locutus est.

Exercise 106

Nostri se undique cinctos esse senserunt; neque ulla se recipiendi potestate relicta constituerunt spe hostibus terroris injiciendi summa vi impetum facere. Sciebant quidem diutius ante cunctando se in haec pericula adductos esse et jam tandem fortissime pugnando sperabant se hostem coacturos esse cedere. Itaque signo invadendi dato in eam partem aciei quae tenuissima esse videbatur magno clamore procurrerunt. Quo impetu inopinato hostes adeo perturbati sunt ut acie statim inclinata nemo invadentibus resisteret.

Exercise 107

Nuntio ad Gallium misso ad auxilium petendum. Gallicasque copias in Hiberniam invitandas et arma et pecunia juvandi causa exercitus Hibernici promissa sunt; quibus nave Gallica transportatis centum milites ut arma quae expositura erat acciperent ad oram convenerunt. Tempestate tamen duabus lintrium fractis, eas reficiendo (eis reficiendis) tempus teritur. Interim ad rebelles dispergendos turma equitum ex urbe missa est; quibus visis illi in omnes partes diffugerunt nautaeque Gallici ad salutem fuga petendam arma e nave projecere; quae ibi sunt adhuc in portu submersa.

Exercise 108

Dux Gallorum (or Gallicus) nolebat nos comminus aggredi quod milites proeli imperiti erant et putabat eos vallo tectos melius pugnaturos. Praeterea tribus ante annis sui comminus Britannis resistere non potuerant, sed in urbem deducti obstinate (or summa pertinacia) muros defenderant. Et memoria ejus temporis et studio belli ducendi adductus erat ut in loco perstaret. Tamen ut Belgis (pro) custodibus usi sumus, totum enim annum quotidie expectabamus eos a nobis defecturos esse.

Exercise 109

Athenienses sperabant exercitum Lacedaemoniorum in Boeotiam iter facturum esse, nec quidquam fecerant ad familias et bona servanda. Itaque summo metu et pavore senserunt barbaros urbis oppugnandae causa jam omnibus cum copiis progredi. Manifestum erat sex diebus Xerxem Athenis adfuturum esse, quod brevissimum visum est tempus ad populum totius urbis transferendum. Sed sciebant maximi interesse hoc efficere, et ante regis adventum tutos transtulerant omnes qui domos relinquere volebant. Alii Aeginam, alii Troezena ducti sunt; multos tamen haud adducere poterant, ut longius quam Salamina progrederentur.

Exercise 110

1. Dixitine te venturum esse?
2. Utrum tu primus advenisti an frater tuus?
3. Quali in terra habitas?
4. Num speras te eum rursus visurum esse?
5. Unde venisti? Quo tendis? Ubi constituisti habitare?
6. Nonne credis hoc detrimentum pavorem aucturum esse?
7. Quot libri tibi sunt?
8. Quoties eum vidisti? Quando exspectas eum regressurum esse?
9. Utrum has conditiones accipere constituisti annon?
10. Quantas est hostium exercitus et quis ei praeest?
11. Quod jam iniisti consilium?

Exercise 111
1. Utrum imperare facilius est an parere?
2. Vidisti-ne equum quem tuo fratri dedi?
3. Quoties ad Galliam ivisti?
4. Num me culpa dignum ducis?
5. Numte rogaverunt ut Romam ires (viseres)?
6. Quanta est domus in qua habitas?
7. Utrum horum liborum alteri anteponis?
8. Cur Britanniam Galliae anteponis?
9. Quod consilium (or quid consilii) nunc cepisti?
10. Quantas est hostium exercitus et quis ei praeest?
11. Ubi hunc equum emisti? Quo litteras misisti? Unde hae naves venerunt?

Exercise 112
1. Dic mihi cur illud feceris.
2. Non certiores facti sumus quando novae copiae adventurae sint.
3. Dubium erat num ante noctem adventuri essent.
4. Nesciebamus quo amici nostri abiissent et ubi eos reperturi essemus.
5. Incertum est num rursus eum visuri simus.
6. Non certior facus sum utrum manere an discedere deberem.
7. Dic mihi unde veneris.
8. Nescio quomodo hoc facere debeam.
9. Audiistne quod dux inierit consilium?
10. Certior factus sum quam fortiter nostri pugnassent.

Exercise 113
1. Non certior factus sum quando ille advenerit.
2. Dubium est utrum hoc facere debeamus necne.
3. Nescio num (an) vera dixerit.
4. Difficile est dicere num de industria hoc factum sit necne.
5. Non certior factus sum quomodo respondere deberem.
6. Non possum dicere quoties ut veniam rogatus sim.
7. Nemo scire videtur quantae hostium copiae fuerint.
8. Incertum erat quot milites adventuri essent.
9. Non certiores facti eramus qualis vir esset.
10. Potesne mihi dicere num jure poenas dederit?

Exercise 114
1. Nemo scit utrum hoc dixerit necne?
2. Audivistine uter consul creatus sit?
3. Nesciebant milites quid consilii dux cepisset?
4. Negavit se scire num Crassus exercitui praefectus esset.
5. Incertum est quot militibus praesit, et qua consederit.
6. Rogavimus eos qui essent, ubi habitarent, unde venissent, quo tunc irent.
7. haud possum vobis dicere quando se venturos esse promiserint.
8. Dubium est quomodo talia facere possit.
9. Nos senes intelligimus quam beati sint juvenes.
10. Nescio utrum laude an culpa digni sitis.

Exercise 115
1. Scire vult quid cras facturus sim.
2. Maximi interest utrum equites an pedites dimittere in animo habeant.
3. Nesciebamus utrum hostes nos vesperi an multa nocte nos aggressuri essent.
4. Dubium erat quid novi nintius adlaturus esset.
5. Rogemus num una cohors satis futura sit.
6. Admodum incertum erat quando domus hostes flumen transituri.
7. Dic mihi num pater tuus mortuus sit.
8. Multum interest utrum equum vili emerit necne.
9. Certior-ne factus es num ei persuasum sit ut redeat?
10. Dubium est num nos impedituturus magis quam adjuturus sit?

Exercise 116
1. Dux cognoscere conabatur quot hostes essent quidque in animo haberent.
2. Potuistine cognoscere cur hoc fecerit?
3. Nemo intellegere videbatur quo consilio tales conditiones rogarent.
4. Haud scio an nos recipere debeamus.
5. Non audierant quid rex constituisset.
6. Incertium erat ubi amici nostri essent et quando nobis obviam ituri essent.
7. Haud scio an ut discedat monitus sit.
8. Me misit ut qualis insula esset reperirem.
9. Incertum est unde profecti sint et quando ad urbem adventuri sint.

Exercise 117
1. Non potui cognoscere quo consilio id dixisset.
2. Non possumus reperire quanta sint hostium castra.
3. Non ei dixi qua via iter facturi essemus.
4. Duces non milites certiores fecerunt quid constituissent.
5. Speculatores praemissi sunt ut (qui) cognoscerent quid in castras hostium ageretur.
6. Potesne mihi dicere quot millia passuum Veii oppidum Roma absit?
7. Non facile cognoscere potuimus quot essent hostes.
8. Scis-(ne) quo hi viatores cant?
9. Haud scio an se recipere coacti sint.
10. Non potuimus cognoscere quo consilio (quamobrem), domum redissent (redirent).

Exercise 118
Dicitur vates quaedam novem libris ad Tarquinium regem Romanum allatis num vellet eos emere rogasse. Illi autem quanti vendere velit roganti cum se velle trecentis nummis respondisset, discessit, postea tamen cum sex libris regressa roganti Tarquinio ubi ceteros reliquisset respondit se ceteros quidem incendisse, hos autem velle eodem pretio ei vendere. Negavit Tarquinius rursusque illa abiit. Rursus tamen regressa cum tribus modo libris rogat num eodem pretio hos jam velit emere.

Exercise 119
Rex igitur cur toties regrederetur miratus jam patres consuluit num eos servare deberet. Illi primum rogabant quales essent libri, num vates eos ostendisset. Ad quae respondit rex eam nihil dixisse sed incensis sex de novem libris jam tres modo eodem pretio offerre. Patribus dubium esse videbatur quid agere deberent; tandem tamen suadebant ut libros emeret. Deinde illa, pecunia accepta, Romanisque ut libros diligentissime servarent admonitis abiit.

Exercise 120
De tarquinio rege narrant eum aliquando constituisse novas centurias equitibus Romanis addere. Attius augur negavit hoc fieri posse; ex quo ira commotus petit ut quid dei velint signo aliquo demonstret. Attius respondit se posse quid in animo rex haberet ei dicere; sed Tarquinius 'Dici potius mihi' inquit 'num possit fieri id quod in animo habeo (habeam).' Attius 'posse fieri' dixit; quo audito rex eum jussit cotem discindere: nam illa de re se putare. Ilaud moratus Attius, ut ferunt, novacula discidit.

Exercise 121
Proximo anno Cleon Macedonian missus est ut urbes a lacedaemoniis captas reciperet. Primo quidem Amphipolim contendit et (in) loco edito prope urbem consedit. Interea Brasidas, dux Lacedaemonius, qui qualis esset Cleon sciebat, constituit eum dolo decipere. Imperavit igitur suis ne se in muro ostenderent sed pone vallum se celarent. Interim speculatores misit ut (qui) cognoscerent quantae copiae essent Cleoni et num novae copiae venturae essent. Qui cum rettulissent exercitum hostium parvum esse neque diligenter instructum, Brasidas suos jussit portis patefactis hostes statim adoriri. Tunc Athenienses, duci non (parum) confisi se fugae mandarunt et plerique occisi sunt.

Exercise 122
Captivus ad regem adductus et ab eo rogatus ubi pecuniam celasset respondit se olim quidem divitem fuisse, jam autem pecunia omni a militibus adempta nihil sibi esse relictum. Tum rex num haec vera essent milites rogavit, qui affirmabant omnes se neque aurum ademisse neque scire quo loco id captivus servaret. Rex autem dixit se per cruciatus cogniturum quis verum diceret, sed captivus metu perculsus rogavit num rex pecunia tradita sibi parcere vellet. Quod cum rex promisisset se facturum, captivus dixit se eis quo pecuniam portasset statim monstraturum esse.

Exercise 123
Olim domum praeclari cujusdam viri me contuli, qui antea amicus mihi fuerat, ut rogarem num in re quam susceperam vellet me adjuvare. Servus quidem negavit eum domi esse, ego autem meum amicum conspicatus pro certo habui hominem mentitum esse. Aliquot post diebus cum ille domum meam mentitum esse. Aliquot post diebus cum ille domum meam venisset, ego, cui nullus erat servus, ipse portam ei patefeci. Quem cum vidissem vultu immoto clamavi, "Domi non est." Amicus autem attonitus rogavit num fuerem; ad quae respondi, "Equidem servo de te mentienti credidi, nonne tu vis mihi credere de me ipso loquenti?"

Exercise 124
faliscis mos erat liberos magistro committere ut cum eo habitarent. Gerentibus bellum Romanis cum Faliscis magister putabat si liberos obsides dederet (dedidisset) Romanis se placiturum esse; itaque insciis civibus de industria illos ad castra Romana ductos duci obtulit; qui tamen rogabat quo consilio liberos qui sibi commissi essent hostibus tradere ausus esset et grave supplicum ei minabatur: deinde liberos jussit sumptis virgis qualibus ipse magister uti soleret ad urbem illum agere.

Exercise 125
Nuntius Romam allatus est exercitum Romanum victum esse consulumque qui praeessent alterum esse interfectum, alterum in fugam se dedisse. Primum tota urbs metu et dolore erat plena: mox tamen patres ut reipublicae consulerent convocati decreverunt ut qui pugnare possunt omnes cum mulieribus liberisque in capitolium se conferrent: (affirmarunt autem) se ipsos, qui ob senectutem arma ferre non possent in urbe mansuros. Quos Galli silentio sedentes, togis laticlaviis vestitos invenerunt. Primum quidem attoniti sunt: tandem autem cum appropinquarent barbam longam senatoris Gallus quidam manu mulsit; quo ab irato Romano percusso reliqui omnes senatores interfecerunt.

Exercise 126
Solon, Atheniensium sapientissimus, Sardes quondam ivit ut Croesum viseret. Num quis ignorat quomodo illi amici facti multa inter se disseruerint? Fabula tamen digna est quae rursus narretur. Croesus enim existimabat eum felicissimum esse cui magna potentia et divitiae essent, et qui facere posset quaecunque vellet. Auro igitur argentoque omni Soloni ostensis, cum eum certiorem fecisset quot gentes regeret, rogavit quis ei mortalium beatissimus videretur. Pro certo enim habuit Solonem responsurum illum beatissimum esse qui urbem Sardes et tantum regnum regeret. Solon autem respondit duos juvenes Cliobem et Bitonem beatissimos esse.

Exercise 127
Croesus autem negavit se unquam de his audisse et Solonem qui essent rogavit. Qui respondit eos juvenes esse magna pietate, quorum mater sacerdos esset. Quae cum vellet ad templum ire, bobus qui carrum trahere solerent mortius filios eam pro bobus eo traxisse. Qua fabula Solon vult demonstrare eos qui vivant quum omnes rebus adversis obnoxii sint beatos non esse ducendos; sed illos qui mortem honestam obierint revera beatissimos esse.

Exercise 128
Me sceleris paenitebat.
Te-ne captivi miseret?
Taedet eos vitae.
Eum facti pudebat.
Decet nos hoc facere.
Te loqui oporet.
Te loqui oportuit.
Licet nobis uti armis.
Ne te facti paeniteat.
Licet tibi discedere.
Licuit tibi discedere.
Nobis placet reges exigere.
Accidit ut rex interficeretur.
Omnibus mori contingit.
Non oportet te amici tui pudere.
Deis placere tibi licuit.
Nos pugnare oportet.
Accidit ut adessem.

Exercise 129
1. Me miseret tui doloris.
2. Meae patriae me pudet.
3. Judici placebat captivos interficere.
4. Dixit se mei miserere.
5. Credo te tui sceleris paenitere.
6. Respondit se taedaere in urbe habitare.
7. Non cuivis contingit Corinthum adire.
8. Te oportet quid facias scire.
9. Te oportuit hoc tua sponte parere.
10. Liberos decet parentibus parere.
11. Ne talis facti te pudeat.

Exercise 130
1. Ne te taedeat ruri habitare.
2. Dixit nos oporttere domum relinquere.
3. Eum qui a proelio fugit (fugiat) mox ignaviae paenitet.
4. Accidit ut tunc (eo tempore) adessemus.
5. Me ejus malorum miseruit.
6. Dixit se facti pudere.
7. Non puto te illud facere oprtuisse.
8. Ne te tui erga nos benefici paeniteat.
9. Accidit ut imperator cum legatis adesset.
10. Licuit tibi ante pugnam (commissam) effugere?

Exercise 131
1. Ob mortis metum (vel) fortissimi virtutis obliviscuntur.
2. Multarum rerum inscius est quarum debet esse peritus.
3. Cura rerum alienarum difficilis est.
4. Me omnium miserebat ex pugna regredientium.
5. Peritia milites alloquendi duci Romano necessaria affert.
6. Memoria vitae praeteritae alii laetitiam, alii dolorem affert.
7. Cura tua mei me patris admonet.
8. Cupidus sum tibi gratias agendi ob benevolentiam tuam cujus nunquam obliviscar.
9. Omnium laborum quos eum postulas peritus est.
10. Pro certo habeo eum nostri absentium memorem fore.
11. Sub imperatoribus Romani honoris causa, non reipublicae administrandae causa consules facti sunt.
12. Consuetudo mea Caesaris cupidum ejus amicitiae me facit.

Exercise 132
1. Neminem vitae bene actae paenitebit.
2. Dux vobis est memor aliorum, sui immemor.
3. Viri miseremini (vos miserat) indigna patientis.
4. Accusatus est proditionis.
5. Amor patriae plus apud eum valet quam mortis timor.
6. Optimi magis studiosi sunt agendi quam loquendi.
7. Misericordia (miseritus) feminae consilio destitit.
8. Imperitus est natandi.
9. Laboris quidem imperiti erant sed spernebant periculum.
10. Spero te patriae non obliturum esse propter studium res novas videndi.
11. Caesaris erga me amicitiam maximi aestimo.
12. Hi barbari pontes aedificandi periti videntur.

Exercise 133
Quum autem aliquot dies navigassent forte navem longam conspexerunt ad se appropinquantem, quamobrem territi quidam reverti volebant, dux tamen se pudere reverti dixit: fortes enim oportere hostibus audacter se offere nec se credere fuga tantam navem vitare posse. Appropinquante tandem nave multos milites in ea vehi viderunt, quorum unus vultu superbo vestituque insigni rex esse videbatur; qui magna voce ut in suam navem conscenderent invitabat. Quo facto unde essent profecti et quamobrem domos reliquissent rogabat.

Exercise 134
Responso audito ut secum navigarent precatus, quod fortes viderentur esse milites seque tantorum malorum misereret, se in sua patria illis agros daturum pollicitus est; qui tamen se qualem in terris longinquis di sibi daturi essent fortunam velle experiri affirmavere. Ad quae rex se respondit ejus consilii paenitere nec tamen invitis ut se sequerentur diutius suasurum. Interrogavit quidem num vel pecunia vel commeatu illis opus esset: locutus se talibus rebus nullo modo indigere benigne dimisit cursumque suum tenebat.

Exercise 135
Multa nuper diligentia fabulas mirabiles quibus ab hujus regionis incolis creditur repperi et in libro conscripsi. Inter alia credunt eum qui in rivum prope oppidum fluentum vestem suam injecerit morbo totum annum carere. Cur credant rogati deum affirmant in rivo habitare: non tamen intellegunt cur talia dona ille cupiat. Credunt etiam fontem quendam qui extra urbem cooritur divitem eum facere posse qui certa nocta aestatis viserit; qua tamen omnium aestatis noctium oporteat eum visere nemo potest dicere neque unquam quequam hoc modo divitem factum repperi.

Exercise 136
Brutus vir magna fortitudine diu obsessus ubi (quando) novae copiae adventurae essent volebat cognoscere. Duas igitur naves, quibus legatum praefecit, dimisit eo consilio ut ducem Romanum quanto in periculo esset certiorem facerent. Fractis tamen navibus nuntii ab hostibus circumventi sunt: qui quum ex legato qui essent quaque ex regione venissent quarerent Romanosque esse illos cognossent et salutem daturos et se ipsos duces fore promiserunt: ductos tamen duo modo milia et circumventos interfecerunt. Qua re per exploratores cognita dux Romanus constituit et ipse haud diutius cunctari et quam celerrime duas legiones praemittere.

Exercise 137
Cum Gallorum Amstelodamum obsideret, cives perterriti consilio convocato deliberabant quid agendum esset (agere deberent). Plerique negarunt spem ullam esse hostibus diutius resistendi, et suadebant ut claves urbis regi traderentur. Animadverterunt autem unum e sensibus formire neque sententiam tulisse; quem igitur somno excitatum rogarunt quid de clavibus tradendis moneret. At ille rogavit num rex eas postulasset, et cum negassent eum hoc fecisse, "Exspectemus saltem," inquit, "dum ei placeat eas poscere" — Quae verba urbem servasse dicuntur.

Exercise 138
Miles autem hoc modo agnitus mox a turba civium cintus est rogantiur, quis esset, unde venisset, quo iret, qua de causa in urbe esset, quare per portas non ingressus murum noctu scandisset. Qui haudquaquam territus respondit se neque tot rebus simul respondere posse neque privatorum esse cognoscere aut quod nomen sibi esset aut quo consilio venisset. Tunc multa vi ad magistratus tractus rursus rogabatur quo consilio haec egisset. Qui cum respondere nollet, deliberabant utrum eum retinere an liberare deberent, sed miles quidam aggressus simulavit se captivum agnoscere et nonne in castris conjuratorum visus esset rogavit.

Exercise 139
Puer quidam et soror ejus quondam ab incolis vici prope aditum speluncae inventi sunt. Ili forma quidem ceteris similes erant sed cutis colore dissimiles quae viridi erat colore tincta. Nemo potuit ea quae dicebant intellegere, et domum ad equitem quedam adducti vim lacrimarum effundebant. Cibum autem oblatum tangere nolebant, quamquam manifestum erat eos magna fame cruciari. Tandem fabis domum latis, petierunt signis ut hae sibi darentur; quas cum magno gaudio edissent diu nullum alium cibum edere voluerunt. Puer tamen qui semper languidus erat et tristis, brevi mortuus est.

Exercise 140
Puella tamen ad omne genus cibi assuefacta tandem illum viridem colorem amisit. Multos quidem annos cum equite habitavit ad quem illa et frater ejus primo adducti erant. Saepe de patria rogata affirmabat incolas viridi esse erant. Saepe de patria rogata affirmabat incolas viridi esse colore neque solem ullum videre sed tali luce frui qualem nos post solis occasum videmus (videamus). Rogata quomodo in hanc terram venisset, respondit se fratremque greges sequentes ad speluncam venisse unde sonum jucundum tintinnabulorum audirent. Quo adductos diu per speluncam vagatos tandem ad ostium pervenisse. Yunc (ex ea) egressos nimio solis calore stupefactos ab incolis vici captos esse.

Exercise 141
1. Caesar exploratores dimisit qui ubi supplementum sit cognoscant.
2. Hi adsunt qui dent responsum.
3. Partem exercitus Hannibal reliquit quae Tarentum obsideret.
4. Quo celerius contenderent cibum secum portabant.
5. Pauci mihi sunt quos mittam.
6. Mitte equites quo facilius hostem cohibeamus.
7. Quo sapientor fias libros lege multos.
8. Promittit se libros quos legam missurum esse.

Exercise 142
1. Quo brevior esset fuga aciem prope castra instruxit.
2. Nemo est cui credere possim.
3. Postero die quidam missi sunt qui Ciceronem interfecerent.
4. Custodes in viis sunt qui turbam cohibeant.
5. Rus ivit quo tranquillius viveret.
6. Quo meliorem facias filium tuum debes ipse melius vivere.
7. Caesar delectos in silvis disposuit qui in hostes pugnantes inciderent.
8. Labienum reliquit qui castris praeesset.

Exercise 143
1. Non is est qui de inimici morte gaudeat.
2. Dignus est qui interficiatur.
3. Ea consul facit quae non reipublicae prosint.
4. Fortemne satis militem qui mecum veniat reperiam?
5. Erant qui magnas pecunias Caesari dare vellent.
6. Nemo est qui tantam arrogantiam ferat.
7. Num dignus est qui tantum praemium accipat?
8. Num is est cui pecunia credatur?

Exercise 144
1. Non is sum qui fracti meo argentum recusem.
2. Mitte copias quae mihi subvenire possint.
3. Sunt qui eum furti accusent.
4. Non digni eramus qui in vincula conjiceremur.
5. Non facile reperiuntur qui dolorem patienter (acquo animo) ferant.
6. Num is est qui domum meam admittatur?
7. Erant qui celerius currere possent.
8. Naves non aptae sunt quae deucantur.

Exercise 145
1. Nemo repertus est qui pro illo mortem obiret.
2. Non is sum qui periculum detrectem.
3. Sacerdotes quinque Delphos miserunt qui deum consulerent.
4. Talia dicam qualia ei persuadeant.
5. Quinque homines hac nocte castra intraverunt qui urbem traditum iri nuntient.
6. Caesar quo Romam celerius adveniret impedimenta Ravennae reliquit.
7. Dignus est qui Romanus fiat.
8. Sunt qui non divitias cupiant.
9. Decimam legionem eduxit quae in hostem a tergo invaderet.
10. Iloc modo aciem instruxit quo majores copiae esse viderentur.

Exercise 146
1. Ab imperatore missi sunt qui locum castris idoneum deligerent.
2. Quo facilius flumen transiret imperavit ut pons fieret.
3. Non is erat qui milites temere in periculum adduceret.

4. Sub vesperum recentes advenerunt qui confectis vulneribus succederent.
5. Sunt qui putent nos oportere castris motis ad locum editum (superiorem) procedere.
6. Illi qui patriam servitute liberent digni sunt qui ab omnibus laudentur.
7. Tumulus factus est et scalae actae quo facilius moenia ascenderemus.
8. Non is sum, inquit qui velim periculum vitare.
9. Speculatores missi sunt qui comperirent num hostium copiae progederentur.

Exercise 147

Hannibal cum exercitu peditum quinquaginta milium, equitum novem milium primum Pyrenaeos nulla difficultate transcendit neque erat exercitus Romanus qui progedienti obstaret. Ad Rhodanum etiam advenit, neque hic quidem se offerebant Romani: Galli tmaen transitum prohibere parati sunt, Scipioque dux Romanus Massiliam advenerat: quibus rebus cognitis Hannibal constituit in flumine transeundo non cunctari. Eas igitur lintres quae paratae essent jussit ad se colligi arboreque succidi quibus plures aedificarentur. Duos intra dies lintres sunt paratae: sed Galli in altera ripa ut egressum prohiberent instructi sunt. Itaque magnum numerum suorum Hannibal in adversum flumen aliquot milia missum jussit transire Gallosque signo dato a tergo adoriri.

Exercise 148

Poeni quum ad summos montes pervenissent castra in magna planitie posuerunt ubi aliquot dies se reficere possent. Sed locus fuit frigidus et desertus neque is ubi diu manere possent, praesertim cum hicmus appropinquaret. Multi quidem inopia ac laboribus confecti ex itinere relicti erant, et eis qui ex Hispania et africa venissent frigus terrible visum est. Hannibal autem suis animo confirmatis ostendit viam inde deorsum ducere et mox ad terram ducturam ubi amicos inventuri essent (invenirent). "Illic," inquit, "patet Italia; illa est via quae ducit Romam."

Exercise 149
1. Nobis statim proficiscendum; castraque vobis custodienda sunt.
2. Omnia Caesari simul agenda erant.
3. Inter omnes constat legibus parendum esse.
4. Ab omnibus bonis civibus legibus parendem est.
5. Crasso imperatum est ut classem reficiendam curaret.
6. Pontem in Rheno aedificandum suscepimus.
7. Non hoc agendum fuit.
8. Cupidus nos juvandi non nocendum est.
9. Caesar castra munienda curavit.
10. Non nobis proditionis accusandi sunt.

Exercise 150
1. Haud diutius hic nobis manendum est.
2. Alterum pontem aedificandum curent.
3. Puto locum ad castra nobis deligendum esse.
4. Quindecim diebus illis regrediendum erit.
5. Statim proficiscendum est et usque ad vesperum faciendum iter.
6. Caesar ostendit obsides omnibus civitatibus tradendos esse.
7. Reipublicae a nobis consulendum est.
8. Putasne hoc Crasso agendum fuisse?"
9. Promisit se reficiendam classem curaturum esse.
10. Hic nobis novae copiae exspectandae sunt.

Exercise 151
1. Pauperes nobis adjuvandi sunt.
2. Dux constituit diutius sibi non esse cunctandum.
3. Duno legiones nobis praemittendae erunt.
4. Caesar Labieno naves reficiendas mandavit.
5. Diu eis ubi erant manedum fuit.
6. Hiberna eis vere relinquenda erant.
7. Hoc ei non dicendum fuit.
8. Promiserunt se delectum habendum curaturos.
9. Nescierunt ubi castra sibi ponenda essent.
10. Sociis a nobis subveniendum est.

Exercise 152
1. Mare nobis transeundum est.
2. Nobis diutius (nimis diu) non est cunctandum.
3. Milites jussi sunt curare castra munienda.
4. Crasso in Asiam non eundum fuit.
5. Legibus a nobis omnibus parendum est.
6. Patria nobis relinquenda erit.
7. Delectus nobis habendus mandatus est.
8. Socii eis adjuvandi erant.
9. Hannibal castra in summo monte ponenda curavit.
10. Illi nobis proditionis non accusandi sunt.

Exercise 153

Bellum gerentibus Romanis cum Samnitibus Postumius dux Romanus per angustos saltus exercitum in Samnium ducere conabatur. Medio in saltu est campus latus et apertus, quo tamen ut exercitus adveniat intrandae sun angustiae, posteaque aut eadem via regrediendum est aut arctioibus angustiis in Samnium evadendum. Ad apertum campum Romani progressi contique ultra progredi evadere non poterant: nam interea Samnites utrasque angustias obsederant. Romanis igitur ut effugerent montes transcendendi erant; quod facere saepe nequicquam conatis castra munienda erant eodem loco.

Exercise 154

Postumius igitur legatos misit qui conditiones qequas peterent. Pontius Samnis respondit obsides dandos esse et arma tradenda, ipsosque sub jugum mittendos. Tandem tam turpibus conditionibus acceptis discedere sinuntur. Sed ut domum pervenirent per fines sociorum Campanorum eundum fuit qui etiam cibum et vestitum rogandi erant. Senatus autem Romanus noluit foedus accipere et consulem ipsum remisit qui se Samnitibus traderet.

Exercise 155
1. Hoc facere timeo.
2. Metuo ne hoc faciat.
3. Timebam ne non hoc faceres.
4. Vereor ne mortuus sit.
5. Verebar ne non me vidisset.
6. Ne timueris redire.
7. Num times loqui?
8. Timebamus ne videremur?
9. Metuo ne nos videant.
10. Vereor ne non (ut) nos videant.
11. Timebant vera non dicere.
12. Vereor ne mentitus sit.

Exercise 156
1 Timentibus illis sequi solus abii.
2. Milites timebant ne hostes se circumvenirent.
3. Nondum munitis castris timebant ne barbari se aggrederentur (or a barbaris oppugnarentur).
4. Quum mori non timeret, volebat tamen quam diutissime vivere.
5. Veriti ne non (ut) naves cursum tenere possent in portum regressi sunt.
6. Timebat ne consilia sua ab hostibus cognita essent.
7. Veriti ultra progredi milia (milibus) passum decem ab urbe consederunt.
8. Quum muri urbi essent centem pedes, alti, cives tamen ne non oppugnationi possent resistere timebant.
9. Timebant ne non possent profectionem hostes celare.
10. Ventus ne ab suis proderetur se interficere constuit.
11. Adeo patriam diligebant ut pro ea mori non timerent.
12. Timeo ne captivi effugerint.

Exercise 157
1. Non debes timere vera dicere.
2. Timeo ne non vera dixeris.
3. Nostri metuebant ne ab hostibus cingerentur.
4. Plerique metuunt mori.
5. Timeo ne non signa sequi possint.
6. Dux timuit signum dare progrediendi.

7. Nonne metuisti ne milites filium tuum captum interficerent?
8. Veriti ne caperentur in silvas confugerunt.
9. Dux suis imperavit ne flumen transire timerent.
10. Veriti sumus ne urbs capta esset.
11. Timui ne non ad castra ante solis occasum perveniremus.
12. Prima luce profecti sunt, veriti ne hostes se consequerentur.

Exercise 158
Nuntitato Caesaris adventu Arverni veriti ne in suos fines invaderet pontes in flumine factos constituerunt rescindere. Caesar transire vehementer cupiebat quam celerrime nam timebat ne flumine totam aestatem arceretur. Quod tali dolo effecit. Praemissa copiarum majore parte hostibusque quod universum esse exercitum existimabant, hos secutis, Caesar paucos quibuscum ipse manserat jussit quam celerrime pontium unum reficere, veritus quidem ne non ante hostium reditum opus conficerent.

Exercise 159
Agricola quidam moriturus filius arcessitis dixit finem vitae adesse, "Filii," inquit, "non metuo ne jussa mea negligatis neve mei mortui obliviscamini. Itaque vos jubeo diligenter in meo vineto laborare, quo facto magnas divitias reperietis, "Sene autem mortuo filii, verborum ejus memores, solum summa vi effodiebant sperantes (cum sperarent) se maganas divitias ibi celatas reperturos esse. Mox tamen veriti sunt ne decepti essent, nam neque aurum neque argentum reperire poterant, et primo eos laboris paemtuit. Tandem autem cognoverunt quid pater in animo habuisset, namque solo diligenter effodiendo)effesso) id tam fertile fecerunt ut egregras vites ederet.

Exercise 160
1. Quum de hac re certior factus sis, omnibus nuntianda est.
2. Quae quum ita sint ab urbe discedam.
3. Quae quum ita essent, nemo volebat manere.
4. Gaudeo quod venire constituisti (*or* te venire constituisse).
5. Affirmabant se hoc fecisse quod reipublicae prodesse videretur.
6. Certiores facti sumus eos, quod regi displicuissent, capitis damnatos esse.
7. Quum miles fieri nolit ignavus existamandus est.
8. Quum nox appetat (appropinquet) omnes ad tabernacula discedant.
9. Quae quum ita essent nostra intererat (e) concilio excedere.
10. Quod tu exercitusque tuti estis, gaudeo.
11. Simulabant se quod tuti estsemus, gaudere.
12. Tui maxime me miseret quod nemo te amare videtur.

Exercise 161
1. Servus culpatus est quod serius (seto) venisset.
2. Laude dignus es quod patriae bene servisti.
3. Quae quum ita essent dux receptur canere constituit.
4. Capitis damnati sunt quod urbem incendissent.
5. Gaudeo quod tales capitis damnati sunt.
6. Dixit eos supplico afficiendos esse quod ex acrie fugissent.
7. Majestatis accusati sunt quod mortem regi minati essent.
8. Quae cum ita sint nobis statim progrediendum est.
9. Qui quum se fortes milites praebuerint praemium promissum accipiant.
10. Nostri amici affirmarunt se gaudere quod tuto (incolumes) advenissemus.
11. Quae quum ita sint vobis in exsilio manendum est.
12. Rei facti sunt quod contra civitatem conjurassent.

Exercise 162
Triumphus Camilli, captis Veus, quod nimis superbiae praestaret. Romains displicebat. Nam alia inter crimna accusates est quod patem se dis faceret, curru enim tracto albis equis quattor, qui Jovi Solique sunt sacri, urbem intraverat. Milites etiam iratos fecit quia partem spoliorum, quam Apollini dedicaret, jussit reddi. Postremo autem accusatus quod thesauros quosdam, qui plebi essent donandi, celasset, in exsilium exactus est.

Exercise 163
Hiberna quidam rei facti quod seditionem in patria sua fecissent negarunt se quicquam contra jus gentium fecisse quod (quum) Britannis suos servitute oppresos tenetibus ipsi tantum conarentur eam dominatu injusto liberate. Quae quum ita essent negarunt se ullo modo facti paenitere, praesertum quod demonstrassent haud facile esse Hibernos regere invitos. Quae verba multus qui aderant displicuerunt, sed quoriam captivi juvenes erant neque antea ullus sceleris erant accusati, eis parsum est.

Exercise 164
Delphus autem quum quanto essent in periculo cognossent magna cepit formido; qua inductis de thesaurus sacris oraculo consulto quaerebant utrum in terra eos abdere oporteret an in aliam civitatem transportate. Quabus deus respondit theasauros integros esse relinquendos: sine auxilio se sua servare posse. Itaque Delphi, accepto hoc responso, quomodo se ipsos servarent deliberabant Primum mulieres liberosque trans sinum in Achaiam miserunt: deinde plerique virum quum in summum Parnassum ascendissent bona in spelunca abdiderunt. Hoc modo Delphi omnes praeter vatem virosque sexaginta (ex) urbe excesserunt.

Exercise 165
Magna pestilentia in urbe coorta multisque et divitum et pauperum amissis, multitudo corum qui superarent, quibus nec mulieres nec liberi essent, relicta urbe constituerant navem solvere et novas domos reperire. Eorum quos relinquebant miserbantur, quibus tamen sciebant non se posse succurrere. itaque noctu nave soluta secundum nacti ventum multa ab urbe milia passum ante primam lucem aberant. Nesciebant quidem quas regiones tenderent: id solum constitutum ut ad occidentem navigarent.

Exercise 166
Alter exercitus jamdudum alterum spectabat. Tandem senex quidam progressus rogavit ut juvenis ex utroque exercitu deligeretur qui pro civibus suis pugnaret. T. manlius igitur ex altero exercitu et pater ejus Q. manlius ex altero processit; neuter autem sciebat quis alter esset. Accidit enim ut patre absente natus T. Manlius a Scythis abriperetur. Primo quidem superabat filius; pater enim hastam tanta vi conjecit ut lapsus ipse humum ceciderit. Sed celeriter ortus filio vulnus funestum inflixit; ille enim hostem proruentem nomen suum clamare audiverat, et quum sciret eum patrem esse suum ne manum quidem ad se defendendum movit.

Exercise 167
Exercitus Octaviano numero quidem multo major erat qual L. Antonio, sed tanta negligentia illa nocte consedit (locum cepit) ut paene ab hostibus oppressus deleretur. Casu enim duces quibus L. Antonius confidebat eum certiorem non fecerant fossam viginti quinque pedes latam esse quae castra regis a fronte defenderet. Itaque rebelles cum jam proruerent ad vallum oppugnandum hac fossa impediditi sunt. Duces suos jusserunt plaustra eo (in eam) conjicere, sed custodibus alterius exercitus jam excitatis, ballistae saxa in eos ingerere coeperunt. Antonius quidem dicitur, suos hortatus ut fortiter pugnarent et in loco locum ubi tutus esset reperiret.

Exercise 168
1. Non est dubium quin de industria hoc fecerit.
2. Negare non poteram quin nocens essem.
3. Nemo est quin saepe peccet.
4. Ne prohibueris qun proficiscantur.
5. Non possum facere quin ad te scribam.
6. Non dubitabamus quin a nobis ille staret.
7. Non fieri potest ut nocens effugiat.
8. Haud multum abfuit quin fame perirem.
9. Non dubitandum est quin fidem praestaturus sit.
10. Nemo in urbe erat quin aut filium aut fratrem in exercitu haberet.

Exercise 169
1. Non negant quin pacem aequis conditionibus cupiant.
2. Nemo fuit nobili genere (ortus) quin Catilinam contemneret.
3. Haud multum (miniem) abfuit quin urbem vi et armis caperent.
4. Non dubito quin jam consul sit.
5. No answer given in original answer key

6. Noli prohibere (impedire) quin Roma discedat.
7. Non fieri potest quin illi credamus.
8. Dubitare non possumus quin hoc plebi (volgo) placeat.
9. Nulla navis est quin tempestate laesa sit.
10. Facere non potui quin te consulerem.

Exercise 170
1. Per te stetit quominus ecercitus deleretur.
2. Quis te impediebant quominus nobis subvenires?
3. Nive impediti sunt quominus Alpes transirent.
4. Te classem prohibere oportuit navem solvere.
5. Milites deterrere non poteramus quominus (or quin) in hostem impetum facerent.
6. Per nos stetit quominus domus incenderetur.
7. Prohibere eos debemus nos aggredi.
8. Milites non poterant prohiberi in flumen procurrere.
9. Per me credo stetisse quominus vinceremur.
10. Vix iis obstare poteram quominus (or quin) naves incenderent.
11. Recusaverunt quominus urbem relinquerent.

Exercise 171
1. Per Horatium stetit quominus Roma caperetur.
2. Milites prohibendi sunt urbem intrare.
3. Dux suos vix prohibere potuit quominus (or quin) domos incenderent (or domos incendere).
4. Ne timor te deterreat quominus (or quin) vera dicas.
5. Debes vetare classem solvere.
6. Nonne per regam nostrum stetit quominus periremus?
7. Tribuni prohibere poterant quominus leges juberentur.
8. Per legatos stetit quominus pax fieret.
9. Urbe hostibus tradita prohibuimus quominus cives fame morerentur.
10. Illos minis prohibuisti vera dicere.
11. Nonne recusavisti quominus cibum (rem frumentariam) exercitui praebere?

Exercise 172
1. Nemo est quin sciat hoc fieri oportere.
2. Prohibendi sunt hostes flumen transire.
3. Haud dubium est quin manere debuerint.
4. Loqui dubitabant; nec mihi dubium erat quin irati essent.
5. Haud multum abfuit quin urbs deleretur.
6. Nemo adest quin te mentiri sciat.
7. Per Themistoclem stetit quominus Athenienses Salamina relinquerent.
8. Nemo est quin pro patria pugnasse sciat.
9. Ne hos prohibere conatus sis effugere.
10. Non est dubium quin nos prodiderint.
11. Non possum facere quin nos servatum iri sperem.

Exercise 173
1. Fieri non potest quin haec audiveris.
2. Non est dubium (dubitandum) quin vixerint fortes ante Agamemnona.
3. Quis tam turpis est quin patriam amet?
4. Per deos stat omnibus fame mortui simus.
5. Ne recusaveris eos adjuvare (quominus adjuves) qui civitati profuerint.
6. Non dubitavi quin me decipere vellent.
7. Nostri vix prohiberi poterant quominus statim oppugnarent.
8. Facile impedivi quominus servi haec Caio nuntiarent.
9. Non est dubium quin hic nuntius magnum civibus pavorem sit injecturus.
10. Fieri non potest ut civitatem servemus.

Exercise 174
Nemo est quin audiret quam fortiter pontem quo hostes Romanorum se urbem intraturos sperarent Horatious Cocles defenderit. Primum cum comitibus duobus, deinde solus omnem in is factum impetum sustinens hostes prohibebat transire: neque dubium est quin saluti reipublicae Romanae fuerit. Identidem aggressi hostes semper magna strage sunt repulsi. Tandem, quum haud multum abesset quin pons ab Romanis rescinderetur, civibus ut rediret exclamantibus, deum fluvii prcatus in aquam se projecit. Verentur amici ne submergatur: sed praeter opinionem et suorum et hostium tututs in alteram ripani evadit.

Exercise 175
Hoc anno Galli duce Brenno cum Alpes transissent bellum Romanis minabantur. Dicuntur autem a legatis quibusdam Romanis lacessiti esse, qui jure gentium violato, proelio inter Gallos et Etruscos facto interfuissent. Quos quominus puniret quum senatus recusasset, Galli jurati se eum dis hanc injuriam ulturos Romam profecti sunt. Ad Alliam flumen Romanos magno proelio vicerunt neque postea quisquam eis obstitit. Magnopere quidem mirati quod nemo prohibere conatus est (conaretur) quominus Romam intrarent, aliquamdiu extra muros manserunt.

Exercise 176
Quo tempore Scythis tot hostes quot vicini erant rex Suevorum Forum Novum obsedit brevique tempore eo potitus est. Non est dubium quin per oppidanorum negligentiam hoc accideret: sunt autem qui dicant (ex) proditione effectum esse. Erant tamen civium qui ad ultimum resistere constituissent. Inter hos erat sacredos quidam qui cum paucis comitibus se in aedibus conclusit; et ceteri, ejus fortitudine confirmati, conditionibus recusatis in hostes tela immittebant. Nuntiis qui se dedere juberent ad hos identidem missis tandem hostes aedes incenderunt: sed summa constantia in aedibus incendi quam cedere malebant; constituerant enim liberati patriae non superesse.

Exercise 177
Antiochus legatos Romanos, quum advenissent, salutabat manumque ad Popillium porrigebat; qui tamen oblatas litterae jussit primum legere. Rex quum perlegisset respondit se, quid agendum esset, amicos consulturum esse: sed Popilius virga quam manu ferebat rege circumscripto "Priusquam hoc circulo excedas," inquit, "responsum dato quod senatui Romano referam." Primum haud multum abfuit quin rex ne legato pareret recusaret: haud tamen ignarus quantum sibi prodesset amicitiam Populi Romani servare, tandem se quod vellet senatus acturum esse respondit. Quo facto tandem Populius ad regem velut ad amicum sociumque manum porrexit.

Exercise 178
Hannibal, quum legati qui cum Carthaginem revocarent in Italiam advenissent summa ira iis acceptis vix ab lacrimas temperabat (prohibitus est quin lacrimas effunderet). Exclamans, "non est dubium" inquit, " quin mei cives odio invidiaque, non ipsi Romani me vicerint. Quo vultis me ducite. Italia quum relinquenda sit haud multum quo abeam mea interest." Legatis autem timentibus ne reipublicae diutius servire nollet et maxime interesse Carthaginem defendere persuadentibus, urbem repsondit quae suis ducibus confidere timeret non dignam esse quae ab illis defenderetur.

Exercise 179
Poeni quod tam celeriter classis Romana ab Africa discessisset elati, plus etiam exitio ejus audito gaudebant. Jam vero jactare poterant se mari quidem amicos esse sed hostes omnibus qui in eo navigarent. Quae quum ita essent Romani eos prohibere non poterant quominus bellum ad Siciliam transferrent cum omnibus copiis terrestribus et centem quadraginta elephantis et classe quae exercitui subveniret. Hac insula recto cursu petita et copiis eductis, locos campestres vastare paraverunt. Romani tamen constantia invicta novam classem instruendam susceperunt, ot tribus mensibus ducentae (et) viginti naves aedificatae ad certamen paratae sunt.

Exercise 180
Imperium Xanathippo mandatum est, qui omnibus is visus est cui optime contidere possent. Clamatum est proelium statim committendum (esse), nemo enim dubitabat quin Xanthippo duce victuri essent. Ille igitur dux hoc modo constitutus (creatus), exercitu in campum educto, proelium cum Romanis committere paravit. Primo imperavit ut elephanti impetum in mediam aciem Romanorum facerent et equites utrimque in alas inciderent. Quo facto equites Romani, multo inferiores numero, re integra fugiunt, et elephanti in primos ordines peditatus Romani invecti hostes passim prosternunt. Legionarii tamen, quos simul aggressi sunt a fronte pedites et a latere equites et a tergo elephanti, plerique fortiter resistunt et in loco (ubi stant) moriuntur.

Exercise 181

Decem post annis Caius, frater natu minor Tiberii, ratus se opportere fratris mortem ulcisci, leges tulit quae rem publicam everterent. plebem enim Tiberii mortis nondum oblitam patres auctoritate sua non prohibere potuerunt quominus Caium tribunum plebis crearet. Tiberius vero leges tulit quod eum plebis miseruit, Caius autem suas quo facilius ulciscendi libidini indulgeret. Regni quoque appetendi accusatus est. Tunc biennium multis oratioonibus apud populum habitis omnes eas leges ferebat quae potestatem senatus diminuerent, quarem iniquissima fuit illa quae effecit ut panis plebi vili daretur.

Exercise 182
1. Simulac nos cnspexerunt discessere.
2. Sciebam eos simulae nos conspexissent discessuros esse.
3. Postquam quid actum sit audieris, quid te agere opoteat scies.
4. Discedere prius noluit quam decem vidisset.
5. Ex quo tempore de clade exercitus certiores facti fueramus omnem spem salutis abjecimus.
6. Simulatque signum datum est milites omnes simul procurrerunt.
7. Quoties nuntii adveniunt omnes ad portas currimus.
8. Donec stipendium accepissent discedere nolebant.
9. Caesar omnes copias prius in naves imposuerat quam Pompeius Brundisium adveniret.
10. Priusquam Pompeius Brundisium advenit Caesar omnes copias in naves imposuerat.

Exercise 183
1. Prius fere victi sumus quam pugna est commissa.
2. Galli castra oppugnabant priusquam nostri muros complerent.
3. Milites postquam e navibus egressi sunt eas incenderunt.
4. Certiores facti sumus ducem postquam stipendium slvesset suos dimisisse.
5. Turba prius convenit quam ad templum advenirem.
6. Simulac rex visus est est omnes cives clamorem sustulerunt.
7. Quum regressus eris quid actum sit audies.
8. Ferte signa, milites, priusquam nos hostis conspexerit (conspiciat).
9. In via manebant donec rex praeterierat.
10. Hic nobis manendum est donec amici nostri advenerint.

Exercise 184
1. Ad te veniam quum hoc opus perfeccero.
2. Simul atque opus perfeci ex urbe excessi.
3. Castra ab hostibus prius oppugnata sunt qua, nos arma capere possemus.
4. Caesar apud suos ante contionatus est quam hiberna reliquit.
5. Nuntiatum est equites praemissos esse antequam exploratores regressi essent.
6. Manes Romae donec alias litteras acceperis.
7. Constituerunt non ante discedere quam litteras nostras accepissent.
8. Simulac bellum indictum est imperator suos eduxit.
9. Captivi in silvas prius effugerunt quam milites eos consequi possent.
10. Nostri conferto agmine progressi sunt donec senserunt hostes pedem referre.

Exercise 185
1. Horatius restitit donec pons rescissus est.
2. Exercitum relinquam quum primum novus consul adveniet (advenerit).
3. Cicero recusavit quominus ad provinciam iret postquam abiit consulatu.
4. Adero quum primum me arcesses.
5. Recusavit quominus exercitum dum novus consul adveniret.
6. Postquam Pompeius ex acie effugit milites ejus statim dispersi sunt.
7. Non tibi ante in navem conscendendum est quam ego jussero.
8. Non prius accusabitur quam ipse Romae aderit.
9. Consul negavit P. Scipionem ante accusatum iri quam Romam redisset.
10. Milo in senatu erat donec dimissus est.

Exercise 186

Simulac Demosthenes cum copiis Syracusas attigit Niciaeque cum exercitu se conjunxit urbs acrius obsidebatur. Primo quidem inertia Niciae ipsum Demosthenem directam oppugnationem facere prohibebat: tandem tamen illi persuasem est ut noctu oppugnare suos sineret. Qui impetus infeliciter evenit: Athenienses enim, priusquam ad Achradinae muros advenerunt, inter se turbanantur nec multum abfuit quin ob tenebras, secum ipsis confligerent. Itaque recepti ab Demosthene anedum fuit posteaque rursus superante Niciae consilio fame urbem redigere constituere.

Exercise 187

Haraldus, simul ac nuntius allatus est Gulielmum e nave egressum esse, ad meridiem magnis itineribus contendit. Milites ejus, qui recenti victoria elati spem victoriae non abjecerant, noctem ante proelium commissum epulando ac bibendo egerunt. Ancipiti proelio totum diem dimicatum est et vesper jam appropinquabat priusquam satis certum fuit utri victuri essent. Tandem fuga simulata Gulielmus hostes e loco elicuit et equites Normannorum magnam stragem ante mandarunt quam regem, oculo sagitta transfixo, occidere viderunt. Quo mortuo fusi passim (in omnes partes) diffugerunt.

Exercise 188
1. Quum ver redierit ex hibernis discedemus.
2. Quum se occisum iri pro certo haberent tamen progressi sunt.
3. Jam ad urbem appropinquabant quum novas copias advenisse nuntiatum est.
4. Quum quid agendum esset ignorarent nuntios exspectare constituerunt.
5. Quum potueram rure semper vixi.
6. Quum nullam esse spem salutis scirent fortiter constituerent mori.
7. Quum redieris mutatam urbem invenies.
8. Vix iter inceperamus quum ut consisteremus imperatum est.
9. Quum prope ab urbe abessemus constitimus.
10. Quum se posse resistere crederent se tradere nolebant.

Exercise 189
1. Nos obviam tibi veniemus quum tu advenies.
2. Dux quum se suos conservaturum speraret receptui cecinit.
3. Nos Veiis eramus tum quum tu Romae eras.
4. Quum scirent se victum iri tamen nolebant se dedere.
5. Cives fame paene mortui sunt quum auxilium advenit.
6. Nos quum sciremus hostes adesse conati sumus quando nos aggressuri essent cognoscere.
7. Signum datum est quum navis appropinquaverat.
8. Quum credas nullam spem salutis esse, cur diutius utimini?
9. Qui cum Athenas venissent amicos suos invenerunt.
10. Quum existimetis me vos decepisse cur alio nuntio non utimini?

Exercise 190
1. Dum silvam succidunt eos hostis adoritur.
2. Dummodo accusatus sit sine dubio in vincula conjicietur.
3. Dum dormimus clam hostes nos circumvenerunt.
4. Dum Camillus revocatus sit non rem propsere geremus.
5. Dum (quamdiu) reges Romae regnabant nemo libertate fruebatur.
6. Dum collem transeunt nulli hostium visi sunt.
7. Dum transfugae traditi essent de pace agere noluerunt.
8. Nos ipsos celabamus dum flumen transiissent (transierant).
9. Dum tu manebis, ego etiam manebo.
10. Minucius promisit se dum dictator abesset (abest) non proelium commissurum esse.

Exercise 191
1. Dum nos tempus terimus Galli nos consecuti sunt.
2. In carcere retentus est dum rex victor rediret.
3. Dum conjurati Caesarem cingunt Antonius a Trebonio clam deductus est.
4. Ne eum rogaveris dum irascitur.
5. Dum Romam ad tempus perveniat, consulatum petet.
6. Milo dixit se in senatu mansisse dum dimissus esset.
7. Dum hi colloquuntur Galli visi sunt furtium progredi.

8. Adveniebant transfugae dum exercitus Manlii minimus fuit.
9. Vincemus dum (modo) eos ad proelium eliciamus.
10. Negavit se pugnaturum esse dum novae copiae advenirent.

Exercise 192
1. Placuit dum ver appeteret non ex hibernis excedere.
2. Sciebant dummodo ne frumentum deficeret se oppidum defendere posse.
3. Dum (quamdiu) frumentum suppetebat, omnibus oppugnationibus resistebant.
4. Obsidionem omittere coacti sunt dum novae copiae advenissent (advenirent).
5. Et ab hostibus lacessiti sunt et ne sui ad hostem transirent timebant.
6. Plerique homines, quum periculum patriae instat, se fortes praebent.
7. Quum quid actum sit audiero ad te scribam.
8. Jussi sunt dum hostis sibi pugnandi occasionem daret castris se tenere.
9. Nos pedem referre oportet, inquit, praesertim cum hostis novas copias acceperit.
10. Dum pugnatur nemo loco cessit.
11. Dummodo socii paullo diutius resistere possint, poterimus proelium redintegrare.
12. Milites, quum signum recepti datum esset, tamen loco cedere noluerunt.

Exercise 193
1. Dum consul aberat periculum augebatur.
2. Quum hostes duos modo millia passum abessent nobis e castris vagari non licuit.
3. Answer missing.
4. Romani cum sacerdotes re infecta redissent, muheres miserunt quae Coriolanum conciliarent.
5. Pompeius quum fini tantum belli interesset tamen plus laudis inde cepit quam Crassus.
6. Major pars ei suaserunt ut proelium committeret dum copiae integrae sunt (or essent).
7. Cum nuntius redierit certius intellegemus quid hostes facturi sint (in animo habeant factere).
8. Quum homines magno numero conveniunt facile in tumultum incidunt.
9. Ego quum pacis cupidus sim tamen hanc rcentem injuriam aegre fero.
10. Dum (modo) arma tradant, consentiemus.
11. Quum bellum confectum erit, tribunus Caesarem reum factet.
12. Circiter meridiem fuit quum Patres convenerunt.

Exercise 194
Et Demothenes et milites ob hanc cladem metu sunt commoti, quum Nicias eam paene exspectasse videretur. Hic jam, quum dis auxilium denegentibus identidem cladem acciperent, ut obsidione desisteret censebat. Dum autem de re disceptatur, Syracusani, pugna in portu aliquoties commissa totaque deleta Atheniensium classe, ultimam fugae facultatem abstulerunt. Omnes tandem vehementer cupiunt dum adhuc fieri potest ad socios in partem insulae quae ad deterruit dum nova luna orta esset. Interea consilio ab transfugis prodito Syracusani saltum quo solo ad interiorem partem insulae evadere possent obsederunt.

Exercise 195
Tandem die constituto aliquot milia progressi ad funestum saltum advenerunt: quem quum ab hostibus obsessum invenissent neque quicquam incursionibus suis efficerent primum tramitem quo montes ascenderent contabantur repirire, deinde spe fere abjecta, quum per medios hostes ad oram maritiam perrumpere constituissent, hoc consilio copias bipartio distribuerunt Demosthenem quidem hostes celeriter consecuti intercluserunt. Niciam sexto post die quam Syracusis profectus intercepturunt flumen transeuntem cujus autem milites, quum aqua multas horas caterent, non sibi temperabant (cohiberi poterant) quin in flumen ipso comitum sanguine rubrum proruerent. Itaque confusis signis et ordinibus. Nicias nullis conditionibus factis se dedidit qui cum Demosthene captiis damnatus venero necatus est; reliqui autem Athenienses Syracusis in lautumiis custoditi sunt.

Exercise 196
Superatis omnibus his difficultatibus Gallisque deviictis haud multum abfuit quin Hannibal non acie sed insidus omnia perderet. Nam ad summas Alpes paene ascenderat quum legatorum more senes quidam cum aggressi profitebantur se alienis cladibus monitos amicitiam quam vim Poenorum malle experiri paratosque esse quod vellet agere, quos Hannibal duces quidem accepit, neque iis a se temere credendum ratus neque omnio aspernandos eos esse, parato tamen ad pugnam exercitu sequebatur. Simulatque autem saltum angustum intraverunt ex insidus undique hostes coorti et a fronte et a tergo, et eminus et comminus aggrediebantur.

Exercise 197
Atheniensibus Sphacteria insula potiri frustra conatis cives ut quid agendum esset deliberarent convocati sunt; inter quos Cleon, qui privatus modo erat neque omnio belli peritus, se (eos) nunquam talibus usos ducibus insula potituros esse affirmavit. "Me duce" inquit, "non viginti dies fore ut hostes resistant pro certo habeo." Non quidam est dubium quin ceteros duces aspernandi causa hoc dixerit: summa tamen imperii statim ab Atheniensibus ei commissa, sine mora ad sedem belli profectus, adjuvante fortuna, praeter omnium opinionem quod susceperat confecti victorque viginti post diebus Athenas rediit.

Exercise 198
Jam illuceescebat quum dux signum dedit, magnum praemium ei pollicitus qui primus moenia ascenderet. Nemo quidem eis ubi muri proruti erant urbem intrantibus restitit, aut muros per scalas (scalis) ascendentibus. Simul atque clamor demonstravit urbem captam esse, barbari omnes loco relicto in arcem confugerunt. Dux autem hostium suos sivit urbem diripere, partim quod ipse civibus iratus erat, partim quod, milites adhuc semper prohibitos quominus urbes captas spoliarent voluit tandem aliquod praemium virtutis habere. Accusatus quidem est quod hoc fecisset ut suae invidiae satisfaceret.

Exercise 199
Vidit quidam somnio ovum a summo cubili suspensum. Qui quum postero die amicum quendam visisset interrogatum quid hoc somnium significaret, certior factus est se magnam auri copiam sub cubili celatam inventurum esse. Quum aliquot horas fodisset multum aurum argento cinctum invenit; argenti igitur parvam partem ad amicum misit. Ille autem iratus quod tantulum praemium acceperat nuntium misit qui rogaret nonne partem sibi vitelli dare posset; namque, quum aurum argento opertum esset, deum vitello quidem aurum, reliqua autem parte argentum significare voluisse. Equidem tamen pro certo non habeo hanc fabulam veram esse.

Exercise 200
Hic, quum patria falso crimine expulsus esset, tamen non destitit quum facultas oblata erat (facultate oblata) ei pro virili parte servire. Non enim is fuit qui suum commodum reipublicae anteponeret, et affirmabat cives suos se, cum opus esset, revocaturos; quod ad tempus (ad id temporis) se velle in exsilio manere. Mox autem potestas facta est studii monstrandi. Conjuratio enim a nonnullis perditis facta est, qui magistratibus interfectis ipsi summam imperii usurpant. In hoc discrimine cives exsulis memores nuntios mittunt qui eum rogarent ut sibi subveniret. Qui omnium injuriam quas passus erat oblitus adventu suo civibus qui sese tam injuste usi erant salutem attulit.

Exercise 201
Rutilius non dignus fuit qui proconsul fieret. Profectus enim ex Asia, dum Ephesum visit, cujus urbis cives Dianam colunt, templum illius deae spoliaverat; et multa alia fecit quae omnibus Romanis morum antiquorum displicerant. Verum etiam quum furtum admiserat id joco excusabat (jocum habebat quo id excusaret). Dixit quidem se libenter parva aurea pocula capere quae statuae deorum manibus porrectis tenebant (tenerent). Comitibus autem rogantibus nonne existimaret se aliquando poenas daturum esse, respondit deos eum non esse punituros qui commoda precatus ipse caperet donum quod primum offerent. Senex quoque eadem quae juvenis faciebat — moriturus enim, "Unius quidem rei," inquit, "me jamdudum paenitet quod aureum pallium, quo Jupiter in templo suo Messenia vestitus est, non abstuli. Potui enim laneum pro aureo reddere."

Appendix

Exercise 202
1. Si hoc facere potes, statim faciendum est.
2. Si hoc facere possem, statim facerum.
3. Pauperibus, si indigere videbantur, semper pecuniam dederunt.
4. Si captivi effugerint, nos poenas dabimus.
5. Si tibi meo consilio opus esse existimarem, te juvare conarer.
6. Si statim profecti essent, inprovidos hostes invenissent.
7. Non jam adessem si amicorum consilio paruissem.
8. Nisi jussero, ne domum reliqueris.
9. Si auxilium rogabantur, libenter id dabant.
10. Si auxilium rogati essent, libenter oportuit dare.
11. Semper si digni eramus qui juvaremur nos juvabant.

Exercise 203
1. Ne promiseris unquam nisi fidem praestare potes.
2. Si ad castra pervenerimus, tuti crimus.
3. Nisi flumen tam altum esset potuimus id pedibus transire.
4. Se prudentiores praebuissent si copias statim exposuissent.
5. Erres si me hoc de industria fecisse putes.
6. Si quis irae moderari non potest oneri est amicis.
7. Sive te laudat sive culpat, scis te jure egisse.
8. Si novae copiae venissent hostes coacti essent obsidione desistere.
9. Si arma sument contra patriam digni erunt qui capitis damnentur.
10. Si quem videbat (vident) indigna patientem semper eum adjuvare conabatur.
11. Si modo tacuissemus, non talia mala jam pateremur.

Exercise 204
1. Nisi mihi irrisisset, forsitan ei ignossem.
2. Dummodo me timeant, oderint.
3. Si Caesar pontem in Rheno fecisset facile Germani in potestatem ejus essent redacti.
4. Si statim hostes adoriemur sine dubio eos vincemus.
5. Meus si frater esset nihilominus eum damnarem.
6. Nunquam bellum L. Scipioni commissum esset nisi P. Scipio se eum comitaturum esse prmisisset.
7. Nisi tributum esset impositum, Macedones feliciores nunc quam sub suis regibus essent.
8. Si quis mihi injuriam fecit, legibus, non vi poenas de eo sumo.
9. Si modo Italiam intraverimus, recto itinere Romam vos ducam.
10. Nisi quis ambitu utitur consulatum petere minime ei prodest.
11. Seu Romam ieris seu hic manseris, ego non urbe excedam.

Exercise 205
1. Poetae fame moriuntur Romae nisi divites eos sublevant.
2. Si recto cursu Romam petemus hac nocte in Capitolio epulabimur.
3. Antiquitus si quis se aptum ad regendum praebebat, plerumque consul creabatur.
4. Sive hic nuntius verus est sive falsus, nobis ubi sumus manendum est.
5. Certo nuntium tibi ad tempus attulissem si modo potuissem.
6. Si hostes statim nos aggredientur, metuo ne non eis resistere possimus.
7. Si hoc rogem jure irascaris.
8. Si (quum) domum redieris multos amicos invenies.
9. Nisi quondam pauper fuissem non jam divitiis fruerer.
10. Si Gracchus regnum petit jure interfectus est.

Exercise 206
1. Nos primae aciei, si occisa erit, succedemus.
2. Si adessem, quid agendum esset scirem.
3. Nisi eum admonueris, tribus diebus oblitus erit.
4. Si adesse posset, hanc rogationem jam profecto suaderet.
5. Si cras adsit, hanc rogationem suadeat.
6. Si Fabius majorem in republica auctoritatem habuisset, nunquam Varro consul creatus esset.
7. Si quid contra leges egerit, de eo poenas sumite.
8. Si quis contra leges quid agit, puniendus est.
9. Si quis eum conspiciat, comprehendatur.
10. Jam in carcere esset si modo eum comprehendere potuissemus.

Exercise 207
1. Si contra rempublican conjurarunt digni sunt qui supplico afficiantur.
2. Nisi conjurassent jam in urbe viverent.
3. Si ad litus perveneris, poteris in navem conscendere.
4. Si meo consilio paruisses, tuas divitias servasses.
5. Si eos scelerum paenitebit, eis ignoscetur.
6. Nisi huic parces, odio eris omnibus.
7. Si sibi consuluisset, Caesaris amicitiam non amisisset.
8. Si auxilium Poenis submittamus odium Romanorum subeamus.
9. Si tui visendi causa venerint, jube eos manere donec ego adveniam.
10. Oportet te divitiis bene uti si vis beatus esse.
11. Sive voluisti sive non, hoc facere debuisti.

Exercise 208
Multos et fortissimos proditione, commilitones, amisimus et ab amicis sumus relicti. Non tamen desperandum est et si vincere non poterimus mori saltem summa laude malimus quam in potestatem venire barbarorum qui nos summis doloribus afficient. Si majores nostri maximos illos Persarum exercitus sustinere noluissent, adhuc penes barbaros Graecia esset. Nos autem, si talibus nos praestiterimus dignos, haud minus patriam juvabimus. Di ipsi, laesae fidei ultores, a nobis stabunt: quin immo, quum violatum foedus aegre ferant, in aciem nos sequentur, pro nobis certabunt.

Exercise 209
Imperator ita apud suos contionatus est: "Videtis, milites, quantae sint hostium copiae et quam inexpugnabilem locum teneant. Si eos statim adoriemur, sine dubio magnam cladem accipiemus. Sin autem illi loco relicto nos aggrediantur, bonam spem victoriae habeamus, namque flumen altum eis prius transeundum est et collis praeruptus ascendendus quam ad nostras munitiones pervenire possint." Ilis verbis summa difficultate suis persuasit ut intra munitiones manerent; quod consilium saluti fuit exercitui. Nam si Romani hostes adorti essent, qui et numero et loco superiores erant, sine dubio victi essent.

Exercise 210
Mortuo Tib. Graccho C. Blosius miro modo amicitiam praestitit. Quum enim Senatus decrevisset ut si quis cum Graccho consensisset puniretur Blosius, apud consules accusatus, amicitiae excusatione puniretur Blosius, apud consules accusatus, amicitiae excusatione utebatur. "Seu judices" inquit "me damnabunt seu me absolvent semper guadebo me Gracchi fuisse amicum. Si vos, consules, me jubeatis me ipsum ea lege servare ut Gracchum accusem, non ita me incolumem faciam. Si moriendum erit, moriar amicis fideles." Dubitant consules; tandem rogenti alteri "Num si Gracchus templum Jovis incendere jussisset id fecisses?" Blosius repondit, "Non ille jussisset."

Exercise 211
Adventu ducis conjuratorum cognito, praefectus castelli suis convocatis ita locutus est: "Si quidem omnia proficerent non existimarem me oportere eos quibus praesim consulere. Quum vero hostes jam adsint, neque nos satis frumenti comparaverimus, si quis timidus adest (aut) si quis non animo paratus est usque ad mortem pro rege nostro pugnare, abeat neve nobis hic obsessis oneri sit. Si potero eum incolumem in Celtica fluvii ripa exponam." Si rex ipse milites allocutus esset, non potuerunt plus studii praestare quam hac oratione audita praestiterunt, nec si quis abeundi cupidus fuit ausus est fateri.

Exercise 212
1. Si optimus quisque periit, quis ad rempublicam administrandum superest?
2. Si suos unquam laborantes viderat ipse eos adjuvare conabatur.
3. Imperatum est ut quisque suam salutem peteret.
4. Maxime nostra interest num quis nobis absentibus adfuerit cognoscere.
5. Diu equus amissus est neque quisquam eum reperire potest usquam.
6. Negavit quemquam sibi ut pecuniam acciperet persuasisse.
7. Si capta fuerit urbs, hostis opinor nemini civium parcet.

8. Nostri quum, aliquamdiu munitionibus se tenuissent tandem in hostem excursionem (eruptionem) fecerunt.
9. Philosophus quidam dixit ignem omnium rerum originem esse.
10. Haud dubium est quin nonnulli hostes nos a tergo adoriri conentur.

Exercise 213
1. Ego regressus certior factus sum aliquem mei visendi causa venisse.
2. Quam celerrime regressus sum nec quemquam apud me reperire potui.
3. Ecquis te rogavit quid faciendum esset?
4. Si quis neget spem ullam esse, a civibus interficiatur.
5. Volo quemvis (quemlibet) mittere gognitum quid agitur.
6. Nescio quis dixit vitam longam summum esse malum.
7. Aliquamdiu affirmatum est optimum quemque nostrorum militum periisse.
8. Non dubium est quin perierint, neque unquam corpora usquam reperta sunt.
9. Quum Romam rediero, comperiam num quis meam domum emerit.
10. Imperatum est ut si quis domos diripuisset (diriperet) interficeretur.

Exercise 214
Si post tantam victoriam Galli statim fugientes persecuti essent, Roma profecto fuisset capta, adeo regressis iis qui ex acie effugerant cives erant metu perculsi attoniti. Galli tamen haud tantam esse victoriam rati quanta revera fuit epulando castrique spoliandis se dediderunt. Multis igitur qui ex urbe voluerunt excedere, occasio fugiendi data est, ii autem qui manebant se parare ad urbem defendendam poterant; qui reliqua urbe deserta in Capitolium se contulerunt quod firmo vallo muniverunt. Pro certo enim habebant, si Galli oppugnarent (oppugnassent), sibi opus fore omnium virium.

Exercise 215
Parum quidem dubitari potest quin hujus cladis, seu proditione seu inscientia, auctores in primis fuerint duces. Exercitus enim si solita via iter fecisset advenisset incolumis postridieque aequo Marte contendere potuit. Breviore tamen usi tramite per agros ducente iter invenerunt ex alia parte palude, ex alia rupibus obsaeptum. Quo cognito dux, legatis convocatis, "Si ultra progressi erimus" inquit, "in periculum adducemur ut ab hostibus inopinantes opprimamur: sin pedem rettullerimus serius fortasse adveniemus. Si modo certum iter tenuissemus, jam ad urbem appropinquaretur." Ad quae nemo statim respondit: et priusquam consilium captum esset clamor est sublatus hostes instare.

Exercise 216
Juvenis quidam Lacedaemonius, nomine Isadas, hoc in certamine praeter omnes entuit. Neque arma neque vestem induerat, hastam solam altera manu, altera gladium ferebat. Ita armatus summo ardore domo egressus primus in pugnam procurrit. Qui quum omni ictu mortiferam plagam infligeret omnes qui impetum ejus sustinebant ipse incolumis prostravit. Seu tam miro spectaculo hostes attoniti sunt, seu ipsi dei ob egregiam virtutem cum servaverunt, constat neminem unquam tam mirifica praestitisse. Proelio autem confecto Ephori, ut ferunt, virtutis causa coronam ei decreverunt, quod tamen inermis tanto periculo se objecerat (objecisset), mille drachmis eum mulctavere.

Exercise 217
Ipso die quo patres num magistrum equitum deberent Romam revocare deliberabant nuntius allatus est eum eductis copiis quae in castris relictae essent proelio que eum Samnitibus commisso gravem cladem accepisse. Itaque dictator ne moratus quidem ut patrum sententias cognosceret ad castra quam celerrime rediit. Magister equitum, ad tribunal arcessitus et rogatus cur ille, cui salus Populi Romani commissa esset, injussu dictatoris legiones quas castris tenere esset jussus, in aciem eduxisset, hoc solum respondere poterat: se existimasse legionibus quibus praeesset, si quando data esset facultas, pro bono Populi Romani uti oportere.

Exercise 218
Princeps quidam Indicus ab Hispanis captus est; qui quod ille inter suos pollebat, utramque manum desecuerunt eo consilio et eum rursus in se arma ferre prohiberent. Ille tamen hanc injuriam ulciscendi cupidus domum regressus suos incitabat ne solitam virtutem se defecisse Hispanos existimare sinerent; qui quum crudelitatem qua Hispani in eum comitesque ejus usi erant viderent, incensis domibus, ne quis regredi vellet, obstinatis animis aut Hispanos expellere aut in acie perire in colonias Hispanicas invaserunt. Saucius autem princeps, dum res geritur, sagittas quas pugnantibus praeberet ore suo ferebat.

Exercise 219
Romani quidem certiores facti de clade quam acceperat Regulus, magnam classem ad superstities reducendos instruxerunt. Poeni autem jure rati constantiam Romanorum una victoria non fractum iri, ipsi novam classem aedificare coeperunt quae se (ab) alia incursione defenderet. Verum frustra conati sunt Clypeam ante redigere quam Romani ad eam pervenire possent. Praesidium enim exiguum, mira quadam virtute, omnibus oppugnationibus repulsis usque ad proximam aestatem restiterunt, quo temporo classis Romana advenit. Proelio navali contra promontorium Hermaeum facto victores Romani Clypeae defensores, qui salutem tam bene meruerant, in naves exceperunt.

Exercise 220
Si quidem Hanno, cui imperium jam permissum est, exemplo Hamilcaris usus esset, Romani sine dubio victi essent. Hic autem quum imperium paulisper modo obtinuisset fide omnio se indignum praebuit. Nam si quando ex parte rem prospere gesserat, non potuit fortuna uti; et quum certam victoriam, se judice (ut existimavit ipse), reportasset, castra ex inopinato ejus negligentia capta sunt. Tanto in discrimine Poeni, quum non possent sperrare virum, quo tam injuste usi essent, sibi subventurum esse, summam imperii Hamilcari iterum detulerunt; qui, patria omnibus rebus anteposita, eam recipere non recusavit. Deinde et disciplina severa et studo et auctoritate apud principes Numidicos, hostibus justo proelio victis, aliquot urbes quae defecerant recepit.

Exercise 221
Ulysses Phaeaciam insulam ejectus omni hospitio affectus est quo illis temporibus hospites ubique utebantur. Ab Nausicaa enim regis filia, quae ei prima occurrit, ad patris regiam ductus vestibus quas optimas texuerant puellae donatus est, epulisque quas optimas hospites praebere poterant acceptus. Postridie ludis celebratis, rogatus ut eis interesset, eum honorem primo recusavit; postem autem injuriis regis filii lacessitus, qui solus officii sui erga hospitem oblitus est, tantas fere vires quantas bello Trojano praestitit, et Phaeaces suis ludis superavit.

Exercise 222
Tib. Gracchus si quis alius dignus fuit qui a suis civibus beneficiis afficeretur. Natus enim patre qui Hispaniam pacaverat — id quod multi alii consules re infecta reliquerant — et natu conjunctus cum utroque Africano, facile potuit principatum usurpare, si voluisset legibus parere neque conatus esset eas mutare. Sed iter ei per Etruriam ad primam suam provinciam faciendum fuit; quae terra tunc deserta, liberis nedata, a servis culta eum tantum conmovit, ut constitueret aut remedium aliquod reperire aut in conatu (conatus) perire. Optimus quisque Romanorum legibus quas tulit favebat, et nisi tribunus quidam ei obstitisset opus plerisque — ne dicam omnes — approbantibus perfecisset.

Exercise 223
1. Quanquam non majestatis damnati sunt, magnas injurias reipublicae intulerunt.
2. Etiamsi hoc neges, nemo tibi credat.
3. Quamvis magnus sit hostium numerus, non nobis desperandum est.
4. Etsi consilia sua comperta esse sciebant, simulabant tamen se insontes esse.
5. Te hoc facere volo etsi non ipse fecissem.
6. Dux, quanquam saepe rem prospere gesserat, copiis suis disclicebat.

7. Certum est mihi vera dicere, etiamsi inimici mihi mortem minentur.
8. Caesari, quamquam jam maximas pecunias mutuatus erat, nihilominus credebatur.
9. Quamvis quinquies me decepisset, nihilominus ei confisus essem.
10. Satis sim contentus etiamsi paulisper in exsilium ire cogar.

Exercise 224
1. Etsi magnum pretium mihi offerat, non fundum vendam.
2. Romam hodie adveniendum est, quamvis multa impediant.
3. Quanquam eum nocentem esse pro certo habeo, id agam ut eum absolvam.
4. Quamvis exercitus ejus magnus sit, una acie non omnia periclitabitur.
5. Etiamsi totius Galliae princeps esset, non ei parcerem.
6. Quamquam totius hujus regionis ditissimus erat, exiguam pecuniam pauperibus dedit.
7. Quanquam dei a nobis stant, gladio opus erit.
8. Etsi optimae essent legionum mearum, tamen ad Pompeium eas remitterem.
9. Caesar duas legiones a Pompeio missas, etsi suarum erant optimae, ad eum remisit.
10. Quamvis magnum periculum subirem, non tali causa id vitare conarer.

Exercise 225
1. Quivis tacere potest etiamsi iratus est.
2. Constituerant tacere quamvis malti cruciatus sibi infligerentur.
3. Aliquamdiu restiterunt quamquam pro certo habebant spem nullam salutis esse.
4. Quum credam te velle mihi prodesse, tamen non possum tuum auxilium accipere.
5. Nunquam tibi credam etsi te jurejurando obstringas.
6. Hoc discrimine socii defecerunt quamquam promiserant se in officio mansuros.
7. Etiamsi exercitus dimissus erit milites tamen erimus.
8. Diu ferociter pugnatum est, etsi numero hostibus multo inferiores fuimus.
9. Non debos talia coram aliis dicere, quamvis ea vera esse existimes.
10. Etsi conatus est dolorem celare, tamen non est dubium quin hoc aegre tulerit.

Exercise 226
1. Quanquam jamdudum in externa terra habitabant.
2. Recusarunt quominus hoc facerent, quamvis sibi prodesset.
3. Hostibus non cedemus quamvis magnae eorum copiae sint.
4. Etsi hostibus numero inferiores erant, locum summa constantia tenebant.
5. Quum callidus esset, tamen nos decipere non potuit.
6. Non possum ei confidere etsi promittat se fidem praetaturum esse.
7. Quanquam tam pauperes erant, non potuimus eis auxilium offerre.
8. Quamvis magna sit imperatoris potestas, tamen ratio ab eo reipublicae semper est reddenda.
9. Etsi rei fiantm sine dubio absolvantur.
10. Ad necem deducti sunt etsi dux promiserat se eos conservaturum esse.

Exercise 227
Lucullus, quanquam saepe rem prospere gesserat, non potuit bellum cum Mithradate gestum conficere. Rex enim, postquam Triarium justo proelio Zelae vicit, hac victoria contentus in montes se receperat. Jussit quidem Lucullus suos perequi: qui tamen, quamvis magna duci cupido esset regis capiendi, eum sequi noluerunt. Plerique enim ab Italia viginti fere annos abfuerant et ex quo tempore Lucullus imperium obtinuit multa erant passi. Nam Lucullus, etsi bonus imperator erat, nihil ejus comitatis praestabat quae militum studium conciliet: idem, dum inopia sui afficiuntur, magno luxu ipse usus erat. Evenit igitur ut exercitus defendere quidem Pontum a Mithradate vellet, haud tamen omnio alterum bellum suscipere.

Exercise 228
Caesar, etiamsi exercitus sibi oppositus multo major fuisset, nihilominus ex hoc bello victor evasisset. Tanta enim erat et disciplina et in re militari usus suorum ut, quamvis adversa esset fortuna, nunquam animum demitterent. Quod in bello Dyrrhachino praesertim manifestum erat. Quanquam enim oppugnatis munitionibus quas tanto labore fecerant defensores inde expulsi sunt, nihil tamen erat pavoris, neque milites passim per regionem diffugerunt; sed ii qui cladi supererant via in montes ducente conferto agmine se receperunt. Postridie igitur Caesar exercitum habuit restitutum, qui, quamvis deminutus, pericula fortiter obire paratus est.

Exercise 229
Quamvis omnibus diversae sint sententiae de moribus Scipionis, nemo potest dubitare quin miram quandam auctoritatem apud suos qcquisiverit. Si quidem nonnunquam de ejus jussis clam querebantur, tamen nemo fuit quin vellet, proelio commisso, capitis periculum pro eo subire; idque etsi manifestum fuit se ipsum (pro sua parte) nunquam conari suos conservare, sed obstinato esse animo, quamvis multi suorum occiderentur, hostes profligare. Qua de causa accidit ut Romani, quanquam multi et potentes hostes eis simul obsistebant, victores tot proeliis evaderent.

Exercise 230
Athenienses, quum tot civitates defecissent, tamen immotam constantiam praestabant; qui quanquam ipsi duas totius classis partes praebebant, libenter Lacedaemoniis summam imperii non solum terra sed etiam mari permiserunt. Themistocles ille conatus est aliquid ejus studii quod in Atheniensibus excitaverat ceteris etiam Graecis injicere. Qui nisi tantum sapientiae quantum virtutis praestitisset, de libertate Graeciae actum esset. Ejus autem consilio socii se jurejurando obstrinxerunt fore ut usque ad mortem resisterent, et si res prospere evenissent, Delphico deo decimam partem bonorum voverent omnium civitatum Graecarum quae se Persis sua sponte dedidissent (in deditionem venissent).

Exercise 231
1. Se gessit quasi fureret.
2. Sicut meritus est praemio est affectus.
3. Pugnabat velut salus civitatis in se uno poneretur.
4. Omnia providi perinde ac evenerunt.
5. Sicut tu putabas, id solum egit ut nos deciperet.
6. Rempublicam administrat non sicut res postulat sed quasi ceteris ipse futurus esset exemplo.
7. Non aeque ac putas nobis studet.
8. Haud cadem facit ac promittit.
9. Ut magni meam ipsius salutem, ita civitatis multo pluris aestimo.
10. Tibi invideo ut rebus publicis vacuo.
11. Ut in tali discrimine, diu quidem dubium erat utri essent victuri.
12. Ut saepe fit, opere nondum perfecto defessus erat.

Exercise 232
1. In flumen irruerunt quasi insani essent.
2. Nostri victi sunt sicut ego praedixi.
3. Oportet nos uti aliis perinde ac volumus eos nobis uti.
4. Animadversum est eum (visus est) saepe se convertere tanquam si quis se sequeretur.
5. Ut in tanto discrimine tantam prudentiam quantam poterant praestiterunt.
6. Videre aliud est ac credere.
7. Non dubium est quin nobis minus sit otii quam nostris majoribus.
8. Non eadem semper fecerunt ac promiserant.
9. Proelium commiserunt quasi nullo cladis timore afficerentur.
10. Graeci non eisdem virtutibus ac Romani insignes erant.
11. Se in flumen projecit quasi revera vellet inimicum servare.
12. Ut in tanto discrimine dux solus immotus permansit.

Exercise 233

Proelio Zamae facto Hannibal eandem constantiam atque aciei instruendae peritiam quam quattuordecim ante annis pugna Cannensi praestitit. Fortuna tamen jam adversa erat, et in proelium iniit quasi hoc ipse non ignoraret. Elephanti autem, qui saepe Poenis saluti fuerant, jam Romanorum clamoribus territi in suos conversi primam aciem turbaverunt. Mercenarii milites in prima acie constiterunt; quos se recipientes Poeni secunda acie instructi inter ordines suos nolebant admittere et in eos velut in hostes impetum fecerunt. Quod non praeter opionem Hannibalis factum est. Tertiae igitur aciei, veteranis ex Italia deductis, imperavit ut impetu facto turbam tumultuariam ex acie pellerent. Quo facto tandem cum Romanis redintegratum est.

Exercise 234

Nuntii, sicut jussi sunt, cives certiores fecerunt tribus diebus domos illis relinquendas atque in alium locum discedendum esse. Hi primo nihil responderunt, quasi quid postularetur non intelligerent; princeps autem, qui ut in tali re, se intrepide gerebat, nuntios rogavit ut qua de causa haec postularent certius exponerent. Ad quae illi responderunt se ea solum quae sibi mandata essent agere. Tunc ex toto vico magni clamores gemitusque coorti sunt velut (si) poenam mortis subirent, universique nuntiis circumfusi sunt tanto furore iraque usi quantum si hi ipsi malorum fuissent auctores praestare potuerunt.

Exercise 235

Antiochus incursionem in Aegyptum primo vere fecerat. Accidit autem perinde atque aliqui suorum praedixerant; nam simul atque Alexandriam appropinquavit, legatus quidam Romanus, nomine Popilius, eum aggressus litteras a Senatu missas porrexit. Quibus perlectis rex respondit se, suis amicis ad consilium convocatis, de re deliberaturum. Popilius tamen regi virga circumscripto imperavit ne eum locum prius relinqueret quam responsum sibi dedisset. Nec rogitanti regi quicquam respondit, sed tacitus adstitit quasi non audiret, donec rex audacia legati perterritus promisit se omnia quae Senatus decerneret facturum. Eodem modo Romani, quocunque ierant, se gerebant quasi ipsi imperium orbis terrarum obtinerent.

Exercise 236

Cicero certior factus se ab Antonio proscriptum esse, quum ad villam quae haud procul ab mari erat confugisset, in navem conscendit eo consilio ut in Macedoniam transiret. Sed aliquoties in altum evectus et adversis ventis repulsus tandem professus se in patria quam toties servasset moriturum esse ad villam regressus est. Tunc quum cubitum iisset bene ut in tanto periculo dormivit. Servi tamen, quasi periculum ejus providerent, excitatum eum et in lectica positum per silvas ad mare vexerunt. Mox autem milites, qui ad hoc missi erant, eum consecuti sunt; qui quum advenissent vetuit ille servos resistere, et cervicibus e lectica porrectis milites opus perficere jussit.

Exercise 237

1. Sibi obsides traderent quos postulasset.
2. Cur ei illum sequi noluissent.
3. Se nolle eos prodere qui suam fidem sequerentur.
4. Num ille putaret se solum hoc scire.
5. Si hoc faceret omnes illum laudaturos esse.
6. Si se secuti essent, ad urbem tutos eos perventuros fuisse.
7. Progrederentur ut in hostem invaderent.
8. Sui se sequerentur: se facile hostem victuros esse.
9. Non semper sibi consulendum esse.
10. Eos tempestate prohibitos esse ad portum pervenire.
11. Illo die insignem victoriam se reportasse.

Exercise 238

1. Cur sociis persuasissent ut deficerent.
2. Statim discederent neve unquam ad illum locum redirent.
3. Se illis antea dixisse qualis eventus pugnae futurus esset.
4. Modo sibi darent quae eos rogasset, se discessurum esse.
5. Quando sperarent novas copias quas exspectarent adventuras esse?
6. Se muros expugnasse; non tamen arcem in suis manibus esse.
7. Ne illi de salute desperarent.
8. Illos debuisse auxilium sibi celerius submittere.
9. Num eum furere qui talia diceret?
10. Quod si verum esset se recusare quominus eos diutius adjuvaret.
11. Nisi auxilium pervenisset omnes cives fame morituros.

Exercise 239

1. Cur illi in suam patriam invasissent.
2. In patriam illi redirent.
3. Poenis se adortis, eorum septingentos, ducentos suorum interfectos esse.
4. Ne sociorum injurias obliviscerentur sed ulciscerentur celeriter.
5. Illo die majorem virtutem illos praestitisse quam eos.
6. Quum Romam redissent se de illis rebus quaestionem habituros esse.
7. Se non posse jam illos adjuvare. Si postridie venissent, se quid agere posset deliberaturum esse.
8. Tribus ante diebus se castra relinquere potuisse; jam, seu vellent, seu nollent, illic cogi manere.
9. Cives illum orare atque obtestari ut regressus rempublicam servaret.
10. Si domi suae maneret, certo ab iis illum oppugnatum iri.

Exercise 240

1. Ubi ea nocte manere possent?
2. Se pro certo non habere se ad eos tempore perventurum.
3. Se duas legiones quas habuisset ad Pompeium misisse.
4. Illic nullam esse salutem aut sibi aut illi.
5. Si fidem praestaret eum jam (tunc) ibi adfuturum esse.
6. Omnes meminissent libertatem sibi in illo uno proelio positam esse.
7. Ne argentum unquam darent ei qui sibi non esset notus.
8. Non facile esse simul civibus simul sibi consulere.
9. Num amicum suum negligendum esse quod abesset?
10. Cur se oportet morem homini gerere qui patris sui libertus esset?

Exercise 241

Deinde Labienus locutus est de Caesaris copiis contemptim. Ne illum esse exercitum arbitrarentur qui Galliam Germaniamque devicisset. Se quidem ipsum omnibus in iis regionibus factis proeliis adfuisse nec temere quod non cognosset affirmare. Minimam vero partem illius exercitus superesse. Multos enim pestilentia periisse, multos domum esse regressos. Nonne audiissent factas esse Brundisii legiones ex sauciis illic relictis? Copias quas coram viderent tirones esse et plerasque ex coloniis Transpandanis conscriptas. Robur autem exercitus duabus pugnis Dyrrhachii factis periisse. Se denique juraturum nunquam se nisi victorem in castra regressurum esse: ceteri eodem consilio uterentur.

Exercise 242

Apud Livium scriptum invenimus Appium patribus convocatis affirmasse se surdum esse velle ne turpia consilia quae illo die nomini Romano dedecori essent audiret. Se maxime deplorare mutatum illorum animum, qui longe alius esset ac priore tempore. Quo tanti spiritus, quo virtus fugisset? Nonne olim jactassent se Alexandro ipsi, si juventute sua in Italiam ausus esset invadere, non cessuros fuisse? Ne Lucanis jam Graeculisque id traderent quod patres sui gladio nacti essent.

Exercise 243

Pacis conditiones, quamvis graves, eae solum erant quas in tali exspectarent. Hannibal autem suis manibus de rostro oratorem detraxit qui ut bellum duceretur suadebat. Quamobrem irato populo, quod ita oratorum libertatem deminuisset, respondit sibi ignoscendum esse si postquam sex et triginta annos in castris meruisset, institutorum fori obliviscretur. Apud Livium scriptum invenimus conditiones ab Scipione et magistratibus Carthaginiensium constitutas et Romam ad senatum relatas ab illo acceptas esse, et quod satis severas esse existimabat et quod verebatur ne illis rejectis Poeni bellum renovarent.

Exercise 244

Deinde convocato concilio dux ita locutus: sibi jam constituendum esse num in loco perstare magis prodesset alidum jam est facultas se recipere. Novas enim copias quas diu exspectassent nondum advenisse: quod ad se attineret. se credere non parem esse hostibus exercitum suum. Scire tamen se virtuti patientiaeque suorum posse confidere et si illi voluissent se paratum esse quam diutissimo resistere. Sententias aperte dicerent; se enim nihil invitis illis facturum esse. Cujus orationis quum dux finem fecisset, alia ab alio sententia edita tandem constituerunt, quum tot essent hostes, prudentius esse (consilium) se recipere neque gravis cladis periculum subire.

Exercise 245

Caesar, quum de actis Senatus nuntius allatus esset, apud milites contionatus est. Quid patres egissent, qua causa egissent exposuit: Novem annos se suosque reipublicae fideliter servisse, et multas victorias reportasse. Germanos se ultra expulisse, Galliam fecisse provinciam Romanam; senatum jam violatis legibus munus abrogasse tribunis quod oratione se defenderent, affirmavisse rempublicam periclitari Italiamsque in arma convocasse, quum ipse nullam is injuriam intulisset. Deinde milites, quos Pompeius seditiosos esse putabat, consensu affirmarunt se ducem tribunosque secuturos esse. Toto ex exercitu unus solus legatus se infidelem praebuit.

Exercise 246

Sulla, devictis inimicis imperioque sumpto, Senatum convocatum summo ardore postulavit ut C Marius hostis decerneretur. Neque quisquam ei se opposuit donec Scaevola sententiam rogatus dicere recusavit. Qui quum Sulla eum voce minaci sententiam rogitaret respondit illi quidem licere manus militum ostentare quibus curiam cinxisset, licere mortem sibi identidem minari; nunquam tamen se coactum iri dicere Marium a quo respublica Romana servata esset Romae esse hostem.

Exercise 247

His temporibus sunt qui cupere videantur non modo leges mutare — id quod forsitan laude dignum sit — sed totam rempublicam evertere. Talis viri orationem heri audiebam apud turbam artificum in foro ita contionantis: Quid esset qui inter se dominaretur? Quis esset cui divitias congererent dum ipsi pecunia panis causa emendi carerent? Illos ipsos responsum posse dare nec sibi opus esse declarare. Patres satis valere ut aequas leges fieri prohiberent; M. Crassum quotannis consulatum sibi suisque amicis emere. Unum solum esse remedium. Ex urbe eos expellerent. Flammis et sanguine eos remedium. Ex urbe eos expellerent. Flammis et sanguine eos docerent quantam plebi injuriam intulissent.

Exercise 248

Tertio jam die postquam copiae Roma profectae sunt, tristis nuntius allatus est hostes, exercitu Romano a. d. IV Id. Mart. (ante diem quartum Idus Martias) profligato, jam urbe Coriolis et omnibus agris bonisque sociorum potitos esse. Nuntius quidem rettulit se solum ex acie supresse; hostes recenti victoria elatos instare neque amplius tria millia passuum jam sine dubio ab urbe abesse. Adeo autem feroci eos esse ingenio ut pro certo haberet fore ut nemini quamvis seni infirmoque parceretur. Quo audito patres legatos mittere constituerunt qui aggredienti hosti obviam irent et pacem peterent.

Exercise 249

Victoriam haud ancipitem jam reportaverat, et pro certo habebat bellum mox propsere eventurum, cum spes omnis perdita est quod milites bellum continuare recusarunt. Affirmabant enim se laboribus confectos esse, neque in meliorem spem belli conficiendi venire. Quare patria et si quid cordi esset relinquenda, mala omnia subeunda essent ut imperator victoriae irritae laudem adipisceretur? Si quidem hostes sequerentur se non posse eos in castellis montanis consequi, et ipsas victorias quas jam reportassent multo Romanorum sanguine stetisse.

Exercise 250

Imperator autem respondit neminem quidem magis quam se suis consulere, stultorum tamen esse commoda victoriae paene exploratae perdere. Ne arbitrarentur se bellum modo suscepisse ut laudem sibi adipisceretur, illos enim secum fructus victoriae aeque participes fore et hostibus profligatis posse, spoliis hostium auctos, domum satis redire. Praeterea hostes etsi in montes confugerent nondum eo pervenisse, et signis confestim motis fore ut eos priusquam ad locum tutum se recepissent facile consequeretur.

Exercise 251

Ne crederent, id quod vulgo in urbe jactaretur, se consulatum eo consilio petere ut provinciam acquireret divitiasque quas tot senatores civitatibus imperio Romano subjectis abriperent. Num eos putare se, Catoni quondam conjunctissimum, adeo animo mutatum esse? Immo se malle spem omnem honorum abjicere quam tantae infamine occurrere. Se nuper audisse publicanos Ciliciae amicum suum Ciceronem rogasse ut sibi legionarios traderet per quos vectigalia colligerent. Eum primo quidem recusasse, postea tamen precibus superatum esse. Quin ipsos milites nisi Romani essent quominus tam crudeli operi interessent recusaturos. Verum conarentur philosophiae studere et malorum oblivisci quae sanare non possent.

Exercise 252

Hac nocte rex parvam comitum manum circum se collectam paucis verbis valere jussit. Fortunam illorum tamdiu cum sua conjunctam esse ut non nisi ultima necessitate coactus talia verba ederet. Si quid spei jam restaret se fide et auxilio eorum ultra usurum, neve crederent se parvi ea facere. Paucos enim illos esse qui secum rebus properis fructi jam rebus se adversis oppressum descrere nollent, cujus rei summas se eis gratias habere. jam vero saluti eorum consulendem. pro qua postero die se traditurum esse. Cur eos secum perdere oporteret? Cum rebelles se ipsum in potestate habuissent fieri posse ut illos sincerent quocunque vellent effugere.

Exercise 253

Imperator de ingenti hac multitudine certior factus consilio legatorum convocato ita locutus est: "Illos jam cernere quantum sibi periculum instaret. Colles armis signisque opertos esse et imperatorem Graecum bellis et victoriis esse assuetum: salutem suam in consensu esse positam: sibi modo imperarent, se paratum esse imperium duci meliori concedere." Cum in tanto discrimine etiam inimici plausu demonstrarent se ei confidere, haec addit: "praemio victoriae confisi ne locum fugae ignavis relinquerent. Navibus et impedimentis ustis in illo loco proelium committerent." Qua sententia consensu omnium probata, dux acie instructa hostium impetum exspectavit. Fortasse nesciebat in eo loco Caesarem et Pompeium olim de imperio orbis terrarum decertasse.

Exercise 254

Se potuisse in Hispaniam ire ubi fratrem participem laborum habiturus fuerit et Hasdrubalem hostem pro Hannibale. Sed cum oram legens audisset hostes in Galliam advenisse, se statim egressum equitibus praemissis castra usque ad Rhodanum movisse. Experiri se jam cupere num Carthago illis viginti annis novum genus civium edidisset, an eidem essent quos Eryce dimissos tam parvi aestimassent. Se quidem velle pro honore modo dimicari neque ipsa pro vita; sed pro Italia ipsa et pro domibus certari; neque alterum exercitum a tergo esse qui illis victis (nisi illi vicissent) hosti obstaret. Reputaret quisque Senatum se spectare, et fortunam Romae in sua virtute constare.

Exercise 255

Interea Poeni, qui sciebant quam exiguae sibi copiae navales Lilybaei essent, neque dubitabant quin locus defendi non posset nisi auxilium ferretur (latum esset), novas copias statim mittere constituerunt. Hannibal igitur, Hamilcaris filius, quam celerrime ad Siciliam cum quinquaginta navibus et decem milibus militum missus est. Qui, cum classe inter Aegates insulas contra Lilybaeum sitas navigans, tempus opperitur quo per scopulos et saxa portum cingentia se insinuare possit. Tandem ventum nactus secundum navem solvit, suisque ad certamen confertis, audacia successu digna per aditum angustum penetravit. Interim Romani, quorum naves in ancoris stabant, ejus temeritate attoniti pro certo habebant eum in scopulos allisum iri.

Exercise 256

Atrociter et tumultuose pugnatum est. Primo impetu pelluntur oppugnatores atque e ducibus fortissimis dum strictis ensibus castellum expugnant, nonnulli occiduntur. Mox iterum, fortuna secundiore, adgrediuntur. Ex alio in alium locum pulsi sunt Indi, et summa ferocitate certantes pedem gradatim rettulerunt. Plerique veteranorum occisi sunt et post pugnam et longam et cruentam Philippus et dux sociorum cum globo bellatorum, qui adhuc supererant, e castello regressi ad virgulta silvae vicinae confugiunt. Incendunt victores casas et castella: mox omnia flammis corripiuntur: senum mulierum, infantium, multi inter flammas perierunt.

Index

A

Ablative 59
  absolute 43
  manner 43
  of agent 6
  of association 98
  of cause 15
  of comparison 59
  of instrument 6, 72
  of manner 100
  of orgin 98
  of price 72
  of quality 59
  of respect 100
  of separation 98
  without preposition 58
  words governing 12
Accusative 53, 107
  verbs governing 9
Adjective 107

D

Dative
  of purpose 96
  possessor 13
  predicate 96
  verbs 83

Deponents 45
Direct command 85

G

Genitive
  partitive 74
  value 72
Gerundives 107
Gerunds 107

I

Indirect statement 61, 90
Infinitives 38
  future 61
  indirect statement 65
  tenses 65

N

Noun
  verbal 107, 112

P

Participles 43
  passive 45
  perfect 43
  present 47, 107
Place 53

Prepositions 53, 107
Price 72
Pronouns
  reflexive 64

S

Sentences
  consecutive 26
  final 22
Space 53
Supines 112

T

Tenses
  historic 21
  primary 21
  sequence 21
Time 53

V

Value 72
Verbs
  finite 38
  intransitive 45, 83
  of saying or thinking 61

Also Available from Alacrity Press

Lays of Ancient Rome
Thomas Babington Macaulay

Now in the public domain, the *Lays of Ancient Rome* by Thomas Babington Macaulay were originally published in 1842. The Lays were immensely popular in England during Victorian times and to this day are a popular subject for recitation. Winston Churchill memorized them as a student to prove his mental capabilities. This edition includes all four lays, with introductions, verse numbers, and explanatory footnotes (from the 1891 edition).

Latin for Beginners
Benjamin L. D'ooge, Ph.D.

Now in the public domain, *Latin for Beginners*, by Benjamin L. D'ooge, Ph.D. was originally published in 1909. The *Latin for Beginners: Centurion Edition* celebrates the 100th an-niversary of the publication of the Latin classic. The text has been retypeset and formatted to a slightly larger size. All the original illustrations and plates have been included (in black and white). Special vocabularies have been moved from the appendix and placed with their respective lessons. As a bonus for the Latin scholar, included after the reading material, is the ballad of *Horatius* from *The Lays of Rome* by Thomas Babington Macaulay.

With Lee in Virginia
G.A. Henty

The debate over States rights has reached a boiling point. The Rebel states are planning an attempt to secede from the Union, and war is imminent! Share a fictional young Virginian's experience as, Vincent Wingfield, joins the Confederate army. During this adventure, you will learn why the Confederates were blessed with great leaders and how they confronted incredible odds as they fought against the economic advantage and sheer manpower of the Union. With a backdrop of the U.S. Civil War and Lee in Virginia, this tale is a wonderful mix of adventure and history. This is a story of excellent reading for older children or adults. Included in this edition are geographical, historical, and explanatory footnotes which will help the modern reader to savor this G.A. Henty classic.

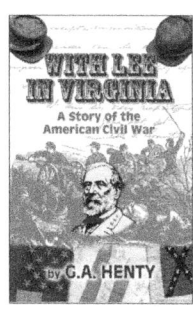

The Young Carthaginian
G.A. Henty

The year is 218 B.C. and Rome and Carthage are locked in a life-or-death struggle for control of the ancient world. Join a fictional young Carthaginian noble, named Malchus, as he travels with the famous General Hannibal across the Alps and into Italy, the heartland of the Roman republic. During this adventure you will learn why Hannibal was a great leader and why Rome ultimately won the struggle in spite of Hannibal's genius. Included in this edition are geographical, historical, and explanatory footnotes to aid the modern reader.

At Aboukir and Acre
G.A. Henty

The year is 1798 and the French armed forces are on the move. Napoleon has formed an audacious plan to protect French trade interests and undermine Britain's access to India by invading Egypt. Join a fictional young man, Edgar Blagrove, as he witnesses famous historical events including *The Battle of the Nile*, *The Battle of the Pyramids*, and the defense of Acre. Along the way you will learn about great figures of history including Napoleon Bonaparte, Horatio Nelson, Sir Sidney Smith, and Sir Ralph Abercrombie. Included in this edition of *At Aboukir and Acre* are geographical, nautical, and historical footnotes to aid the modern reader.

Made in the USA
Las Vegas, NV
15 November 2021